DESIGN INNOVATIONS FOR
Aging and Alzheimer's

DESIGN INNOVATIONS FOR
Aging and Alzheimer's

Creating Caring Environments

ELIZABETH C. BRAWLEY

WILEY

John Wiley & Sons, Inc.

Published by John Wiley & Sons, Inc., Hoboken, New Jersey
Published simultaneously in Canada

For general information about our other products and services, please contact our Customer Care Department within the United States at (800) 762-2974, outside the United States at (317) 572-3993 or fax (317) 572-4002.

Wiley also publishes its books in a variety of electronic formats. Some content that appears in print may not be available in electronic books. For more information about Wiley products, visit our Website at www.wiley.com.

Library of Congress Cataloging-in-Publication Data:
Brawley, Elizabeth C.
  Innovations in design for aging and Alzheimer's disease / Elizabeth C. Brawley.
       p. cm.
  Includes bibliographical references and index.
  ISBN-10: 0-471-68118-0 (cloth)
  ISBN-13: 978-0-471-68118-2
1. Long-term care facilities—Design and construction. 2. Older people—Dwellings—Design and construction. 3. Alzheimer's disease—Patients—Dwellings—Design and construction. 4. Aging—Environmental aspects. 5. Architecture—Psychological aspects. 6. Interior decoration—Psychological aspects. I. Title.
  RA998.5.B73 2006
  725'.56—dc22   2005010714

Printed in the United States of America

10 9 8 7 6 5 4

Dedication

It is with extraordinary gratitude that this book is dedicated to my family, my sister Mary, her husband Ed, and the two boys in my life, Jason and Walker, who have brought me such joy.

I also owe a debt of gratitude to the doctors, nurses, technicians, and nursing assistants who took such good care of me during the most frightening fight of my life. These dedicated and extraordinarily caring healthcare professionals have allowed me the opportunity to become an older adult.

I owe more than I can ever repay to my wonderful and extraordinary circle of friends, who overwhelmed me with their generosity. The spontaneity of my "best buddies"—my support group who began arriving as if by magic from all over the country when I needed them most. Kathy Laurenhue came to spend Thanksgiving week with me, and like a true friend she brought adorable hats to distract from my rapidly balding head. When Kathy left, my sister Mary arrived from North Carolina and made sure there was a small Christmas tree in place before she departed. Jan Olofson took her place, followed by Kate Walker. I'll never forget Katie's relentless efforts to find something that would work to remind me to take medication on a prescribed schedule when I couldn't remember anything for longer than 15 seconds. When check-off charts, timers, and all else failed, she brought my medication every six hours. When she left she resorted to the always reliable personal touch. She faithfully called—and waited on the phone to ensure that I took the medication.

My longtime friend and Christmas angel, Lynn Stedman, left her family in Washington at Christmas to be with me until after the New Year. Knowing that Christmas is my favorite holiday season, she and Donna Fletcher somehow managed to bundle me into the car for a magical twilight tour of San Francisco's Christmas lights, and they were truly the most beautiful I have ever seen. To my forever friend Marty, for providing someone to keep the house clean and making it Christmas all year, thank you. And to Mary and Ed, Janis and Jim, Leslie and David, and Becci and Larry, thank you for the wonderful Christmas in July when I finally made it back to North Carolina.

You, my friends, indulged me with heartwarming cards and messages and have enriched my life with comfort and caring far beyond anything I could have ever imagined. You gave me courage, and I continue to be deeply touched and appreciative and so grateful that each of you is in my life. From the bottom of my heart—

Thank you.

Contents

Preface

In a society where youth is glorified and television and advertising constantly remind you of this, it's tough to admit you're getting on in years and tougher still to prepare for it. Most seniors recognize but don't want to confront the realities of aging or imagine the possibility of their own impending frailty. The aversion to even thinking of the likelihood of living somewhere other than home, even in an assisted living community, stems less from the issue of the quality of such facilities than from an unwillingness to face the reality that many of our bodies and body parts don't seem to support us as well as they used to.

The reality of aging is that chronic conditions must be addressed. Over 50 percent of older adults are affected by arthritis, followed by hypertension, hearing impairment (which affects more than 36 percent), heart disease, cataracts, and other vision impairments. Even more frightening for nearly everyone over 40 is the possibility of Alzheimer's disease and cognitive impairment.

Studies suggest an important element of successful aging is a person's ability to age in place in a stable living environment.[1] The American Seniors Housing Association (AHSA) identified 20,920 senior housing properties in its 2004 study, which included 5,250 senior apartments, 6,200 independent living properties, 7,270 assisted living and 2,200 continuing care retirement community properties which comprised in total over 2,323,600 housing units.[2] As the aging population grows in number and the average life expectancy increases, long-term-care alternatives will be in increasingly greater demand. Continuing care retirement settings are appealing because they emphasize housing and the advantages of community living, rather than focusing on the frailties and illnesses that accompany aging. While care is part of the package when needed, the focus is on living.

There is an important lesson here. If we are to meet tomorrow's challenges of providing care, our assisted living facilities and nursing homes must change to become real homes, with neighborhoods and a sense of community designed to appeal to the evolving tastes of the baby boom generation. There is no question that baby boomers will demand different and probably unprecedented forms of healthcare and social activity. One of the challenges for providers and design professionals is how to offer these services within the community in a place they call home. The smart choice is to become more determined in our push for person-centered care, organizational culture change, and a better quality of life for our elders. As our population ages the need for long-term care is increasing dramatically. Culture change is long overdue. In fact, it is critical if facility-based long-term care is to survive.

Open minds, open communication, and cooperative planning between design professionals and healthcare providers is fundamental to creating caring environments. Innovative designers can do more than create new buildings and new building designs; they can build awareness about life-enhancing design. We have so much to learn from each other, and everyone stands to benefit, especially the residents.

Guided by a philosophy of caring, the term *life-enhancing environment* describes the physical and cultural atmosphere created to support older residents. The major environmental factors influencing physical health and emotional well-being are sound, light, and sense of touch. The significance of the physical environment increases if judgment and mental competence fade. Older adults rely on their senses to interpret information about the environment. Inadequate light and the presence of glare and noise are particularly aggravating and significantly affect comfort levels and behavior.

Every day we are facing new challenges, and healthcare providers are looking for design professionals who have the insight to "diagnose" current problems and the vision to creatively work together and solve them. One of the biggest roadblocks we face as design professionals is forgetting we are designing for individuals—real people whose physical abilities are very different from our own, and whose cognitive skills may be declining as well. Residents may be our mothers, fathers, grandmothers and grandfathers, sisters, brothers, uncles, aunts, neighbors—even our best friends. This is an opportunity for design professionals to take the initiative and develop person-centered design to support person-centered care in very meaningful ways.

Though our training teaches us there are many solutions to a problem, we may need to be reminded that aging involves a large range of physical and mental experiences. It is wise to remember that any solution that meets a need is likely not the only solution and may not even be the best one. Working together with healthcare providers in a strong spirit of mutual cooperation, we will be challenged to learn more from and about the people for whom we are designing. We will be challenged to become more personally involved with older adults who can open our minds as we continue to explore better and more appropriate ways to solve problems.

Staying abreast of current research and applying it to practice is more important than ever before. Studies have shown that the environment strongly influences behavior, particularly the behavior of those with Alzheimer's disease and related dementias. It is also showing with some consistency that well-designed physical environments can maintain and enhance the ability to function and improve quality of life.[3] Diminished memory and declining capacity for reasoning and judgment cause these individuals to respond more intensively to the immediate environment than cognitively intact persons, making good design an important treatment factor. If we are to develop the environment as a legitimate method of treatment, its design and use must be founded in sound research and distinguished by much more than personal likes, dislikes, and opinions.

Volume, good intention, and great taste are not necessarily indicators of good quality or design for aging adults. Design professionals must rely more strongly on evidence-based design, critical research findings, and postoccupancy evaluation as essential elements of the design process. There is still too little research on the effects of the environment on older users and too few rigorous independent postoccupancy evaluations.

Activity should be the heart of long-term care and is an area that needs and deserves open minds, open communication, and cooperative planning between design professionals and healthcare providers to create the very best caring environment. Activities define who we are. Depression and anxiety often result when a person loses the ability to drive, work, mow the grass, cook, or do other meaningful tasks. One of the important lessons we've learned through adult day care is how important it is to substitute old cherished activities with similar simpler activities. Many older adults derive a high degree of satisfaction and good exercise from pets, gardening, and music.

The mistake that most often hampers the planning process is having no strong activity program and waiting to hire an activity director after the building is complete. This strategy has proved only moderately successful at best.

In the absence of strong resident-centered programming, buildings are designed with generic activity spaces. These are far less successful than spaces designed to accommodate successfully operating programs with specific needs and flexibility built into the design. An activity space with no running water, for example, inhibits the range of activities. Incorporating a country kitchen or simply designing for running water greatly expands activity options to allow for cooking, painting, and a variety of other crafts and activities that require cleanup. Storage space is rarely optimal or adequate when there is no prior thought to specific use and needs. Generic storage is usually shelves, which don't accommodate large balls and sports equipment. No one who enjoys entertaining would design and build a home without serious thought about how it might be used for entertaining. With the greatest respect for those in my profession, architects and interior designers should not be directing care and programs, but all too often, without the benefit of good direction and the opportunity to experience the program in action, that is exactly what is happening.

Robert Butler, the founding director of the National Institute on Aging and the International Longevity Center USA, suggests in the recent reissue of his landmark book *Why Survive: Being Old in America,* "In order to make a wider impact, each of us in the field of aging needs to add flesh and blood, tears and laughter to the data and statistics by listening to the human stories of older people themselves. Through the words of older Americans, we learn who among them are and are not doing fine."[4]

I include architects and interior designers in the "each of us in the field of aging." There is virtually no curriculum or academic training to educate architects and interior designers about designing environments for aging adults and long-term healthcare. Applying criteria for designing and building hospitals to senior housing has already proved flawed. Taking part in programs for aging adults rather than relying on documentation might stimulate changes in design and design outcomes as well. This kind of hands-on research put into practice is likely to produce more successful outcomes. Providers can help design professionals to gain a better understanding of activities by taking part as well, so that all three groups—providers, architects, and designers—work side by side with residents. This is a more comfortable experience and also provides time to hear older adults tell their own stories.

As the pioneers of culture change in long-term care work to ensure organizational commitment to person-centered care, design professionals should be engaged in learning more about this movement—what it is about, its mission and goals. Changes in the architectural environment must be endorsed and driven by the appropriate organizational, staff, and social changes to be successful. It is a rare opportunity from the beginning to support current changes in aging, wellness, and healthcare with good design and to contribute to their success.

An example of the significance of research for design is found in the recent Maryland Assisted Living Study conducted by the Division of Neurobiology and Division of Geriatric and Neuropsychiatry of the Johns Hopkins School of Medicine. This study of older people in assisted living facilities revealed a high rate of dementia but a lack of recognition by caregivers. It found that nearly 68 percent of the randomly selected residents had dementia, but only half had been adequately evaluated and treated.[5]

While at first glance this study may not appear to impact building design, the need for supervision is one of the reasons people seek supportive housing, including assisted living. Yet assisted living is commonly seen as a setting for people who are simply experiencing minor functional difficulties. This study indicates that almost 70 percent of assisted living residents have dementia, while we are designing housing primarily for cognitively intact persons who may have mobility problems.

Existing care settings are still too often inappropriate design models for care of the frail elderly. With better understanding of the aging process, the challenges posed by frailty and dementia, and the unique problems associated with dependence, we will be better able to provide responsive care environments. Information from studies such as this might have a very strong impact on the design process for assisted living environments if more design professionals were aware of it.

There is no question that we need accredited educational programs in design for aging. We need more research on the impact of the environment on behavior, on specific design elements and interventions and their impact, and a more effective means of making crucial research easily available to architects and design professionals in understandable language. These would be giant steps toward translating research into practice and creating caring environments that are about life and the living, about vitality and the dignity of human beings—caring environments (an atmosphere of living) where residents are encouraged to enjoy everything of which they are capable.

Elizabeth Brawley, IIDA, AAHID
Sausalito, CA

Contact Elizabeth Brawley at:
Design Concepts Unlimited
PO Box 454
Sausalito, CA 94966
Phone: (415) 332–8382
Fax: (415) 332–9022
E-mail: betsybrawley@attglobal.net
Web site: www.betsybrawley.com

Acknowledgments

Perhaps because this book almost didn't become a reality, I am particularly grateful for the contributions and generosity of many. My hope is that it will prove to be a resource of information and inspiration for creating caring environments that we can all comfortably live in. For even though we don't ever expect to be frail or believe we will need the care and services provided in assisted living, nursing homes, adult day care, home care, or hospice, it's inevitable that some of us will. Today there are those who benefit from supportive long-term care and special Alzheimer's care in many settings, and their numbers are growing. I hope this book will inspire providers and designers to improve and expand our care choices. I am particularly hopeful that it will encourage and motivate architects and designers to create exceptional caring environments, and to find solutions that better meet the needs of older frail adults, many of whom have dementia. Good architects and designers can thrive on these challenges.

Powell Lawton was not only a giant in the field of aging and environment, he was one of those rare people who made a difference in the lives he touched. A kind and caring man and an inspiring teacher, he encouraged me to dream bigger dreams and tackle more difficult problems and to trust myself. Thank you hardly seems adequate.

To the many healthcare professionals who care, care for, and contribute so much, and to design professionals who are proving that we can improve quality of life through better design, thank you. Together, particularly in the last ten years, we have proved that we can deliver better design and better care. More importantly, we are proving every day that better design can make it significantly easier to deliver better care.

I gratefully acknowledge the Hula B. and Maurice L. Rothschild Foundation for their generosity. Through their generous assistance, and the support of American of Martinsville, Collins & Aikman, InVista, and the InPro Corporation, this work was possible. Thank you.

Acknowledgment and special thanks are due to many colleagues who were kind enough to contribute their expertise and to review much of the content of this book. First and foremost, my gratitude and appreciation to my longtime friend and colleague Eunice Noell-Waggoner, director of the Center of Design for an Aging Society, past chair of the Illuminating Engineering Society of North America's Committee on Aging Vision and Lighting, and a constant source of inspiration and encouragement. She provided illustrations, insights, and a review of the chapters on vision and lighting.

Thank you to Helen Luey, senior program director of the Hearing Society; Kathleen O'Brien, senior vice president of the National Alzheimer's Association; John Zeisel, president of Hearthstone Alzheimer's Care; and Mark Taylor, director of healthcare markets for Shaw Industries for sharing their time and expertise to ensure the accuracy of this work. And to David Kamp, thank you for designing the beautiful gardens that inspire me to dream greater, more beautiful and colorful dreams.

Special thanks to Rose Marie Fagan, national executive director of the Pioneer Network, for her patience, her many contributions to my work, and the continuing contributions of the Pioneer Network in promoting long-overdue culture change in long-term care. To Jude Rabig of the Green House Project, and to Laura Gilpin and Marc Schweitzer of Planetree, thank you for your help and your continued diligent work in changing the culture of resident and patient care for our elders.

A very special thank you to Suzi Kennedy and the wonderful staff and participants of the Life Enrichment Adult Day Care Centers in North Carolina. They really lived up to their motto, "We do whatever it takes." When Suzi asked me to be part of the design team for their new adult day care center, she said they would wait until I was healthy enough to travel. She assured me that whenever I could get there, they could take care of me if I needed anything. And they did! I was still suffering with some memory loss and unsure whether I could do the work I loved. She couldn't have known what a gift she gave me. What a way to return to work, in the loving arms of the most caring and supportive staff and warm and welcoming participants. There will always be a special place in my heart for the Life Enrichment Centers (and they truly are) of North Carolina.

I especially want to thank the many care providers, architects, and designers who are doing such good work and so willingly contributed photographs and images to bring this book to life. I am constantly touched by the remarkable courage and strength of so many people who in quiet, unassuming ways make such a difference in the lives of others.

Thank you to Debra Levin and the board from the Center for Health Design, who have always provided such good examples of leadership in healthcare and encouraged innovation and good, evidence-based design; and to Mark Goodman and Richard Peck at MedQuest Communications for their continued support. A special thank you to Cynthia Leibrock, who encouraged me to write and introduced me to Amanda Miller at John Wiley and Sons, who has always provided expert advice, help, and encouragement. A special thank you to John Czarnecki, my editor, and to Laura Arnold and Leslie Anglin for all their patience and hard work.

I would like to acknowledge Ruth Blank, whose friendship and constant encouragement during the many years we served together on the national board of the Alzheimer's Association have been so genuinely appreciated, and Elayne Brill and David Troxel for their expertise, their encouragement, and their constant phone calls and support. Ours is a very special friendship that I value more than you can imagine.

And lastly, I would be remiss not to acknowledge Anastasia Dellas, with very special thanks. Her experience, persistence, special talents, and above all her generosity of spirit enabled the completion of this book.

Aging and Alzheimer's Disease

Implications for Design

As health outcomes for elders improve, the extra years offer opportunities for leisure activities, second careers, and volunteer service.

Aging in the Twenty-First Century

Aging and Age-Related Changes

Aging can make your skin sag, your pants bag, your joints hurt, your blood pressure rise, and your risk of disease increase, and that's just for starters. Because old age is often portrayed as an inevitable, steady decline in physical and mental abilities, many of us worry about the possibility of increasingly long periods of frailty. Perhaps the greatest fear that comes with having another birthday is the terror of dementia—everyone's shared nightmare about massive cognitive failure and the eventual loss of self-identity. But longer lives have, for the most part, been accompanied by better lives, and contrary to public perception, fully 60 percent of people over 80 years of age live independently in the community.[1]

The dramatically changed distribution of age in our population as a whole raises important questions about the nature and quality of life in the twenty-first century. At the time most current social policies were put into place, American life was far different from what it is today. Not only was life expectancy shorter, but divorce rates were low, serial marriage was unusual, and the average number of children born to each woman was double what it is today. Influenza, pneumonia, and tuberculosis were the leading causes of death, and life expectancy after retirement was relatively short.[2]

Today, life for older adults presents a very different picture.

Demographics

Just as the overall demography of our society is changing, the demographics of aging are also changing dramatically. Both the number and the proportion of older people, relative to the rest of the population, are increasing, and the aging of the "baby boomers," born between 1946 and 1964, will accelerate this growth. The population age 85 and older is growing rapidly.[3]

For much of human history the average life expectancy at birth was less than 30 years. By 1900, the average was 48 years in the United States; then in the twentieth century, nearly 30 more years were added.[4] Today life expectancy has risen roughly 60 percent—adding nearly 19 years to our lives. Overall it is now 77 years of age in the United States—80 years on average for women and 74 years for men. By 2030, an estimated 20 percent—one in five Americans—will be 65 or older.[5] Mortality rates may continue to decline, particularly for those in higher age groups, which could add as much as 24 years to the remaining life expectancy of 65-year-olds by the end of the twenty-first century.[6] Minority elderly will increase far more quickly than the general population.

Declining infant mortality, longer lives, and falling fertility rates are the three primary factors responsible for our aging society. Over the last century, 43 million Americans have celebrated their sixtieth birthdays, thanks to strides in medicine, and each day about 5,000 Americans turn 65. Over the next 30 years, the number of older Americans is expected to double, growing by over 35 million people. By the year 2030, the population of those 60 and older will more than double to 85 million, while the number of those 85 and older will triple to 8 million.[7]

But the often overlooked good news is that due to cultural changes and biomedical advances, many Americans are not only living longer, but coming to old age healthier and better educated than ever before in history.[8] Over the last century, 43 million Americans have celebrated their 60th birthdays due to the strides in medicine, and each day about 5,000 Americans turn 65!

Just as important is new evidence of links among health, socioeconomic status, and mental sharpness in later life, underscoring the potential to modify aging outcomes.[9] Seniors are an ever-growing segment of the U.S. population. As we improve health outcomes for elders, the extra years offer opportunities for leisure activities, second careers, and volunteer service; however, many older adults, including three million who are 85 and older, are still at risk of losing their independence. The effects of the aging population will be most strongly felt between 2010 and 2030, when one in every five Americans will be 65 or older. There will also be 2 million fewer 25- to 40-year-olds in 15 years, a drop of 4 percent.[10,11]

Figure 1.1 As we improve health outcomes for elders, the extra years offer opportunities for leisure activities and fun. *Courtesy of The Life Enrichment Center, Shelby, NC.*

Global Aging

Global aging is also occurring at a rate never seen before. The world's population age 65 and older is growing by an unprecedented 800,000 people a month, and has increased from 131 million in 1950 to a record 420 million in 2000. The numbers and proportions of older people are continuing to rise in both developed and developing countries.[12] This means that more people age 65 and older are alive today than ever; the United States ranks thirty-second on a list of countries with high proportions of people age 65 and older.

Italy has replaced Sweden as the world's oldest country, with 18 percent of Italians having celebrated at least a sixty-fifth birthday. By 2030, Italy and Japan are predicted to have the greatest percentage of older people, 28 percent, and they are on target to have more citizens over 80 than under 20 in the next 50 years.[13] More than one-third of the world's oldest people (80 and above) live in three countries: China (11.5 million), the United States (9.2 million), and India (6.2 million).[14]

Aging, Diversity, and Health

There is great variability in health and the quality of people's later years, influenced by such things as access to medical care, behavioral patterns, educational background, and working conditions. Most people are healthy most of their lives, but advanced age is associated with poorer health. Not only are older people more likely than the young to develop diseases that require healthcare interventions, but they are also more likely to suffer concurrent chronic conditions such as arthritis, Parkinson's disease, and diabetes, which require ongoing management. People are living longer than they once did after the onset of illness, but they are not necessarily healthier. Better treatment of chronic diseases such as heart disease means that individuals may live long enough to develop age-related conditions such as arthritis and diabetes.[15] Prevalence of chronic diseases among adults age 70 and older varies by race and ethnicity. Members of ethnic minority groups are at disproportionate risk of developing disabling disease. For example, nearly 60 percent of elderly African Americans report high blood pressure, and a growing share of both African Americans and Hispanics report problems with diabetes.

As our society ages, the ranks of the elderly are becoming more diverse. In 2000, 16 percent of those 65 and over identified themselves as being from one of the four minority populations (American Indian/Alaska native, Asian/ Pacific Islander, African American, or Hispanic). It is projected that by midcentury over one-third (36 percent) of all older Americans will come from these groups.[16] Older people of color not only have higher rates of chronic

Figure 1.2 Ethnic minority groups are at a disproportionate risk of developing disabling diseases such as high blood pressure and diabetes. *Courtesy George G. Glenner Alzheimer's Day Care Centers, Inc., San Diego, CA.*

Figure 1.3 Following the old-fashioned advice of eating right, staying active, and getting plenty of rest can go a long way toward keeping not only our bodies but our brains healthy as we age. *Courtesy of Francis E. Parker Memorial Home, Piscataway, NJ. Landscape Architect: DirtWorks PC, New York, NY.*

diseases (such as diabetes, hypertension, and cancer) but also shorter life expectancies.[17]

New technologies offer impressive new ways to extend and improve life in old age. Medications and procedures that could not have been imagined a few years ago have radically changed the way some diseases are treated and have limited the threat they pose.[18] While heart disease remains the number one cause of death in the United States, patients have a much greater chance of surviving a heart attack and receiving treatment to control heart disease because of new procedures and approaches to cardiac surgery, and new medications. Laser and ultrasonic technology have also led to new, less invasive surgical techniques.[19]

The old cliché, "feeling old is a state of mind," may just be true. Experts say that only about 30 percent of the symptoms of physical aging can be traced to our genes; the rest is up to us. Some of the body and mind changes normally associated with aging may be the result of treatable health conditions or a lifetime of poor health habits.[20] Along with a few insights from aging research, following the old-fashioned advice of "eating right, staying active, and getting plenty of rest" can go a long way toward keeping not only our bodies but our brains healthy as we age.

Most of us would like to live our lives to the fullest every day—to maintain our day-to-day activities and enjoy the things that bring us pleasure, no matter what our age. We don't want to be crippled by health problems or overly dependent on others. Living well in old age is more important than just living to old age. And there is good news. The National Institute on Aging confirms that older people today are living longer and that the rate of disability among older persons is declining at an accelerated pace. There is a lot we can do to improve our quality of life, no matter how old we are.

Age-Related Changes

If you are living with a chronic health condition, you are not alone. Estimates are that one in four Americans lives with more than one illness and that half (125 million people) suffer from at least one chronic condition. Chronic conditions are growing more common as people live longer, and while these diseases are among the most common and costly health problems, they are also among the most preventable. Many chronic diseases can be controlled with exercise, diet, and medication. While we continue to search for ways to prevent and cure diseases, we also need to manage them better so people can live better lives.

Chronic, by definition, means long-lasting or recurring. Examples of common chronic health conditions include arthritis, cancer, diabetes, Alzheimer's disease, depression, and heart disease.[21] As baby boomers age and people live longer, the number of people who are most vulnerable to and most affected by chronic conditions will increase. Currently, chronic conditions are the major cause of illness, disability, and death in the United States.[22] Although chronic diseases are becoming more prevalent in the older population, disability rates for older Americans have been declining in recent years.[23]

No one is immune to chronic conditions, but the type of chronic conditions that are most common varies considerably with age. Age is one of the risk factors for chronic conditions that cannot be modified. Risk factors related to behavior and environmental conditions, however, can be modified. This underscores the importance of promoting healthy behaviors, creating safe and healthy environments, and promoting access to appropriate healthcare services. The time is right to find out what we can do to promote a healthy population now and in the future.

MOST COMMON CHRONIC CONDITIONS AGE 75+

- Arthritis
- Hypertension
- Hearing Impairments
- Heart Disease
- Cataracts

National Academy on an Aging Society[24]

The chronic conditions most common among older adults require more care and are more disabling than conditions in younger age groups, and those that also involve chronic pain present a significant obstacle to maintaining mobility, function, and independence. The continued growth in the number of older people will probably cause an increase in the number of people most affected by chronic conditions.[25]

Arthritis

Arthritis is inflammation of a joint—any joint—due to such varied causes as injury, infection, a chemical imbalance in the blood, or a malfunctioning immune system. One in three U.S. adults is affected by arthritis—an increase of more than 60 percent over estimates from five years ago. This puts the number of adults with chronic arthritis symptoms at 70 million.[26] It is the most common chronic condition in older adults. In 1995, about 58 percent of persons age 70 or older reported having arthritis.[27] There are many forms of arthritis, but the most common are osteoarthritis (OA) and rheumatoid arthritis.

Osteoarthritis, the most common form, is caused by an injury or simply by wear and tear to the joints, affecting hips, knees, neck, and lower back. The joint pain or stiffness is usually worst when awakening in the morning, then improves quickly. More than 20 million Americans are affected by osteoarthritis, which is the leading cause of disability in this country. Preliminary findings from a 24-month trial with older adults with lower-extremity OA found use of a multiple-component intervention to be helpful, and such treatments may hold promise as a public health strategy for older adults.[28]

Almost every adult over 40 has some degree of osteoarthritis, particularly in joints that are repeatedly stressed—and obesity makes it worse, especially on weight-bearing joints. While there is no way to prevent or cure it, there are many things that will minimize the severity and slow its progress.

TO CONTROL SYMPTOMS OF OSTEOARTHRITIS

- **Lose weight**
- **Exercise**—stretching, strength training, aerobic walking, swimming
- **Modify the environment**
  - Chairs—Make sure chairs have arm supports and backrests. Avoid low seats that are hard to get out of.
  - Bathtub—Apply no-slip finish to the tub or shower. Install grab bars for assistance in getting in and out of the tub or shower.
  - Toilet—Install an elevated toilet seat.
  - Flooring—Avoid slippery surfaces and loose throw rugs. Wall-to-wall carpet is safer.

Hypertension

The rate of hypertension for people 65 and older has increased since the 1990s. Nationally, over half (53%) of the population age 65 and older had hypertension in 2001. Data regarding the extent to which different conditions affect the population are of great value in planning disease prevention activities and anticipating the healthcare needs of the older population.[29]

Hearing Impairment

Hearing loss affects 38 million Americans; almost two-thirds of those affected are over the age of 55. While there are many possible causes of hearing loss, including trauma, repeated exposure to loud noises, side effects of medications, inherited abnormalities, and certain viral or bacterial infections, the most common cause is simply getting older.[30]

Age-related hearing loss, also called presbycusis, may itself have a number of causes, including an inherited vulnerability, natural aging processes that affect hearing, or the cumulative effect of a lifetime's exposure to noise.

The onset of hearing loss may be very gradual, sometimes occurring over a 25- to 30-year period, and many people are not aware of it until someone else brings it to their attention. Because this is a chronic problem that affects most older adults, and because the environment can be modified substantially to increase the opportunity for hearing, I have included a chapter dedicated to the acoustic environment.

Vision Impairment

One in six adults age 45 and older is affected by some type of vision problem, and the risk of vision loss increases with age. Normal changes in the aging eye include losing focus, especially on near tasks; trouble driving at night; and difficulty reading or doing detailed work in low light. Vitamin deficiencies and side effects of medication are culprits, but the most common causes of vision loss in older adults are age-related macular degeneration, glaucoma, and cataracts. Infection or damage to the vision area of the brain due to stroke, head injury, or a brain tumor can also cause problems.

The ability to see can be enhanced substantially with environmental improvements, and there is evidence that some types of vision loss may be prevented or minimized with lifestyle changes. This book includes two chapters dedicated to environmental changes in lighting and daylighting.

Depression

Depression in later life is common, yet some studies show that less than one-fourth of people with depression are accurately diagnosed and adequately treated. The problem may be even worse among the elderly, often because the recognition of depression is complicated by the coexistence of other medical conditions.[31] While it is true that depression is more common in older people than in the general population, it is not an inevitable part of aging. Nor is it something that we can control at will, or something of which to be ashamed. The hallmarks of depression in old age are its coexistence with medical illness and its association with cognitive impairment. Many chronic medical conditions, such as stroke, heart disease, and cancer, may cause changes in the brain that can make one susceptible to depression. People over 65 are more likely to have one of these conditions, which may contribute to the higher incidence of depression in older people. It is often these very factors that can lead to the failure to diagnose depression.[32]

Depression is one of the most treatable health conditions. With so many effective treatments available, there is no reason to allow depression to rob anyone of living with comfort and joy; however, getting the right treatment is critical. Studies have shown that as many as 80 percent of depressed people can find adequate relief with proper treatment. Left untreated, depression wreaks havoc on a person's life, may worsen symptoms of other diseases, and can even be fatal. People who have suffered a stroke or heart attack are more likely to die if they have depression.[33]

Mild depression can weaken the immune system in older people, while treating the depression may help them fight disease more effectively. Researchers at Ohio State University College of Medicine say that people 60 and over often have mild depression, and found that the link between depression and a weakened immune system may explain why older adults are at greater risk for cancer and severe infections.[34]

Diabetes

Approximately 17 million Americans have diabetes, and of these over 7 million are age 65 or older.[35] According to the Centers for Disease Control and Prevention the number of cases of diabetes among adults has climbed 49 percent in the last decade, and as it continues to rise each year, it is expected to increase by as much as 56 percent by 2020.[36]

Recent research published in *The New England Journal of Medicine* (February 7, 2002) shows that diabetes can often be prevented or delayed, even among older adults at high risk for the illness. Results from the disease prevention program led by the National Institutes of Health

(NIH) indicate that simple lifestyle changes can help ward off diabetes, even among older adults. Participants who took a prescription drug reduced their risk by 31 percent. By contrast, those who lost as little as five pounds and took a walk five times a week cut their chances of developing the disease by nearly 60 percent. People age 55 to 60 who exercised and lost weight were able to hold the disease at bay more successfully than any other age group. This counters the myth that only young people can alter the fate of their health.[37] Frank Vinicor, director of the CDC Diabetes Program, commented, "The data show that it's never too late for preventive efforts."

Just as exercise and weight loss can help prevent diabetes in the first place, by controlling cholesterol and blood pressure levels, they play a critical role in preventing complications of the disease such as stroke, blindness, kidney failure, and cardiovascular disease. Losing weight helps lower the body's resistance to insulin, and exercise helps remove extra glucose from the blood and can facilitate weight loss.

Older women and American Indians, Latinos, African Americans, and other racial minority groups groups are at heightened risk for type II diabetes, sometimes called adult-onset diabetes, and its complications. The CDC has partnered with multiple organizations to provide education to diverse groups of older adults about their increased risk for diabetes.[38]

Osteoporosis

More than 10 million Americans have osteoporosis, which means "porous bone," and 18 million more have lost enough bone, in a condition known as osteopenia, to make them more likely to develop the disease. This is a major health threat for more than 28 million Americans, 80 percent of them women. White and Asian women are most likely to get osteoporosis.[39] A woman's risk of hip fracture, the most debilitating side effect, is actually equal to her combined risk of breast, uterine, and ovarian cancer.

Osteoporosis does also affect men, although not with the same frequency as women. This is probably because men have more bone mass than women, and they lose bone more slowly. One out of two women and one in eight men over 50 will have an osteoporosis-related fracture during their lives.[40] While men have only one-fourth as many hip fractures as women, men over the age of 75 are three times more likely to die after a hip fracture than are women.[41]

Bone is living, growing tissue. We can lose bone over many years, but as people age more bone deteriorates and breaks down. Osteoporosis develops when the spaces in the honeycomblike formation inside the bone grow larger because much more of the bone is destroyed than is being replaced. Bone breaks down too quickly and the replacement occurs too slowly, making the bones weaker. Experts do not fully understand how this happens.

Too little exercise and a diet too low in calcium and vitamin D are the major risk factors, while lower hormone levels also contribute to the problem. But osteoporosis is far from being an untreatable consequence of old age. It is preventable, and there is much that we can do to reduce the risk of fracture.

The best ways to prevent weakened bones in later life are a diet rich in calcium and vitamin D and a lifestyle that includes regular weight-bearing exercises. The average American diet falls far below the recommended intake of these nutrients. The body uses vitamin D to absorb calcium, and being out in the sun for a total of 20 minutes every day helps most people's bodies make enough vitamin D. There is much evidence indicating that calcium and vitamin D deficiencies contribute to osteoporosis in elderly individuals.[42]

In a recent (October 2004) report to the nation, Vice Admiral Richard H. Carmona, MD, the U.S. surgeon general, said that bone health is an often-overlooked aspect of health and warned that by 2020 half of all Americans over the age of 50 will be at risk for fractures related to osteoporosis and low bone mass if no immediate action is taken. He made three simple recommendations:

- Get the recommended amounts of calcium and vitamin D.
- Maintain a healthy weight and be physically active. That means at least 30 minutes of exercise a day for adults, including weight-bearing activities to improve strength and balance.
- Take steps to minimize the risk of falls by removing items that might cause tripping, improve lighting, and get regular exercise to improve balance and coordination.[43]

Stroke

Stroke is the number one reason that people move into nursing homes and the third leading cause of death in the United States. Yet many strokes can be prevented.

Strokes are much more common in the elderly, but they can strike at any age. Stroke occurs when the supply of blood that constantly nourishes the brain is somehow altered. As a result, brain tissues either are deprived of oxygen and nutrients or drown in blood. A TIA (transient ischemic attack) is a temporary condition that usually lasts less than an hour and leaves no permanent physical or cognitive effects. But TIAs can be powerful predictors of full-blown strokes. Stroke symptoms usually occur suddenly, coming on within seconds or minutes. The symptoms vary depending on the type (ischemic or hemorrhagic) and location of the stroke in the brain. The warning signs of stroke include:

Stroke is the number one reason that people move into nursing homes and the third leading cause of death in the United States.

- Sudden numbness or weakness of the face, arm, or leg, especially on one side of the body
- Sudden confusion, trouble speaking, or difficulty understanding
- Sudden trouble seeing in one or both eyes
- Sudden trouble walking, dizziness, loss of balance, or coordination
- Sudden, severe headache with no known cause

The American Stroke Association

Time is of the essence—call immediately for emergency assistance, because there is no way to tell if the symptoms will fade or persist once they start[44] and prompt medical treatment can reduce the risk for irreversible complications and permanent disability.

Stroke strikes about 750,000 Americans every year. It is the leading cause of serious disability and the third leading cause of death, killing about 160,000 annually.[45] Seventy percent of the physical decline that occurs with aging is related to modifiable factors, including smoking, poor nutrition, and physical inactivity. By taking advantage of recommended preventive health and screening services and by making healthy lifestyle changes, Americans can improve their odds for healthy aging.

About 80 percent of strokes are *ischemic,* occurring when the blood flow in an artery leading to the brain is somehow blocked. Deprived of oxygen and nutrients from lack of blood, brain cells begin to die within minutes. Another 20 percent of strokes are *hemorrhagic,* meaning they are caused by a ruptured blood vessel, often related to high blood pressure and smoking.[46]

To reduce stroke risk limit saturated fat and cholesterol intake and exercise regularly. Aerobic exercise reduces risk of stroke in many ways. Exercise can lower blood pressure, increase levels of high-density lipoprotein (HDL) also known as "good" cholesterol, and improve the overall health of blood vessels and the heart. It also helps people lose weight and control diabetes and stress.

In reviewing the chronic problems and diseases that affect most older adults, in almost every instance better nutrition and exercise are identified as the interventions most likely to bring about improvement.

Exercise and Better Nutrition

If past trends are any indication, some chronic conditions may become more common in the future. If disease rates rise while the number of older people grows, an increase in the number of people with chronic conditions can be expected. In reviewing the chronic problems and diseases that affect most older adults, in almost every instance better nutrition and exercise are identified as the interventions most likely to bring about improvement.

Using targets set for physical activity, nutrition, weight, pneumonia vaccination, and injuries and deaths due to falls *The State of Aging and Health* report of 2000 found the country was not meeting goals for improving the health of older Americans.[47] This indicates that Americans, though living longer, are not necessarily living in better health during their senior years.[48]

We can improve the odds for healthy aging simply by taking advantage of recommended preventive health services and by making healthy lifestyle changes. In fact, 70 percent of the physical decline that occurs with aging is related to modifiable factors, including smoking, poor nutrition, physical inactivity, and failure to use preventive and screening services.[49] Research shows that simple behavioral changes can improve the health condition of even the oldest old.[50]

The challenge is to encourage people to reduce preventable health risks, thereby increasing the number of additional *healthy* years they can expect to live. The health risks posed, particularly by lack of physical activity, are inescapable. Designing environmental interventions to support greater physical activity—in both the outside and inside environments, as a way to reduce age-related health risks and health costs, will be addressed in several upcoming chapters.

Courtesy of the George G. Glenner Alzheimer's Day Care Centers, San Diego, CA

"Because my memory has problems doesn't mean my feelings do."—Anonymous.

Alzheimer's Disease

With advancing age many people experience some change in cognitive ability, including memory as well as a range of other intellectual functions. How big a change varies greatly, and cognitive decline may not be inevitable as we age.

Memory Loss and Normal Aging

Remembering and forgetting are perfectly normal parts of everyday life. Trying to retain every bit of information we're exposed to throughout life would be overwhelming and inefficient, even for the supercomputer we call our brain, so forgetting may be almost as important as remembering. It isn't clear how the brain sorts out what goes into long-term memory and what doesn't, but it is likely that this process is influenced by many things, including our emotional state, stress level, the environment around us, previous memories, biases, and perceptions.

What we know is that as we grow older, it's not so much that we forget more easily, but that we may take longer to learn information in the first place. Memory studies have shown that about a third of healthy older people have difficulty with declarative memory, memories that can be consciously recalled and described verbally. Yet a substantial number of 80-year-olds perform as well as people in their thirties on difficult memory tests.[1]

Good news: Once something is learned, it is retained equally well by all age groups. It simply takes a bit longer for the older person to learn it. In practical terms this means that as we get older, we may have to pay closer attention to new information that we want to retain, or use different strategies to improve learning and trigger memories.

What Is Dementia?

Dementia is not a single disease; it's an umbrella term for loss of brain function that impairs thinking, emotions, and behavior. Many, but not all, dementia conditions are progressive and irreversible, although most can at least be slowed if identified and treated. Although Alzheimer's disease is by far the most common type of dementia among people 65 and older, there are other causes. Vascular dementia is usually caused by very small strokes over a period of time, which affect blood flow to areas of the brain related to memory and thinking. Some neurological diseases, such as Parkinson's disease and Huntington's disease, can cause dementia because of their effects on brain tissue, and dementia quite often emerges in the later stages of AIDS.[2]

What Is Alzheimer's Disease?

Although Alzheimer's disease is more common in older adults, it is not a normal consequence of aging. The disease process may begin in the brain as many as 20 years before the symptoms of Alzheimer's appear. While the cause remains a mystery, the pace of research has accelerated in the last ten years, yielding a wealth of new information that will lead to better treatments.

When I was introduced to Alzheimer's in the early 1980s, the disease was still very much a mystery. There were no effective treatments for my mother or my grandmother, and diagnosis was an imprecise procedure occurring late in the disease process. Silenced by the disease, people with Alzheimer's relied on friends and family members much like me, and then organizations like the Alzheimer's Association, to speak for them. Thankfully, times have changed, and we now have well-established guidelines that enable physicians to diagnosis the disease much earlier and with better than 90 percent accuracy.

Alzheimer's disease is a chronic neurodegenerative brain disease that usually begins gradually, causing a person to forget recent events or familiar tasks. How rapidly it advances varies from person to person, but the disease eventually leads to confusion, personality and behavior changes, and impaired judgment. Communication becomes more difficult as the disease progresses, leaving those affected struggling to find words, finish thoughts, or follow directions. Eventually, most people with Alzheimer's disease become unable to care for themselves.[3]

The beginning signs of the disease manifest themselves as memory loss, which may appear to be a normal sign of aging. People with Alzheimer's don't simply forget where they put their keys, but are unable to remember routine tasks such as bathing and eating. They forget what time of day it is, what they're supposed to be doing, where they are going, and what they're looking for after they've lost it. They live in a world that becomes more unfamiliar each day, as people and common places become unrecognizable.

Long-term, progressive dementia ultimately makes independent living impossible. This means long-term care is necessary, either in the home, an assisted living environment, or a nursing home. More than half of those with Alzheimer's disease live at home, cared for by spouses and relatives, but many require nursing home care in the most advanced stages. The National Institutes of Health estimate that more than half of the people who live in nursing homes have Alzheimer's.[4]

Because of its enormous impact on individuals, families, the healthcare system, the economy, and society as a whole, Alzheimer's presents a major health problem for the United States. With the immense responsibilities caregivers face and the accompanying isolation from friends and other social contact, which negatively affect their health as well, caregivers often become the "second victims" of Alzheimer's disease.

Age is a key risk factor for Alzheimer's disease in all racial and ethnic groups. While over 10 percent of all persons over 65, and nearly half of those over 85, have Alzheimer's disease, the prevalence, incidence, and cumulative risk appear to be much higher in African Americans and Hispanics than in non-Hispanic whites. The prevalence doubles every five years beyond the age of 65.[5] Too often, among some racial and ethnic groups where cultural or language barriers may prevent people and their families from seeking a diagnosis, it goes unrecognized or is misdiagnosed during its early stages.

The numbers are particularly significant because of the dramatic increase in life expectancy since the early 1900s. Approximately 4 million Americans are 85 years old or older, and this age group is the fastest growing segment of the population. It is also the group with the highest risk of Alzheimer's. The U.S. Census Bureau estimates that nearly 19 million Americans will be age 85 or older by the year 2050, and as more and more people live longer, the number of people affected by diseases of aging, including Alzheimer's, will continue to grow.

With the aging of 78 million baby boomers,[6] one of the reasons that science and research play such a crucial role is that unless science finds a way to prevent or cure the disease, in less than 50 years the number of Americans with Alzheimer's—4.5 million today—will increase to 7.7 million by 2030, and to between 11.2 and 16 million by 2050.[7] Baby boomers will start to enter the age of greatest risk in 2010. If scientists can find ways in the next ten years to delay the onset of Alzheimer's disease and slow its progress, the number of baby boomers who get Alzheimer's will be cut by one-third; and among those who do get the disease, the numbers who will need full-time care could be cut by 60 percent.[8]

The Impact of Alzheimer's Disease

*Ninety-five percent
of what we know
about Alzheimer's
we've learned in the
past 15 years.*[9]

We now know a lot about Alzheimer's—what it is, who can get it, how it develops, and what course it follows. Ninety-five percent of what we know about Alzheimer's we've learned in the past 15 years.[9] There has also been significant progress in the critical area of early diagnosis, and there are some promising leads on possible treatments. All of this research has deepened our understanding of this devastating disease. It has also expanded our knowledge about other late-life neurodegenerative diseases, brain function in healthy older people, and ways to minimize normal age-related cognitive decline.[10]

What We Know About Alzheimer's Disease

In normal aging, nerve cells (neurons) in the brain are not lost in large numbers; in Alzheimer's disease, however, many nerve cells stop functioning, lose connections with other nerve cells, and die. At first, Alzheimer's destroys neurons in parts of the brain that control memory, including the hippocampus and related structures. Then as nerve cells in the hippocampus stop working properly, short-term memory fails, and a person's ability to do easy and familiar tasks often begins to decline. Alzheimer's later attacks the cerebral cortex—the outer layer of neurons in the brain, particularly the area responsible for language and reasoning—and at this point, begins to take away language skills and change a person's ability to make judgments.

Personality changes may also occur. Emotional outbursts and disturbing behaviors, such as wandering, become more frequent as the disease progresses. Eventually, as many other areas of the brain are affected, the person with Alzheimer's becomes less and less responsive to the outside world.

What Causes Alzheimer's?

The most established risk factors for Alzheimer's disease are age and genetics. Most cases of the disease develop in people older than 60; this is referred to as late-onset Alzheimer's. We don't fully understand the cause of late-onset Alzheimer's, but having a positive family history increases the risk of Alzheimer's disease from two to four times.[11] In contrast, in a very few families who develop early-onset Alzheimer's, we know exactly what causes the disease. In these families, affected persons (about half of the children of an affected parent) get the disease in their thirties, forties, or fifties. These individuals have mutations in one of three genes that have been identified. So in the rare cases in which the cause of the disease is known, the genetic findings show that the cause relates to beta-amyloid

10 WARNING SIGNS OF ALZHEIMER'S

1. **Memory loss.**
   One of the most common early signs of dementia is forgetting recently learned information. While it's normal to forget appointments, names or telephone numbers, those with dementia will forget such things more often and not remember them later.

2. **Difficulty performing familiar tasks.**
   People with dementia often find it hard to complete everyday tasks that are so familiar we usually do not think about how to do them. A person with Alzheimer's may not know the steps for preparing a meal, using a household appliance or participating in a lifelong hobby.

3. **Problems with language.**
   Everyone has trouble finding the right word sometimes, but a person with Alzheimer's often forgets simple words or substitutes unusual words, making his or her speech or writing hard to understand. If a person with Alzheimer's is unable to find his or her toothbrush, for example, the individual may ask for "that thing for my mouth."

4. **Disorientation to time and place.**
   It's normal to forget the day of the week or where you're going. But people with Alzheimer's disease can become lost on their own street. They may forget where they are and how they got there, and may not know how to get back home.

5. **Poor or decreased judgment.**
   No one has perfect judgment all of the time. Those with Alzheimer's may dress without regard to the weather, wearing several shirts on a warm day or very little clothing in cold weather. Those with dementia often show poor judgment about money, giving away large sums to telemarketers or paying for home repairs or products they don't need.

6. **Problems with abstract thinking.**
   Balancing a checkbook is a task that can be challenging for some. But a person with Alzheimer's may forget what the numbers represent and what needs to be done with them.

7. **Misplacing things.**
   Anyone can temporarily misplace a wallet or key. A person with Alzheimer's disease may put things in unusual places, like an iron in the freezer or a wristwatch in the sugar bowl.

8. **Changes in mood or behavior.**
   Everyone can become sad or moody from time to time. Someone with Alzheimer's disease can show rapid mood swings—from calm to tears to anger—for no apparent reason.

9. **Changes in personality.**
   Personalities ordinarily change somewhat with age. But a person with Alzheimer's can change dramatically, becoming extremely confused, suspicious, fearful or dependent on a family member.

10. **Loss of initiative.**
    It's normal to tire of housework, business activities or social obligations at times. The person with Alzheimer's disease may become very passive, sitting in front of the television for hours, sleeping more than usual or not wanting to do usual activities.

production. These findings are also supported by knowledge gained from studying Down syndrome.[12] While the only conclusive diagnosis is still an autopsy of the brain of a person with dementia, researchers have made considerable progress in developing accurate diagnostic tests and techniques, and in specialized research facilities, trained clinicians can now diagnose Alzheimer's disease with a very high degree of accuracy.

Mild Cognitive Impairment

Healthy older adults may notice a modest decline in their ability to learn and retrieve new information, such as names. Although this can be frustrating, it does not interfere with their ability to engage in what they need to do or enjoy doing. As some people grow older, however, they develop memory problems greater than those expected for their age, but do not meet all the accepted criteria for Alzheimer's.

Though memory loss is one of the earliest symptoms of Alzheimer's, there are clear differences between what is known as age-related memory loss and dementia—both in the symptoms experienced and in the underlying biological changes in the brain. While dementia involves a broad loss of cognitive abilities, age-related memory loss is primarily a deficit in declarative memory. Forgetting where the car is parked happens to everyone occasionally, but forgetting what a car is—that's cause for concern.

Recently, scientists have been focusing on a type of memory change called mild cognitive impairment (MCI), which is different from both Alzheimer's disease and normal age-related memory change. People with MCI have ongoing memory problems, but they do not have such symptoms as confusion, attention problems, and difficulty with language.[13] Distinct changes in memory that occur over the course of a year or two, and that can be verified with psychological testing, are hallmarks of MCI. Such changes may at first be mild enough that daily functions are not disrupted, and are often noticed first by someone else. Some studies suggest that MCI, a condition marked by repeated lapses in short-term memory, may in fact be early-stage Alzheimer's disease in some individuals—but certainly not in all.

Significant changes in memory or persistent forgetfulness that interferes with work or home responsibilities signals the need for a doctor's help. Stress and fatigue can affect memory, as can depression, side effects from medications, stroke or mini-strokes, or a head injury.[14] In any case, this is the time to work with your doctor.

The goal of MCI studies is to define the features of the very earliest impairment so that when treatments become available to prevent the disease, or forestall its progression, we will be able to identify those who have it at the earliest point and intervene.[15] The objective is early detection and intervention to prevent the disease. Ultimately, researchers hope to develop prevention strategies for persons who are at risk.

The Changing Face of Alzheimer's

The explosion of knowledge that has occurred during the past 25 years and that continues today has set the stage for a hopeful future. It is now possible to diagnose Alzheimer's with a very high degree of accuracy. The Food and Drug Administration (FDA) has approved five medications to treat Alzheimer's symptoms,[16] with more in the pipeline. However, the medications we have now will not stop or reverse the disease and appear to help for only months or a limited number of years.

In addition to these medications, scientists are making great strides toward finding better treatments. Neuropsychological diagnostic tests for Alzheimer's disease, such as those that measure delayed recall, verbal fluency, and overall cognitive status, continue to improve. In one study, researchers at the University of California, San Diego, found that these tests were highly accurate in distinguishing between cognitively healthy individuals and people with mild Alzheimer's.[17]

A number of nonpharmacological approaches are now being used to treat the behavioral and psychiatric problems that occur frequently as Alzheimer's progresses. These help to manage the disease.

A number of nonpharmacological approaches are now being used to treat the behavioral and psychiatric problems that occur frequently as Alzheimer's progresses. These help to manage the disease, allowing individuals with Alzheimer's to live more independently for a longer period. Research has vastly increased our understanding of the transformation from healthy aging to Alzheimer's disease, and the factors that influence the development of Alzheimer's.

Understanding of the fundamental neurobiology of the disease and its impact on the brain is developing rapidly. Three genes that cause rare, early-onset forms of the disease and one risk gene for the more common, late-onset form have been identified. Current research is focused on attacking Alzheimer's disease at much earlier stages, before symptoms begin. Additional strategies for slowing the progression of the disease—to postpone onset of and hopefully prevent full-blown Alzheimer's—are under investigation.[18]

The discovery of neurogenesis and the presence of stem cells in the adult brain has dramatically altered the way scientists think of brain function and its regenerative ability.[19] Though much basic work still needs to be done, researchers are hopeful that effective repair strategies through neurogenesis or other stem cell therapies can one day be developed to restore nervous system functions lost through trauma, disease, or normal aging. The potential to rebuild a damaged adult nervous system may be greater than we once thought possible.[20]

Advanced technology is changing our understanding of Alzheimer's, with state-of-the-art magnetic resonance imaging (MRI), functional MRI, and positron emission tomography (PET) scanners expanding possibilities for early detection and intervention. The PET can spot significant pathology in people who are still functioning normally, by homing in on the glucose that fuels the brain and recording brain activity. A team at UCLA headed by Drs. Daniel Silverman and Gary Small scanned people who had only minor memory problems, and found the images predicted, with 95 percent accuracy, which people would experience dementia within three and a half years.[21]

Lifestyle

The best treatment for Alzheimer's disease is prevention. One factor that is capturing an increasing amount of attention from Alzheimer's researchers is the possible impact of behavior, such as participation in physically and intellectually stimulating activities, on Alzheimer's disease risk. The Alzheimer's Association has initiated a new "Maintain Your Brain: How to Live a Healthy Lifestyle" program, which explores the ways lifestyle choices influence health, especially a healthy brain, as we age. Information on the program can be obtained through the Alzheimer's Association Website (see Resource section) or any of the group's local chapters.

A number of studies in the past few years have provided intriguing hints that challenging activities may be linked to a reduced risk of Alzheimer's disease, and they are consistent with what we know about health benefits associated with being physically and mentally active throughout life. People who tend to age "successfully," with the least decline in cognition and memory, share some characteristics that keep them sharp. Research suggests:

- Physical activity is strongly linked with lifelong brain health. Aerobic exercise in particular seems to sharpen memory skills.
- Mental exercise, especially learning new things or pursuing activities that are intellectually stimulating, may strengthen brain cell networks and help preserve mental function.
- Longer formal education is associated with mental sharpness among older persons, possibly because continued learning creates a "neural reserve" of denser, stronger nerve-cell connections.
- A sense of control or influence over our lives and those of others— believing that what we do makes a difference—seems to prevent cognitive decline, for reasons that are unclear.[22]

If science could delay the onset of Alzheimer's by even five years, the number of individuals with the disease could be reduced by as much as 50 percent over time.[23] For those who are already suffering from the effects of Alzheimer's, the most immediate need is for treatments to control cognitive loss as well as problem behaviors, such as verbal and physical aggression, agitation, wandering, depression, sleep disturbances, and delusions.

The Nun Study

The Nun Study, a long-term research project on aging and Alzheimer's disease, is headed by David Snowdon, PhD, of the University of Kentucky. Six hundred and seventy-eight nuns of the School of Notre Dame have found the means for continuing their service long after they are gone. They have committed to donating their brains to help researchers find clues that will unveil the mysteries of aging; this commitment makes them the largest brain donor population in the world.[24]

Researchers hope to find the causes of and preventions for Alzheimer's disease, other brain diseases, and the mental and physical disabilities that accompany aging. The main question they are trying to answer is at what point the sequence of events leading to Alzheimer's begins to happen. Dr. Snowden explained it this way: "There are many links in the chain—early in life and late in life. We have to find out how to break or weaken those links." The School Sisters of Notre Dame are an ideal population to study because they share so many similarities. They have lived in the same environment, eaten the same food, held similar jobs, have the same reproductive history, and do not smoke or drink.

Perhaps the Sisters of Notre Dame are our greatest examples of aging with grace. Seven of the sisters, nicknamed the Magnificent 7, have lived to be 100 years old. One sister, who pedaled her bike every day, hoped her life would span three centuries. Just a few years ago the oldest Notre Dame nun, Sister M. Matthia Gores, passed away one month shy of her 105th birthday, exhibiting no apparent symptoms of dementia. Whether or not her brain shows the signs of Alzheimer's disease will be confirmed when her gift to science is studied.

Dr. Snowden and other researchers will be learning from the nuns' brains for decades to come. "The sisters' courage is inspiring to me," the doctor writes. "They are doing tremendous things to stop the devastation of this disease."[25] As with the nuns, the real Alzheimer's story is one of courage and faith in the face of adversity, told best by the people with the disease.

Twenty-five years ago there was little to help people with Alzheimer's or those who cared for them. Now there are support groups, day programs, home-care agencies, assisted living facilities, nursing homes, diagnostic centers, and training programs, all specializing in care for seniors with Alzheimer's. It is heartbreaking for the people it afflicts and for the family and friends who witness their steady decline. Helping people with Alzheimer's disease live their daily lives and maintain their cognitive abilities is one of the most important goals of treatment research.[26]

Courtesy of the Life Enrichment Center, Kings Mountain, NC. Photographer: Debbie Vaughan

It never hurts your eyesight to look on the bright side of life.
A hula skirt, a beach ball, and another party at the Life Enrichment Center!

Environment as Treatment

Psychosocial approaches, in particular, are underappreciated, even though these offer some of the best contributions to maximizing quality of life during the course of this tragic disorder. Indeed, thoughtful psychosocial, behavioral and environmental approaches can often have a faster, safer and more effective impact than pharmacological interventions in treating a range of secondary symptoms in Alzheimer's disease.

Gene D. Cohen, MD, PhD
Director, Center on Aging, Health and Humanities
George Washington University

Although there is no cure for Alzheimer's disease there are a range of treatment options for the person with Alzheimer's and the family. A growing number of pharmacological, behavioral, psychosocial, and environmental approaches are available and can be coordinated into a cohesive treatment. Overlooking these treatment opportunities does a great disservice to the person with Alzheimer's disease and to caregivers. Behavioral symptoms such as agitation and frustration, for example, commonly respond to artful distraction. Too often, however, medications—some with distressing side effects—are given when distraction and calm work faster and more effectively.

There is unquestionably a crucial need to find a cure for Alzheimer's disease. Yet with almost five million people already diagnosed, it is time to place a new focus on treating and thus minimizing the symptoms of Alzheimer's disease and related dementias. While prevention and cure are clearly significant goals in combating this disease that steals so many bright minds, our energies can also be positively expended treating those who must cope with the progressively debilitating symptoms until that elusive cure is found.

As John Zeisel and Paul Raia point out in their eloquent arguments for nonpharmacological treatment for many diseases that are unfortunately considered incurable, such as arthritis, multiple sclerosis, diabetes, and Lou Gherig's disease, treatment and medical attention can be provided even when there is no cure.[1] With lifestyle changes, a healthy diet, suitable environmental design, and the use of proper medication, each of these diseases has become treatable. While there is currently no cure for Alzheimer's, we must not lose sight of the fact that incurable does not mean untreatable. Zeisel and Raia stress that Alzheimer's is now at the cusp of the shift from a hopeless condition to a treatable one, and they link nonpharmacological treatments to neuroscience and brain function. Making this vital shift in thinking turns Alzheimer's into a treatable, though incurable disease, rather than the hopeless condition it has been labeled for too long.

The new emphasis on nonpharmacological treatments and our growing understanding of neuroscience is sparking the imagination of caregivers, clinicians, designers, and others concerned with people living with dementia. The recently established Academy of Neuroscience for Architecture combines the best and brightest in science and design. This exciting shift in thinking is creating a new vision as the connection between good design and human behavior is now considered more seriously.[2]

The potential findings of neuroscience and their application to the interior design of buildings bring great possibilities for better, more appropriate building design for those whose needs are greatest. By understanding how brain damage changes perception, we can improve building design for those suffering from neurodegenerative disorders such as Alzheimer's disease.

We can for example, improve mobility and wayfinding in complex buildings by understanding the brain characteristics of people who navigate more easily than others. Complex as such challenges may be, there is great excitement about the reasoning minds of science partnering with the creative minds of architecture and design, exploring pathways to better treatments and solutions. This partnership of science and design is creating excitement and hope that living with Alzheimer's disease is far from a hopeless condition.

As recently as the early 1980s, Alzheimer's disease was still frequently diagnosed as senility, a Latin word meaning merely "old." Scientists and researchers are making great strides, evidenced by the astounding fact that 95 percent of what we know about Alzheimer's today, we've learned in the past 15 years.[3]

Alzheimer's Disease Can Be Treated

Treatment has great potential for improving quality of life at any stage of Alzheimer's disease. In addition to medication for certain symptoms, two courses of nonpharmacological treatment are available: environmental design and staffing/programming (activities, communication, and programs to maximize use of cognitive capacities that remain intact, while compensating for those cognitive capacities that decline). While I have long believed in the power of the environment to affect behavior, particularly for confused persons with Alzheimer's disease, it was during a summer course at Harvard University's School of Architecture that Dr. John Zeisel introduced me to the idea of looking at the environment as a treatment. The goal of this nonpharmacological treatment, he explained, is deceptively simple: to bring about positive emotions and to maintain those positive emotions for as long as possible. Architects and interior designers know that this is possible and that they can help to achieve this end, but we must learn a great deal more about cognitive impairment to do so successfully.

People with dementia face many real frustrations and experience many real losses. They progressively lose their coping abilities and often perceive their environment as more and more stressful. At the same time they have a lower threshold for dealing with stress, resulting in anxiety and inappropriate behavior when the environment becomes too stressful and confusing. In short, persons with dementia are more susceptible to the environment; they are made particularly vulnerable when they perceive normal levels of stimulation as overstimulation.[4]

An important study published in 2003 demonstrated the potential of the environment for contributing to the improvement of Alzheimer's behavioral symptoms. In their summary, the authors suggest that a "balanced combination of pharmacologic, behavioral, and environmental approaches is likely to be most effective in improving the health, behavior, and quality of life of people with Alzheimer's disease."[5]

> *A "balanced combination of pharmacologic, behavioral, and environmental approaches is likely to be most effective in improving the health, behavior, and quality of life of people with Alzheimer's disease."*

They show how the case for environment as an intervention for Alzheimer's disease was made years earlier in the *New England Journal of Medicine*, where it was argued: "Faced with a patient with progressive Alzheimer's disease, physicians may feel they can do nothing to help. This is wrong. . . . Care in a supportive environment can protect function for years."[6,7] Although compelling theoretical and conceptual arguments have long been made for the therapeutic value of appropriate physical environments, until recently little systematic research was carried out to determine if special design features commonly used in Alzheimer's settings are effective in reducing symptoms and enhancing the quality of life for residents with dementia.

Figure 3.1 People with Alzheimer's disease respond on a sensory level rather than on an intellectual level. Familiar and easily recognizable environments reduce aggressive and agitated behavior. *Courtesy of The Sylvestery at Vinson Hall, McLean, VA. Architect: Reese, Lower, Patrick & Scott, Ltd., Lancaster, PA. Photographer: Larry Lefever Photography.*

The 2003 study shows that modification of the living environment can be invaluable in maintaining comfort and dignity. Residential environments that are familiar and easy for residents to understand offer the greatest support. These characteristics are associated with reduced aggressive and agitated behavior and fewer psychological problems.

Provisions for privacy and the personalization of bedrooms also create less agitation. Providing distinctive and varied social spaces was shown to reduce depression, misidentification, and social withdrawal, as did camouflaging exit doors residents are not expected to use.

This latest study correlating behavioral health to the environment in Alzheimer's special care strongly suggests that to reduce agitation, aggression, depression, and social withdrawal, interior environments should be designed in a manner reminiscent of home.[8] Private, rather than shared, bedrooms are quieter and produce less disruption.

Naturally Mapped Physical Environments

Design adaptations work to improve levels of function by reducing demands on the individual's already challenged perception. Most of us use what environmental psychologists call a cognitive map—a mental picture of the environment that allows us to make our way from one place to another. For persons who are no longer able to make and use a cognitive map, a physical environment that promotes safety and reduces fear by directing cognition, even without the person's awareness, becomes treatment.

A pathway through a garden filled with trees, plants, and flowers that returns to the starting point is a design support within a context of multiple cues that reduces demand on the user; it allows one to enjoy walking in a natural environment without the frustration of figuring out how to return. For those with a diminished ability to order their surroundings and get their bearings, sensory awareness of sights, sounds, and smells can help us understand where we are. Donald Norman calls this "natural mapping"—the environment itself contains the information necessary for its correct use, rather than relying on knowledge held in the user's head.[9]

Kevin Lynch identifies the critical link between an environment's image and our ability to map direction of movement. He described how images play a vital role in how we negotiate our way through both familiar and unfamiliar environments, creating a framework by identifying familiar landmarks and recognizing pathways, places, and their boundaries.[10] Landscape designer Martha Tyson uses images and natural mapping in her design of Alzheimer's healing gardens.[11]

With the progression of the disease, persons with Alzheimer's experience increasing difficulty navigating their living space and interpreting environmental information.[12] Calm, structured surroundings can help those with Alzheimer's continue to function as well as possible for as long as possible. Are environmental interventions effective in managing troublesome behaviors associated with dementia, such as agitation, wandering, or loss of function? Evidence suggests that most environmental interventions do accomplish their intended purpose.

Figure 3.2 A pathway through a garden filled with trees, plants, and flowers that returns to the starting point is a design support. *Courtesy of Pleasant Bay Nursing and Rehabilitation Center, Brewster, MA. Landscape Architect: DirtWorks PC, New York, NY.*

Figure 3.3 Calm, structured surroundings can help those with Alzheimer's continue to function as well as possible for as long as possible. *Courtesy of Providence Brookside Manor, Hood River, OR. Architect: LRS Architects, Inc., Portland, OR.*

The vast majority of studies (90%) surveyed by Laura Gitlin and her associates report some level of success, and 10 of 11 randomized clinical trials showed statistically significant improvement for the experimental groups.[13] Special care settings, from adult day care to assisted living to nursing homes, that face major renovation or new construction should carefully consider the value of designing rather than decorating or making constant "quick fixes" to these environments. When the increase in quality of life and the potential decrease in medication costs are weighed, it may turn out that making environmental changes will pay off.

The greatest barrier to environmental nonpharmacologic interventions is the lack of financial resources, or more specifically the lack of reimbursement. Psychotropic drugs are directly reimbursed; employing nonpharmacologic approaches is not.[14] Limited funding for social research has hampered research in this field and, consequently, public understanding of the usefulness of nonpharmacological treatments. In addition, we are still combating the perception that medication is more efficient because it is easier to administer. I have great confidence, however, in the scientists, researchers, architects, interior designers, and other design professionals who continue to work so diligently, and are making important contributions. I believe that ultimately the wisdom of addressing the quality of living for those with dementia from a holistic point of view will be recognized and supported.

Therapeutic Activities and Programming

Activities can also change negative emotions and behavior quickly and promote feelings of purpose, accomplishment, and self-worth. Structured therapeutic activities are the heart of treatment and the motor that drives the nonpharmacologic model. People with dementia who spend long periods of time doing nothing too often experience depression, anxiety, and paranoia. Therapeutic activity can change this, but persons with Alzheimer's

Figure 3.4 Structured therapeutic activities are the heart of treatment and the motor that drives the nonpharmacologic model. *Courtesy George G. Glenner Alzheimer's Day Care Centers, Inc., San Diego, CA.*

can't organize such activity therapies themselves. They lose the ability to initiate activity, often needing a "friend" to get them started. The process of the activity is always more important than the result, and when accompanied by smiles and friendly conversation, it doesn't matter how well the task is completed.[15]

The myth persists that because people with Alzheimer's disease may not remember friends or initiate relationships, they no longer need relationships or social contact. As they lose the ability to make and hold friends, they need more than ever the social interaction, support, and sense of belonging that activities provide. Therapeutic activities and social interaction can work miracles in increasing self-esteem and a sense of belonging.

Habilitation Therapy

Habilitation therapy is a pioneering approach that uses mood to enhance people's ability to live and work to their full potential. The term reflects the conviction that although the brain of a person with Alzheimer's and its function cannot be restored to their prior condition (hence the therapy cannot be viewed as restorative or rehabilitation), the person can be supported to be as independent as possible.[16] In *Learning to Speak Alzheimer's*, habilitation therapy is described as an approach to caring for a person with progressive dementia as one that focuses on validating the person's underlying emotions, maintaining the person's dignity, creating moments for success, and encouraging the use of all remaining skills.[17]

Communication is the cornerstone of nonpharmacological treatment in habilitation therapy, which is radically different from traditional forms of therapy for older adults. Accepting the frame of reference and definition of "reality" of the person with dementia is an essential part of this communication, as is the premise that actions speak louder than words in order to change behavior. Caregivers are expected to change their own behavior or change the environment rather than expecting the person with Alzheimer's to change. This is undoubtedly a more accountable approach with a much higher rate of success.

The physical environment and therapeutic activities become treatment when they are linked to specific brain dysfunctions such as Alzheimer's disease and when they systematically compensate for the functional losses of dementia. When treated consistently in specially planned environments, even those with Alzheimer's disease can achieve higher emotional levels, developing both a sense of self and a sense of belonging to a larger community of residents.[18] Improved quality of life, a slowed rate of progression of the disease, delayed institutionalization, and reduced need for medication are the ultimate measures of success of such a treatment approach.

Design Professionals Can Have a Great Impact

Design professionals who want to create environments that effectively treat Alzheimer's disease must do their homework. Architects and designers of interior environments must understand Alzheimer's disease and the needs of cognitively impaired persons so they can plan public and private spaces that meet those needs. It is difficult to generalize about what a population requires, yet understanding the limitations of those who are cognitively impaired is an important part of developing supportive environments that can help in life functioning over a sustained period. While the need for education is crucial, few academic design programs provide information on the special needs of older adults and those with cognitive impairment.

Design professionals cannot rely on the Americans with Disability Act (ADA) guidelines to define the needs of the growing group of people with cognitive disabilities or other brain-related limitations, such as those related to stroke. For all of its benefits, ADA is not always supportive of the needs of older adults.

Barrier-free and *accessible* are terms that imply design for physical accessibility only. They are used to refer to "special" spaces for the mobility-impaired. *Universal* design is different. Adaptive Environments, a 25-year-old educational, nonprofit organization committed to advancing the role of design, accessibility, and best practices in human-centered and universal design, provides an explanation of universal design:

> Universal design is the design of products, environments, and communication to be usable by all people to the greatest extent possible, without adaptation or specialized design. The concept is also called inclusive design, design-for-all, lifespan design, or human-centered design. The message is the same: if it works well for people at the edges of the spectrum of functional ability, it works better for everyone.[19]

It is hard to imagine a greater challenge than making explicit the power of design as an asset to the performance of the brain. By exploring this link through research and education, architects and designers can provide spaces that meet the needs of all of our society, and have a profound, positive impact on the design of environments for persons with cognitive disabilities. By finding solutions that work for people at the edges of the spectrum who have significant cognitive disabilities, we are likely to end up benefiting everyone. As Zeisel and Raia state, as conceptual and empirical research in the area of environment and health accelerates, it is increasingly clear that a combination of drug treatment, supportive environments, and focused care provides the highest likelihood that persons with Alzheimer's disease can live more satisfying lives.

"if it works well for people at the edges of the spectrum of functional ability, it works better for everyone"

SECTION

II

Good Design
for Living—
At Any Age

Courtesy of the Madlyn and Leonard Abramson Center for Jewish Life, North Wales, PA

Keeping up with e-mail from family, friends,
and grandchildren can be a full-time job for techno-savvy seniors.

Aging Vision and Health

Vision loss is one of the most common and potentially disabling conditions of late life and one that can have serious effects on life quality. Yet vision problems of older adults tend to be overlooked and undertreated. There is a tendency among the public and professional communities to accept vision loss as a "normal" part of aging. Too often this inappropriate acceptance leads to passivity in seeking basic eye care and to needless functional disability.[1]

Vision impairment clearly has a significant impact on the lives of older adults. Approximately 1.8 million noninstitutionalized elderly report some difficulty with basic activities such as bathing, dressing, and walking around the house due to vision impairment. The risk of falls and fractures increases, as does the likelihood of being admitted to a hospital or nursing home or of dying prematurely.[2] Isolation, depression, and poorer social relationships often accompany sight and hearing loss.[3,4,5]

Dimming eyesight and other sensory impairments increase vulnerability and limit the quality of life for all vision-impaired individuals. One-half of those identified as either moderately or severely visually impaired feel their vision problem interferes to some degree with participation in activities of daily living, such as social and leisure activities—the things that provide their emotional and social well-being.[6]

National surveys estimate that as many as 48 percent of all nursing home residents have at least a partial vision impairment.[7] Very often people deny their sight is diminished, making it especially important to be alert for signals that might indicate a problem. Some common behavior signs of vision loss to watch for include:

- lack of eye contact
- unusual head movements
- inability to recognize familiar objects
- inattentiveness
- tripping or bumping into objects
- withdrawal from activities
- losing or misplacing things.[8]

Light and Vision

The decline in both visual acuity and visual performance is a fact of life for older adults. Normal changes in the visual system impact visual ability; age-related eye diseases can cause further impairment. Problems with the aging eye begin with the pupils becoming smaller so that less light enters the eye, which makes it more difficult to adjust to changes in brightness. The lens thickens, becomes less flexible and more opaque, and turns a yellowish amber color. For a 65-year-old these combined changes reduce the amount of light that enters the eye by two-thirds.[9] Older eyes adapt much more slowly to changes in light levels, especially when moving from bright light to dim.[10]

Combined with increased sensitivity to glare and decreased sensitivity to contrast, these insidious changes are a lot for an older person to adjust to. The majority of older persons, including those with dementia, can be expected to have visual impairment. The challenge becomes adjusting the environment to help compensate for vision changes.[11] Higher quality and quantities of appropriate lighting can help minimize the effects of normal aging vision and maximize the abilities of older adults.

Most of us experience normal changes in vision as we age, such as the need for more light or time to adjust to changing light levels. Ninety-two percent of persons 70 years and older wear glasses, and 18 percent also use a magnifying glass for reading.[12] While surgery or medicine may correct or control some common age-related eye conditions, many older adults have impaired vision primarily because of age-related eye diseases such as cataracts, macular degeneration, diabetes, and glaucoma. The prevalence of blindness increases with age, reaching its peak at 85 years of age and older. Not surprisingly, 70 percent of the elderly fear blindness more than other physical impairment.

Visual impairment, defined as vision loss that cannot be corrected by glasses or contact lenses alone, increases with age, and this can mean unnecessary loss of independence and diminished quality of life for far too many older adults. As the older population increases over the next 30

What the World Looks Like to People with Low Vision

Courtesy of Lighthouse International

Figure 4.1.A Normal vision: A person with normal vision or vision corrected to 20/20 with glasses sees this street scene. This area of the photograph is the field of vision for the right eye.

Figure 4.1.B Macular degeneration: The deterioration of the macula, the central area of the retina, is the most prevalent eye disease. This picture shows the area of decreased central vision called a central scotoma. The peripheral or side vision remains unaffected, so mobility need not be impaired.

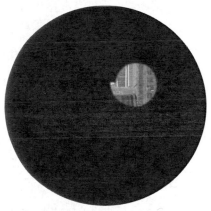

Figure 4.1.C Glaucoma: Chronic elevated eye pressure in susceptible individuals may cause optic nerve atrophy and loss of peripheral vision. Early detection and close medication monitoring can help reduce complications.

Figure 4.1.D Cataract: An opacity of the lens results in diminished acuity but does not affect the field of vision. There is no distorted empty or dark area, but the person's vision is hazy overall, particularly in glaring light.

Figure 4.1.E Diabetic retinopathy: The leaking of retinal blood vessels may occur in advanced or long-term diabetes and affect the macula or the entire retina and vitreous. Not all diabetics develop retinal changes, but the likelihood of retinopathy and cataracts increases with the length of time a person has diabetes.

years, the number of people with vision impairment is expected to increase significantly.

Age-Related Eye Disease

Age-related macular degeneration (AMD) is the leading cause of irreversible visual impairment in the elderly. More common than either glaucoma or diabetic retinopathy, macular degeneration affects roughly one-quarter of people 70 years of age and older, or approximately 3.6 million persons in this country.[13,14] Macular degeneration is the deterioration of the macula (the central part of the retina responsible for detail vision). Central vision becomes blurred and distorted and results in loss of detail vision, making it difficult to distinguish facial features, to read, and increasing the need for light, and reducing color vision. There are two forms of the disease, identified as dry and wet. About 10 percent of those with age-related macular degeneration develop the wet variety, which results in severe and accelerated vision loss.[15]

Currently there is no proven treatment that slows or prevents the development of advanced macular degeneration, though a new treatment, photodynamic therapy, may slow the progression. Laser photocoagulation and photodynamic therapy reduce the risk of either moderate or severe visual acuity loss in some persons with a neovascular form of the disease.[16] It does not, however, reverse the condition, and it is not uncommon for the therapy to require several treatments a year.[17] A recently completed study (2001) involving more than 3,600 people 55 to 80, most with various stages of AMD, looked at the effects of taking different combinations of antioxidants and zinc. Study participants with intermediate and advanced AMD in the group that took zinc and antioxidant supplements experienced the most benefit.[18] For that group the risk of progressive vision loss was reduced by over 25 percent. Although vision wasn't improved, progressive vision loss was slowed. Mayo Clinic ophthalmologists believe the findings offer some hope of slowing the progress of AMD in those with more advanced disease. Persons with AMD for whom supplements might be helpful should discuss treatment options with an ophthalmologist and use recommended supplements only under supervision and follow-up care by their doctor.[19]

Glaucoma is the second leading cause of vision loss in the elderly. According to the Glaucoma Research Foundation more than 3 million Americans have the disease, although only half have been diagnosed. Because the disease causes little pain, it is often not diagnosed in the early stages. Glaucoma is usually caused by increased intraocular fluid pressure, causing irreversible damage to the optic nerve in the back of the eye. Pressure damages the optic nerve that carries the signal from the retina to the brain, resulting in peripheral vision loss. It is estimated that 12 percent of blindness in the United States is caused by glaucoma.

If the condition is detected early, the elevated eye pressure can be treated with eye drops, pills, laser therapy, or surgery. Vision loss resulting from glaucoma is irreversible. Because there are no obvious early symptoms, routine, painless eye examinations are the key to detecting glaucoma at an early stage. A little prevention can help protect vision loss from glaucoma.[20] In 1984 about 5 percent of the noninstitutionalized elderly population reported having glaucoma. In 1995 the rate had risen to approximately 8 percent. Older blacks are as much as twice as likely to have glaucoma as older whites. The prevalence of glaucoma among elderly black persons doubled in the decade between 1984 and 1995.[21]

Cataracts cause a clouding of the lens of the eye that reduces visual acuity and produces an overall haze or blur, an increasing sensitivity to glare,[22] and difficulty reading small print, nighttime driving, and seeing colors in their true brilliance. A cataract is not a film on the outside of the eye, as some people think, but a clouding inside the eye's lens, which is a sealed capsule enclosing a solution of water and protein. The lens focuses available light so that we can see clearly and sharply, but as we mature the crystal-clear lens of our youth progressively becomes more milky and cloudy until it interferes with vision.[23]

Cataracts are the most common cause of vision problems in adults 55 and older; the cause is unknown. The most common risk factor is age. Other contributing causes include long-term exposure to sunlight, smoking (which triples the risk), high blood pressure, high cholesterol, diabetes, obesity, a diet poor in fruits and vegetables, and eye injury.[24,25]

According to the National Eye Institute, over half of all Americans aged 65 and older have cataracts, which are more common in women than men. In the early stages, they do not seriously impair vision, but as vision worsens cataract removal surgery can be performed; in fact, more than 2 million Americans opt for their surgical removal every year. Cataract surgery, generally an outpatient procedure, is one of the most common and successful surgeries today. After recovery 90 percent of patients have improved vision.[26]

Diabetic retinopathy occurs in people with advanced or long-term diabetes and is caused by leaking blood vessels that damage the macula or the entire retina. Each case is unique, but near vision is usually distorted and parts of the visual field may be blurred or obstructed. With diabetes substantially on the rise in this country, we are likely to see a much higher incidence of diabetic retinopathy. Individuals with diabetes must manage their condition and closely monitor blood glucose levels to protect their vision. Laser treatment for localized areas of leakage can sustain the level of vision in the early stages. Severe retinopathy can cause a detached retina. Even with surgery severe vision loss can result.

Vision impairment is not a normal part of aging, but if it occurs due to age-related conditions, injury, or health problems, it directly affects quality of life. While it can reduce independence, mobility, and the enjoyment of seeing, there is much that can be done to ensure those with impaired vision maintain an active, independent, and fulfilling life.

Frequent medical evaluations and the use of special equipment can greatly improve quality of life for older adults and decrease the level of disability associated with these impairments. With the prevalence of age-related eye disorders and conditions of partial sight or low vision it is essential that older persons have regular eye exams.

Lighthouse International, the largest vision research institute in the world, offers numerous information-rich publications on almost every type of vision impairment and vision loss. Practical help is also available in the Lighthouse Catalogue, which features a broad range of easy to see and easy to use products for the home, for the office, and for recreation. This is one of the best and most abundant resources available for reliable information and support in dealing with vision impairment.

Light and Health

The concept of good lighting is changing with recent research findings in neurobiology, chronobiology, and studies in vision and lighting. The science of chronobiology is barely ten years old, but it is slowly demystifying the gift of daylight, exploring the mechanisms by which light governs our sleep, digestion, and immune response, and discovering how biological rhythms can be used to our advantage for health.[27] In the near future, it may become commonplace not only to specify electric light levels for task performance, but also natural or electrical "circadian" light levels, using an entirely new system of circadian photometry.[28]

Until "researchers and practitioners begin to consider, measure, calculate and control the fundamental characteristics of light for the circadian system as well as the visual system" little progress will be made in delivering "healthy" lighting, or lighting that supports human health.[29]

It was once widely assumed that humans were not particularly sensitive to cycled light, but it has become clear in the last 30 years that light/dark cycles regulate many human behaviors, including seasonal depression, sleep/wake patterns, body temperature, brain activity, and subjective alertness. In his opening address to the Fifth International Lighting Research Symposium—Lighting and Human Health Mark Rea of the Lighting Research Center at Rensselaer Polytechnic Institute challenged lighting designers. Until "researchers and practitioners begin to consider, measure, calculate and control the fundamental characteristics of light for the circadian system as well as the visual system" little progress will be made in delivering "healthy" lighting, or lighting that supports human health.[29]

Every time we design or redesign housing for older adults we make decisions that impact the health, safety, and welfare of hundreds of thousands of older individuals. How often is lighting considered as an integral element for achieving the goal of a healthy environment?

Circadian Rhythms

What is circadian rhythm and why is it important to human health, particularly to the health of older adults? Circadian rhythms are physiological cycles in the body that last approximately 24 hours. In mammals, they are driven by a pacemaker located in the suprachiasmatic nucleus (SCN) of the hypothalamus in the brain.[30] Disturbances of these cycles often result from shift work, jet lag, and physiological disorders, some of which are associated with aging. They have become a common problem in today's society, particularly among the elderly. Circadian disturbances are also associated with cardiovascular problems, immune dysfunction, increased mortality, cognitive and functional deterioration, increased risk of institutionalization, and depression.[31]

Light Received Through the Eyes

Light, which is *received through the eyes,* is used for vision and to regulate body functions controlled by the pituitary, pineal, adrenal, and thyroid glands. Altered sleep/activity patterns, body temperature cycles, hunger, and hormone production or suppression are only part of a greater desynchronization of various rhythms in older adults, likely caused by changes in the aging circadian system. Melatonin, seratonin, cortisol, and a host of neurotransmitters such as acetycholine, dopamine, and nonepinephrine are the most significant.[32] In addition to not sleeping well, many individuals are more susceptible to depression and suppressed immune systems. Light is a potent regulator. Environmental light is the primary stimulus for regulating circadian rhythms, seasonal cycles, and neuroendocrine responses in humans.[33,34] Clinical studies have confirmed that light therapy is effective for treating winter depression and selected circadian sleep disorders.[35,36]

Bright light and physical activity have been shown to have restorative effects on cell and rhythm function in humans;[37] however, little has been done to incorporate these finding into practice. The capacity of the circadian system to reset itself using light as an environmental stimulus is reduced in the elderly.

More to the point, many older adults, particularly the institutionalized elderly, don't receive adequate exposure to the bright light so important to the entrainment and synchronization of the circadian system.[38] One study of institutionalized older adults found that they received a median of nine minutes of bright light (>1,000 lux) or 100fc per day.[39] The SCN body clock

Bright light and physical activity have been shown to have restorative effects on cell and rhythm function in humans; however, little has been done to incorporate these finding into practice.

responds only to light intensities which are 20 to 200 times greater than typical interior illumination levels.[40] Common interior lighting does not affect circadian rhythms.

Sunshine Is a Mood Enhancer

It is easy to understand why maximizing healthy circadian function is especially important in an older adult living setting. This explains the new emphasis on creating gardens and "senior-friendly" outside environments.

The best and most affordable source of the bright light necessary for synchronization or entrainment of the circadian system is daylight. Newly discovered retinal ganglion cells—specialized to encode ambient light intensity—communicate directly with the brain. They help to synchronize circadian rhythms and other physiological responses to environmental illumination. This is also true in certain blind persons.[41,42] The recent findings stem in part from the puzzling discovery in the mid-1990s that blind people, with no functional visual system capable of detecting light in the usual

Figure 4.2 Socializing in the garden is an excellent way to receive the bright light exposure necessary for vitamin D and regulating the circadian system. *Courtesy of Hearthstone Alzheimer's Care at Choate, Woburn, MA.*

manner, were still capable of resetting their circadian, or 24-hour, clocks with a shift in day-night cycles.[43]

As days grow shorter in winter months, many people develop depression because they receive less exposure to sunlight. One of the most pleasant effects of sunshine is its ability to cheer people up and make them more alert, as daylight stimulates the production of serotonin, one of the body's "feel good" chemicals. It's like a miracle drug from the sun. When research has given us evidence that bright light and physical exercise can help with depression, sleep problems, and appetite, why are we still using expensive medications instead of the least expensive and most effective prescription available—daylight?

Sleep Disruption

Normal sleep patterns change with aging, but sleep requirements do not change. Insomnia increases. As many as 15 percent of the elderly sleep fewer than 5 hours a night and 25 to 30 percent report frequent night awakenings.[44] When people are light deprived and do not experience the full effect of high light levels during the day and darkness at night, their internal body clock malfunctions. Sixty-five percent of those over 65 experience some problems sleeping.[45] Sleeping pills don't work effectively if taken over a long period of time, and they create daytime drowsiness and mobility problems, contributing to accidental falls and hip fractures.[46]

The majority of research on sleep and circadian disturbances comes from studies of individuals who suffer from Alzheimer's disease, the most prevalent form of dementia, that accounts for 70 percent of those with dementia.[47] The sleep problems associated with dementia are one of the most difficult aspects of the disease for caregivers. The National Institute on Aging indicates that 45 percent of individuals with Alzheimer's are restless and wander at night, one of the leading reasons for placement in a special care setting. Notably, of caregivers forced to institutionalize relatives with dementia, 84 percent say they would take the individual back home if their sleep problems could be solved.[50] Studies are under way to explore whether increased exposure to sunlight might alleviate the characteristic restlessness of persons with Alzheimer's.

Individuals with Alzheimer's are particularly deficient in melatonin.[49] Daylight is known to enhance melatonin levels that decrease markedly with age, in addition to being responsible for resetting the body clock.

Melatonin is currently believed to be the primary hormone associated with signaling circadian photobiological functions. Melatonin levels are high at night and low during the day, and many researchers believe that melatonin can help induce sleep by reducing the "wake-promoting" signals coming from the circadian pacemaker.[48] Daylight is known to enhance melatonin levels that decrease markedly with age, in addition to being responsible for resetting the body clock. Individuals with Alzheimer's are particularly deficient in melatonin.[49]

Researchers have begun to examine the relationship between the agitated behavior of individuals with dementia and exposure to light. Findings indicate that there may be a seasonal fluctuation in frequency of sundowning behaviors which may be related to light exposure.[51,52,53] Bright light treatments have also been reported to be effective for improving sleep in individuals with dementia who experience sundowning.[54,55] Sundowning is a condition common in many individuals with Alzheimer's disease characterized by increased agitation and restlessness in late afternoon.

The sleep and circadian disturbances that affect older adults are associated with a number of other health and physical problems that have a profound negative impact on quality of life. In persons with dementia, age-related circadian dysfunction is more severe and places a significant strain on caregivers.[56] If further research supports the value of light therapy, for older and demented persons, changes in home and facility design should be encouraged.

National Institutes of Health clinical trials are being conducted to determine to what extent therapeutic light, when applied to an institutionalized

Figure 4.3 An NIH research study incorporates a new lighting system designed to combine daylight from skylights with high levels of glare-free diffused electric light. *Courtesy of Rosewood Specialty Care; Hillsboro, OR, and The Center of Design for an Aging Society, Portland, OR.*

population of older persons with Alzheimer's disease, will a) improve nighttime sleep and reduce daytime drowsiness, b) reduce depressive symptoms, and c) reduce agitated behaviors. The research trials at Rosewood Specialty Care for the Memory Impaired in Hillsboro, Oregon, incorporated a new lighting system designed to combine daylight from skylights with high levels of glare-free diffused electric light. To ensure that appropriate therapeutic light levels (250 footcandles measured four feet above the floor) are maintained, photocells record the amount of daylight in the space and send the information to a control panel programmed to either switch on metal halide fixtures or adjust dimmable fluorescent fixtures to maintain the proper light levels. Research indicates the circadian system is much more sensitive to cool light in the blue-green range;[57,58] light sources used during the day are cool (6500 Kelvin). At night warm light (3000 Kelvin) is provided in the common areas at much lower light levels than during the day. The resident bedroom lights are turned off.

This is the largest, most complete study of its kind ever conducted and if the research supports the value of light as therapy for older and demented persons, changes in home and facility design should be indicated. The results will be invaluable in guiding the design of better and healthier lighting systems for use in healthcare settings.

Light Absorbed Through the Skin

Vitamin D is produced by direct sunlight *absorbed through the skin* and has proved to be more important to good health than scientists previously suspected. Vitamin D not only helps absorb calcium, which builds stronger bones, but also protects against a host of other problems, including heart disease, rheumatoid arthritis, multiple sclerosis, and cancers of the breast, prostate, and colon. Vitamin D deficiency has been linked to an increased risk of falls among people over 65 and to persistent and unexplained bone and joint pain. Falls are the leading cause of accidental death in the elderly population,[59] and 90 percent of hip fractures occur as the result of a fall.[60] The risk of hip fractures increases with age

Vitamin D is produced by direct sunlight absorbed through the skin.

It is now recognized that vitamin D deficiency is widespread in the United States and Europe. Young, middle-aged, and older adults are at risk, with African Americans being at particularly high risk for vitamin D deficiency. Vitamin D is essential for efficient absorption of calcium and maintaining bone mass and skeletal health throughout life. A deficiency results in muscle weakness, muscle aches, bone aches, and pains and that can precipitate and exacerbate osteoporosis and masquerade as other illnesses, including fibromyalgia.[61] When mobility decreases, so does our exposure to the outdoors, with its high light levels and full-spectrum sunlight.[62] According to Dr. Michael Holick, head of the Vitamin D Skin and Bone Research Laboratory at Boston University Medical Center, "Probably 40 percent of otherwise healthy adults between 49 and 65 years old and half of all people over 65 are deficient."[63] Though elderly individuals have a diminished capacity to synthesize vitamin D from sunlight, about 15 to 20 minutes of sunscreen-free exposure on the hands, face, and forearms several times a week in the morning or late afternoon should provide adequate vitamin D. For many older adults, that might mean a short walk or morning coffee in the garden. Yet many older people aren't getting enough. The risk of skin damage is managed by limiting the duration of unprotected exposure, as well as choosing the right time of day.[64] Application of sunscreen with an SPF factor of 8 or above reduces vitamin D production by 95 percent.[65] For those who remain outside after the first 20 minutes of exposure, sunscreen is recommended.[66]

> *Vitamin D is essential for efficient absorption of calcium and maintaining bone mass and skeletal health throughout life.*

It is clear that exposure to ultraviolet (UVB) radiation from the sun is our most efficient source of vitamin D. However, those who live in the northeastern part of the United States and in Canada during winter months experience less sun and less outdoor exposure to sunlight than those in southern states. Fortified milk, breakfast cereals, and orange juice are among the most common sources of vitamin D available to those who don't get enough from the sun. Multivitamins can also provide sufficient vitamin D.

Pain Relief

Sunlight may also play an important part in pain relief. Bruce Rabin, medical director of the lifestyle program at the University of Pittsburgh Medical Center, found that patients who were placed in sunlit rooms after surgery reported less pain and took less pain medication than those in darker rooms. Rabin suspects this response is related to serotonin, and that sunlight can also dampen the perception of pain from other conditions, such as arthritis.[67,68]

Research and the Circadian System

Research about the circadian system is ongoing. A growing body of evidence-based research confirms the connection between light, health, and the importance of circadian rhythms.

- Light has been successfully used to treat seasonal affective disorder (SAD).
- We need daily exposure to daylight to reset our biological clocks. A morning walk provides daily exercise and exposure to necessary blue wavelengths found in daylight.[69]

- The natural cycles of light and dark are important for maintaining human health. It is important for older adults to be exposed to bright light during the day, and equally important for them to experience darkness at night.[70] There is growing evidence that exposure to white or bluish light at night negatively affects daily biological rhythms and sleep quality. Older adults should sleep in total darkness to maximize the antioxidant value of melatonin, since light exposure at night will suppress melatonin (sleep hormone) secretion.[71]

- At night red, orange, or amber wavelengths are less disruptive to normal sleep and circadian rhythms than blue wavelengths. For older adults who need night-lights, a potential solution is a night-light with a red filter, which provides enough light to navigate to and from the bathroom, but will not provide enough biologically active illuminance to disrupt sleep cycles.[72]

  Historically, red light has been used to maintain night vision. It was once used to read charts on ships at sea and is used today by pilots to read instruments and charts while flying at night. When we awake at night our eyes are dark-adapted, so that we can see with very little light. Research has shown that falls in the night happen not on the way to the bathroom, when eyes are adapted to the dark, but rather on the way back to bed after exposure to bright lights in the bathroom.[73]

- Exposure to ultraviolet rays stimulates the production of vitamin D.

Extensive research provides a solid foundation to support lighting standards that aid human vision. Research also suggests that the criteria for lighting to support the circadian system are different from those for lighting to support human vision. Appropriate lighting is the foundation of a supportive environment that helps maximize abilities and accident prevention for older adults. Poor lighting profoundly impacts older persons. It decreases their independence, compromises their health, and diminishes their quality of life. We can no longer ignore the photobiological effects of light on the body, and it is long past time that we stopped providing only the minimum light needed for vision.[74] Lighting technologies today are geared toward supporting human vision. Design innovation in lighting technology must begin to address the impact to the circadian system if we hope to impact health and wellness in today's world.

The criteria for lighting to support the circadian system are different from those for lighting to support human vision.

Courtesy of Design Concepts Unlimited, Sausalito, CA

*Watch out, ladies! From 19 to 93, the boys from three generations
are out for their daily exercise and a dose of healthy sunshine.*

Lighting and Daylighting

Healthcare projects are a wonderful challenge for designers. Lighting is an even greater challenge, even for lighting designers, because it can enhance color, texture, and form or just as effectively destroy them. The entrance and lobby of a healthcare setting should convey the message of the healing environment within and set the tone for the rest of the building. Unfortunately, when one moves beyond the lobby to the resident care areas, the vibrant daylight and lighting systems that created the pleasant and visually comfortable environment in the lobby often reverts back to the same old institutional recessed-lensed troffers. This strategy is a poor substitute in terms of communicating the message of a caring or healing environment.

Architects and designers are beginning to better understand both energy efficiency and the impact of the architectural products they incorporate in their designs. As a result, more healthy buildings that minimize long-term environmental damage are being designed, and lighting is becoming environmentally friendly and more focused on sustainability.

Lighting technology has become so sophisticated that there has never been a better time to use a good lighting designer. Good lighting is essential in any healthcare setting, and getting a lighting designer involved early—during the conceptual stage of a project, as buildings are being oriented on the site and as spaces are being designed—ensures that lighting design can be integrated with other systems and functions in the most cost-efficient ways. It is extremely important for the client and the lighting consultant to agree on expectations for how the space will be used, the transitions of light within the space, how color and finishes interact with light, and the physical constraints or opportunities the space offers, such as clearances, natural light, and HVAC needs. If this seems like a less than subtle attempt to encourage healthcare providers to use a qualified lighting designer, make no mistake—it is! Lighting can and will make a greater difference in the success of a healthcare setting than any other single feature except the healthcare itself.

Lighting can and will make a greater difference in the success of a healthcare setting than any other single feature except the healthcare itself.

Daylighting

When the sun is shining brightly, your lighting doesn't have to. Everyone feels better in a bright room with many windows, but sometimes it takes a lot of science to prove the glaringly obvious. An abundance of natural light enhances physical well-being and is a key prescription for designing a healthy building. Daylighting (combining electric and natural light) provides broad-spectrum lighting, has great color-rendering properties, and when used with daylighting controls and occupancy sensors can reduce lighting and energy use during peak demand hours. Although energy savings are important, they must be accomplished within the context of good-quality lighting to achieve the greatest value.

Energy efficiency, sustainability, and the greening of the built environment are on everyone's minds in the design community. Lighting represents 40 to 50 percent of the energy costs of commercial buildings. Recognizing the potential of lighting as a strategy for saving energy, the U.S. Green Building Council's LEED program allocates 40 percent of its points toward building systems and strategies related to energy efficiency. Daylighting fits right into the strategy for energy efficiency by integrating daylight into a space through controls, dimming, and daylight sensing.[1]

Daylighting Strategies

The best lighting solutions avail themselves of abundant natural light— daylight, daylight, and more daylight. Bringing daylight into a building provides both high levels of energy-efficient light and a strong cue as to the time of day. The most common systems that architects use for bringing light into a building and distributing it within the interior spaces incorporate facades with overhangs, awnings, windows, light shelves, skylights, clerestories, and sawtooth ceilings to prevent glare.

Intelligent daylighting means designing buildings with taller ceilings and window openings to help daylight penetrate spaces more deeply. Daylight can be introduced into the building from skylights above or from the sides through windows. Because it is important to balance daylight within the space, the best way to accomplish this is to use a minimum of two sources of daylight, preferably from more than one direction. Successful daylight designs locate large daylight sources out of the field of view.

Figure 5.1 Beautiful clerestory windows flood the entrance lobby at Geer Village with warm sunlight. *Courtesy of Geer Village, a senior living community and regional community center, Canaan, CT. Architect: Heym Dowds and Neeman Inc., Boston, MA. Interior design: Carangelo Commercial Interiors, Old Saybrook, CT. Photographer: Warren Jagger Photography, Inc., Providence, RI.*

Skylights and windows have very different daylighting characteristics and radically different aesthetic qualities, both inside and outside. Windows are glass, but modern skylights can be glazed with glass, acrylic, or polycarbonate plastic. Frosted glass is frequently found in skylights and is double-layered to diffuse light and enhance insulation. The addition of fiberglass fibers between glass layers also provides an attractive diffuse effect.[2] When glass is used it should be specified with a spectral transmittance that admits the blue portion of the spectrum.[3]

Plastics and other materials can be suitable and, in some cases, stronger substitutes for clear glass. Translucent and insulating properties make them ideal for skylights. Inexpensive "bubble" skylight and solar tubes are often considered as alternatives, but unless modified so that the lens or diffuser is deeply recessed at the top of the vertical shaft or lightwell, they produce much too much glare for older eyes. This modification, however, adds substantially to the cost of an otherwise inexpensive solution.

Skylights produce a kind of top-lit architectural drama that windows often can't match, and dollar for dollar, they will usually bring in more light

Figure 5.2 Skylights produce a kind of top-lit architectural drama that is hard to match. *Courtesy of The Episcopal Church Home—Memory Care Center, Louisville, KY. Architect: Reese Design Collaborative, Louisville, KY. Photographer: Bryan Moberly Photography, Louisville, KY.*

than windows and keep the brightness out of the field of view, reducing glare. One important tip to keep in mind is that as long as the light is evenly distributed through the space, a few generous skylights are better than many small ones, in construction cost and the daylight you gain per dollar.

In terms of solar efficiency, well-oriented windows are generally better attuned to seasonal changes than a skylight. Because window openings are vertical, they admit more of the low-angled sun in winter when it's so welcome, while blocking much of the high-angled summer sun to prevent excessive heat gain. Contemporary windows are double or triple-glazed for energy efficiency, and most have low-e coatings to reduce solar heat gain and radiant cooling. As a result their visible light transmittance (VLT) drops to 30 to 65 percent. These large windows will enhance the light in a space for vision but will not allow a resident sitting within 12 inches of a very large window (greater than 3 ft × 5 ft) the necessary light to affect circadian rhythm.[4] Windows and the light they allow into a space do enhance the ambiance of the space, but without question, older adults must get outside for a minimum of 20 to 30 minutes in the morning or late afternoon to receive the required levels of natural light for good health.

The sun is a dynamic energy source for all life and can be our friend, depending on how we treat it. The intensity and duration of natural light not only affects our vision, but also triggers biological, physiological, and psychological responses.

Managing direct sunlight and the resulting solar heat gain is one of the continuing challenges for good interior natural light control. Europeans have practiced energy conservation and shading practices for most of the twentieth century.[5] The ideal shading system permits sufficient natural light without glare, but short of sunglasses there is no one all-purpose shading system that allows optimal light for activities, tasks, and comfort. Interior shading options supply solar protection, ensure diffused light and glare control, reduce interior heat gain, and reduce fading of interior furnishing. Appropriately selected shades conserve energy and reduce associated heating and cooling costs.

Today manufacturers make a large variety of shading products. While shades are available in both vertical and horizontal styles, vertical louvers are not well suited to environments for older adults. Light distribution can produce a bright-dark, bright-dark repetitive pattern of vertical stripes, both confusing and hard on older eyes. Contemporary and traditional vinyl mesh styles with manual or remote controls are highly durable, soil resistant, and excellent for controlling glare. Some vinyl shade products are also designed to control solar heat gain. Privacy sheers, which combine the look of traditional sheer draperies with the functionality of a blind, are now available as an attractive traditional-style window treatment for large verti-

Figure 5.3 The light from the large windows provides a connection to the beautiful gardens outside and brightens the ambiance. *Courtesy of Brookestone, Caring Households for Seniors, Omaha, NE. Architect: Vetter Health Services, Inc., Omaha, NE. Photographer: Ervin Photography, Omaha, NE.*

Figure 5.4 The ideal shading system permits natural light without glare and controls resulting solar heat gain. *Courtesy of Christ Hospital, Cincinnati, OH; and MechoShade Systems, Inc., Long Island City, NY. Architect: NBBJ. Photographer: Tim Griffith.*

cal windows. They can be operated with a remote-controlled operating system. This type of window treatment is quite successful in controlling bright daylight coming into a building when the outside light during the day may be as much as 100 times greater than interior light levels.

Normal glazing admits 88 percent solar radiation. When absorbed by walls and furniture it is converted into long-wave radiation, and when blocked by the glass it creates a greenhouse effect. In a building with 50 percent or more unprotected windows exposed to the sun the temperature in a closed room is 10 to 15 degrees higher than the air outside. Solar shades mitigate heat, require less cooling, and permit visibility. Exterior solar shades can reduce air conditioning loads by more than 60 percent, while interior solar shades can reduce air conditioning loads by more than 23 percent.[6]

The Illuminating Engineering Society of North America (IESNA) guidelines for designing daylighted spaces recommend a maximum 3:1 ratio for general luminance to task luminance. Adhering to this formula helps combat ocular fatigue (tired eyes) and eliminate uncomfortable glare in daylighted spaces.

LIGHT SHELF

A light shelf is a great solution for maximizing daylight from windows and removing glare. Windows with a light shelf, a horizontal surface positioned at 90 degrees to the window glass, divides the window into a light-emitting section above and a viewing section below.

Figure 5.5 Windows with a light shelf infuse daylight into a room while controlling glare. *Courtesy of The Center of Design for an Aging Society, Portland, OR.*

Figure 5.6 The best lighting solutions avail themselves of abundant natural light to provide high levels of energy-efficient lighting. *Courtesy of Geer Village, a senior living community and regional community center, Canaan, CT. Architect: Heym Dowds and Neeman Inc., Boston, MA. Interior Design: Carangelo Commercial Interiors, Old Saybrook, CT. Photographer: Warren Jagger Photography, Inc., Providence, RI.*

Natural daylight bounces upward onto the ceiling and then down into the space. The light shelf acts as an awning to shield the lower window from the brightness of the sky, allowing a comfortable view of the outdoors.[7] Daylight can be supplemented with ambient indirect light fixtures that provide softer, more diffused light. Areas can be zoned and controlled by an intelligent system that dims or brightens the light fixtures as daylight levels increase or decrease.

Daylight in Care Settings

Daylight in living spaces and hallways provides not only "real life cues" as to time of day and the season, but a connection to the natural world. In a

Figure 5.7 Mennonite Village BEFORE the window renovations. *Courtesy of the Mennonite Village Health Care Center, Albany, OR, and The Center of Design for an Aging Society, Portland, OR.*

Figure 5.8 Mennonite Village AFTER clerestory window renovation. *Courtesy of the Mennonite Village Health Care Center, Albany, OR, and The Center of Design for an Aging Society, Portland, OR.*

recent presentation to an international lighting research symposium Eunice Noell-Waggoner, a lighting designer with years of experience in lighting for senior environments and long-term-care settings, described three care settings that effectively incorporated daylighting to the pleasure and delight of their residents.

The Mennonite Home in Albany, Oregon, was built in the 1980s after the energy crisis of the late 1970s.

The high south facing clerestory windows bring ample daylight into the corridor. Many of the residents are in wheelchairs, and the light measurement of 350 fc was taken at the height of their eyes. The director of nurses reported that the residents "may have an occasional bad night, but no consistent problems with sleeping. In fact, she could not understand what "sleep problems" nurses from other facilities were complaining about. The daylight in the corridors remains a very important feature not only for the residents, but for the staff as well. An architect hired for modifications was emphatically told, "Don't change the daylight."

Wiley Creek Assisted Living Facility in Sweet Home, Oregon, was designed with the apartments surrounding a central area topped with a large skylight with diffused glazing. During construction the director changed the original skylight specification from diffused glazing to clear glass, which resulted in a huge problem with glare and heat gain. The problem was solved with the use of adjustable shades, which now filter the light and block the heat during the summer, however, residents prefer the shades open during the winter months. Light measurements taken in late July showed readings of 8,200 fc outside, with readings of 720 fc in one of the neighborhoods and 840 fc in another. Inside measurements were taken in the second-floor sitting area at 4 feet above the floor with

Figure 5.9 The skylight at Wiley Creek Assisted Living Facility, Sweet Home, OR. *Courtesy of Wiley Creek Assisted Living Facility, Sweet Home, OR, and The Center of Design for an Aging Society, Portland, OR. Architect: Christopher Graeff, Portland, OR.*

Figure 5.10 The lovely indoor garden at Alpine Court provides light and a place to walk when weather doesn't permit being outside. *Courtesy of Alpine Court, Eugene, OR. Architect: LRS Architects, Inc., Portland, OR.*

the shades closed. These light levels easily exceed by seven to eight times the recommended minimum light levels in most comparable setting. The residents enjoy socializing in the warmth of the sunlight, and the administrator indicated that the daylight has also proved to be a great marketing feature when potential residents are comparing facilities. She reported only one resident had sleep problems, and they were caused by a physical problem; in addition, she felt the lighting contributed to positive staff morale.

Finally, a lovely indoor garden area was designed at Alpine Court, an Alzheimer's care residence in Eugene, Oregon. The climate in Eugene is wet during the winter months, making an indoor garden an added bonus for residents. Large high windows bring light into the space from three directions. Light measurements in late July recorded readings of 8,800 fc outside and a range from 125 fc to 257 fc within the space. Light was measured at standing eye level (60″ above the floor). The director indicated that residents had few sleep problems, and that there was less sundowning in this setting than in nursing homes where she had worked previously.[8]

Interior Lighting

Should we design healthcare lighting differently? Yes! And we should better utilize daylight as the primary lighting system. The latest research indicates that the health impact of light is related to the length of exposure, duration, quantity, and spectrum, particularly of "morning" light, combined with the relative absence of light prior to sleeping.[9] We should encourage bright light in the morning. Remembering that bright light suppresses melatonin secretion, we should also reduce the amount of electric light at night wherever residents remain for long periods of time, and eliminate light when they are sleeping.[10]

Lighting is a powerful design tool with a powerful impact on many aspects of human behavior and health. Visual performance, ambiance, safety, and security all depend on lighting. With age, the pupil gets smaller, allowing less light to reach the retina, which results in decreased vision. The aging eyes of a 60-year-old person require up to three times more light for tasks than the eyes of a healthy 20-year-old, and by the time they reach age 75 they may require as much as five times more light. Glare becomes particularly debilitating. Physiologically, certain light qualities, such as flicker, associated with old-style magnetic ballasts, can cause headaches, dizziness, and in extreme cases the onset of an epileptic seizure.

The right quantity and quality of light are essential ingredients in an effective lighting system, which should also be "energy effective"—combining the right quality of light with the most efficient lighting system. Energy-effective lighting is essential today, since about 75 percent of the floor space in the typical healthcare setting is lighted 100 percent of the time, and energy efficiency and the life of the light sources greatly impact the bottom line. The good news is that the lighting industry has changed dramatically in the last 15 years—recognizing the great potential for lighting and health. We now have the ability to provide better-quality lighting, with better color, that uses less energy, has a longer life, and for a cost that has actually decreased over the last 20 years in comparison to other building costs.[11]

Lighting is one of the most important design details for supporting the ability of older adults to perform the normal activities of their daily life. In planning care settings it is equally important to use lighting that accommodates residents who are experiencing cognitive difficulties and diminishing physical dexterity. Providing good lighting is a complex task. Understanding that everything we do with lighting has a consequence, often requiring another adjustment, makes it an even more complex task. Simply changing the type of "lightbulb" will not correct poor lighting design. Solving the problem effectively requires providing the necessary light for older eyes to see by raising light levels substantially, balancing natural light and electric light to achieve even light levels, and eliminating glare. That is a beginning.

10 STEPS TO SUCCESSFUL LIGHTING: COMPENSATING FOR CHANGES IN THE AGING EYE

1. **Raise the level of illumination**—Aging eyes need more light. Light levels must be increased to counteract the loss of visual acuity, which occurs throughout the aging process.

2. **Provide consistent and even light levels**—Uneven brightness patterns can produce frightening shadows and/or the illusion of changes in the surface level.

3. **Eliminate glare**—Aging eyes are more sensitive to glare. Glare reduction not only contributes to comfort, it also helps to minimize falls.

4. **Provide access to natural daylight**—The best lighting solutions rely on abundant natural light. Daylight stimulates the circadian and neuroendocrine systems that regulate the body's health.

5. **Provide gradual changes in light levels**—Transitional spaces between outdoor daylight areas and indoor spaces should provide gradual changes in light levels, as well as consistency in moving from one interior space to another.

6. **Increase illuminance at task locations** significantly. Aging eyes function better with high contrast on the task. Good lighting increases the ability to see and enhances task performance.

7. **Use Indirect lighting**—Indirect light sources are easier on the eyes and allow for higher light levels without producing glare.

8. **Improve color rendering**—the yellowing of the lens of the eye impacts older eyes.

9. **Use lighting controls**—Use dimming control technology and motion sensors to control light levels, to harvest daylight and to adjust light levels for day to night variations.

10. **Develop a lighting maintenance schedule**—Lamps (tubes and bulbs) should be replaced when they dim and flicker.

Raise the Level of Illumination

Insufficient lighting is one of the most obvious problems and one of the deficiencies most often cited by surveyors when reviewing healthcare settings. Light levels must be increased to counteract the loss of visual acuity that occurs throughout the aging process. When there is insufficient light, older individuals give up activities—even walking. Fortunately, appropriate lighting can compensate in many ways for poor vision and help to decrease accidents.

The guidelines published by the IESNA were adopted in 2001 as an American National Standards Institute (ANSI) standard. This document, IESNA/ANSI RP-28-2001: *Lighting and the Visual Environment for Senior Living,* describes recommended lighting practice for older adults and should be used as a reference guide. Lighting in the home environment should be specific to the needs of the residents.[12]

Provide Consistent and Even Light Levels

Architects and designers are much more aware today of the need to provide higher levels of even lighting for older individuals. Light levels should be consistent within the space—no dark corners—and also consistent from room to room. Uneven brightness patterns can produce shadows—often frightening shadows for those with dementia, who may not interpret what they are seeing correctly. With changes in depth perception, strong contrast on flat surface levels can cause the eye to perceive a step where one does not exist. Because older eyes take much longer to adapt to change, it is increasingly difficult for the very old to function in suboptimal lighting conditions.[13]

Eliminate Glare

Glare occurs when bright light sources interfere with the viewing of objects or surfaces that are less bright. Overhead glare is caused by excessive brightness from directly above. Aging eyes are more sensitive to glare, and many older adults find it quite painful. Glare and reflection can also contribute to confusion, agitation, and anger, inhibit activity, and compromise safety. Bright light sources are problematic, adding up to eyestrain, headaches, and difficulty for both residents and staff to accomplish tasks.

Most glare can be controlled either by increasing the brightness of the surroundings or decreasing the brightness of the source, or both. Increase the room surface brightness by illuminating the walls and ceiling and using lighter colors. Indirect light sources provide diffused light, eliminating or reducing glare, and contribute to visual comfort. Conceal bright light sources with valances or appropriate diffusers, and windows with translucent shades and blinds on the inside or overhangs and awnings on the outside to reduce glare and minimize accidents.

MINIMUM ILLUMINANCE LEVELS

AREAS	AMBIENT LIGHT	TASK LIGHT
Exterior Entrance (Night)	10	
Interior Entry (Day)	100*	
Interior Entry (Night)	10	
Exit Stairway & Landings	30	
Elevator Interiors	30	
Parking Garage		
Exterior Walkways		
Administration (Active)	30	50
Activity Areas (Day only)	30	50
Visitor Waiting (Day)	30	
Visitor Waiting (Night)	10	
Resident Room		
Entrance	30	
Living Room	30	75
Bedroom	30	75
Wardrobe/Closet	30	
Bathroom	30	
Makeup/Shaving Area	30	60
Shower/Bathing Rooms	30	
Kitchen area	30	50
Barber/Beautician (Day)	50	
Chapel or Quiet Area (Active)	30	
Hallways (Active Hrs)	30	
Hallways (Sleeping Hrs)	10	
Dining (Active Hrs)	50	
Medicine Prep	30	100
Nurses Station (Day)	30	50
Nurses Station (Night)	10	50
Physical Therapy Area (Active Hrs)	30	50
Occupational Therapy (Active Hrs)	30	50
Examination Room (Dedicated)	30	100
Janitors Closet	30	
Laundry (Active Hrs)	30	50
Clean/Soiled Utility	30	
Commercial Kitchen	50	100
Food Storage (Non-Refrig.)	30	
Staff Toilet Area	20	60

* Utilization of daylight is encouraged in entryways to provide a transition between outside and interior illumination levels.

Note: Ambient light levels are minimum averages measured at 30″ above the floor in a horizontal plane. Task light levels are absolute minimums taken on the visual task. For makeup/shaving the measurement is to be taken on the face in a vertical position. It should be understood that the values listed are *minimums*. The optimum solution for task lighting is to give the user control over the intensity and positioning of the light source to meet their individual needs.

Reprinted from IESNA *Recommended Practice for Lighting and the Visual Environment for Senior Living* (RP-28-98), courtesy of the Illuminating Engineering Society of North America.

Figure 5.11 Window treatments—sheers and translucent shades help to reduce and control glare from the windows. *Courtesy of Village Shalom, Overland Park, KS. Architect: Nelson Tremain Partnership, Minneapolis, MN. Interior Design: Tranin Design, Kansas City, MO. Photographer: Design Concepts Unlimited, Sausalito, CA.*

Color, texture, and natural materials are all part of good architecture and interior design. Yet for lighting efficiency, keeping the ceiling and the surrounding vertical walls light in color is best. Lighting the walls and ceiling reduces contrast, shadows, glare, and distractions. Light is absorbed every time it is reflected off a room surface, with light colors reflecting more light than dark colors. Contrast should be effectively provided between the horizontal floor surface and the vertical wall surfaces, however, to give older eyes a clear reference and help with balance.

Indirect light systems require high light reflectance values (LRV) on the ceiling and wall surfaces and medium reflectance values on the floor.[14] The ceiling should reflect at least 80 percent of the light, making the recommended LRV for a flat white paint 80 or above. Upper walls should have light-colored finishes with an LRV of 65 to 85 percent. Rich finishes and other surfaces of low reflectance can be used below wainscot or handrail height with a minimum negative impact. Floor surfaces should have a light reflectance of 30 to 40 percent. This will keep the floor surface color in a medium color value range. Matte surface finishes, rather than highly reflective surfaces, are also a good strategy to control glare.

Provide Access to Natural Daylight

A growing body of evidence suggests that light has nonvisual or photobiological effects on health and wellness. Evidence has also been found of the many benefits of providing access to safe, inviting outside spaces and abundant natural light. Sunlight stimulates and helps to regulate the body's health. Sleep disturbances and depression can both be improved with expo-

Figure 5.12 Pendant indirect lighting illuminates the dining room at High Lookee Lodge. *Courtesy of High Lookee Lodge Senior Housing, Warm Springs, OR. Architect: LRS Architects, Inc., Portland, OR. Photographer: Dave Davidson.*

sure to the higher light levels of daylight. Vitamin D is produced when the skin is exposed to sunlight. Getting outside also offers opportunities for exercise and just enjoying a different view.

Provide Gradual Changes in Light Levels

Because older eyes adapt much more slowly to changes in light levels, it is important to provide transitional spaces between indoors and outdoors.

Figure 5.13 Vitamin D is produced when the skin is exposed to sunlight. Getting outside also offers opportunities for exercise. *Courtesy of the Life Enrichment Center, Kings Mountain, NC.*

Porches and entry lobbies with seating provide pleasant, safe places to sit down while the eyes make the necessary adjustments, a process that can take up to ten minutes. The adaptation time required for the eyes to adjust from bright to dim surroundings is greater than the adjustment time from dim light to bright. For residents transitional spaces are a matter of personal safety. Designers can prevent falls with a combination of good lighting design, skill, good taste, and common sense. It is also important for personal safety to provide even and consistent light levels within the interior space so that residents can avoid moving from brighter spaces into dimly lit environments.

Increase Task Lighting Significantly

Good lighting enhances the ease of performing tasks. Aging eyes see better with high contrast on the project or task. Appropriate lighting helps to reduce agitation, confusion, and anger from being unable to see and allows seniors to continue participating in the activities of their lives that are so meaningful. Articulated task lights allow adjustable, focused task lighting that proves extremely effective at increasing task performance without being expensive. They offer flexibility for different individuals, different task requirements, and for lower levels of ambient light. Articulated task lights with fluorescent lamps, rather than incandescent or halogen lamps, which burn very hot, are a particularly good solution for reading and for craftwork areas. Shielded under-cabinet light sources aid food preparation and cooking, and shielded light fixtures above cabinets add general lighting. Lights in the closet and lighting in the shower increase safety.

Use Indirect Lighting

Indirect light sources—coves and pendant fixtures—are easier on the eyes and allow for higher light levels without producing glare. Today's lighting technologies can provide electronic ballasts, smaller-diameter fluorescent lamps (T8 and T5 types), advanced fixture designs that allow designers to get every lumen possible out of the fixture, and control systems that are the basic building blocks of energy-effective lighting. Fluorescent light using electronic ballasts is the most energy-efficient light source. It produces more light, less heat, and requires less energy to power it.

Skinny tubes rule! Today's top product is the T5 lighting system. The standard 4-foot T5 lamp and ballast system operates at about 89 mean lumens per watt (MLPW).[15] The technology for the new "super T8" lamps with high-efficiency ballasts also shows great promise. While they offer improved efficiency over standard T8 systems,[16] without a dimmable ballast they are not the best choice for older adult care settings.

Use electronic ballasts for all fluorescent lamps. They can boost light output of any fluorescent lamp by about 12 percent more than magnetic ballasts.[17] Today there is an "efficient" electronic T8 ballast that uses 7 to 9 percent less power than a regular electronic ballast.[18] There is evidence that headaches are reduced and task performance increased with the use of energy-efficient electronic ballasts rather than the older magnetic ballasts, which are associated with both flicker and glare.[19]

Ballasts are available in both programmed-start (for long lamp life, especially when motion sensor controlled) and instant-start (for long hours of continuous operation) versions. Lamp burnouts could be reduced by switching to programmed-start ballasts.[20] Motion detectors automatically dim the lights when there is no activity. Too often lighting is an afterthought or considered a small part of a mechanical system. However, the investment in good lighting design results in better lighting, lower energy consumption, and reduced maintenance costs.

Use Lighting Controls

Lighting controls are the most neglected and underused way to save money. Too often control systems are overlooked, especially when the alternative is relying on already overburdened staff to turn lights on and off. These control systems are getting easier to use all the time, and for healthcare settings the simplest system is usually the best. Dimming control technology and dimming ballasts can be used to control light levels and are particularly useful for reducing light levels in the evening. Occupancy sensors that sense body heat or sound emit ultrasonic signals to detect motion. These devices aren't fooled by reflections, oscillating fans, or radiators.[21] Motion sensors, scheduling and time controls, occupancy recognition controls, automated or manual shading systems, photosensors, and photocells for daylight harvesting are available to provide light control. California mandated the use of daylight-sensing photocells over a decade ago. Step level switching can be the answer in some applications.

Improve Color Rendering

The color perception of older adults is altered by the amber tint of the lens of the aging eye. Light sources with a high color rendering index (CRI) of 80 or above will improve lighting quality and maximize color perception. A higher CRI improves visual acuity, depth perception, and perceived brightness,[22] and combined with more vivid colors can make a space visually more pleasant. Lighting designers often recommend replacing low CRI fluorescent lamps with high CRI lamps (tubes) of 80 or above.

"Kelvin" is the unit of a temperature scale that refers to the color temperature of the light source—how warm or cool the light appears. The higher the number, the cooler or "bluer" the light appears. The warm, incandescent-like color of 2700 K or 3000 K can create a more residential atmosphere for resident rooms, dining rooms, and living areas in the evening. The moderate 3500 K, a "neutral" white light, can work in almost any application.[23] Cooler light in the 6500 K range will be needed to augment daylight.

Develop a Lighting Maintenance Schedule

Lamps (tubes and bulbs) should be replaced when they dim and flicker. Flicker, created by old-style magnetic ballasts, causes agitation and headaches and can trigger seizures. It is eliminated with the use of electronic ballasts.

Strategies for Energy-Efficient Lighting and Daylighting

The one-time installation cost for a skylight, combined with energy-efficient fluorescent lighting, dimming ballasts, and photocells, can maximize daylight harvesting, in turn providing much greater light levels on a continuing basis and reducing the amount of electrical energy used to light the space.

The height of the ceiling and width of the space will influence the choice of luminaries (lighting fixtures). Although codes vary, the minimum distance allowed between the floor and the base of the lumenaire is typically 7 ft to 7 ft 5 in. Efficient light fixtures suitable for an 8 ft ceiling height are quite limited.

A better energy efficient lighting strategy to increase flexibility is to maximize the use of indirect fixtures lamped with T8 or T5/HO (high out-

Figure 5.14 Larger spaces are likely to require combining several types of light fixtures, as shown in this room with light valances around the perimeter and pendant indirect light sources. *Courtesy of Alpine Court, Eugene, OR. Architect: LRS Architects, Inc., Portland, OR.*

put) sources by taking advantage of 9 ft or 10 ft ceiling heights. Indirect lighting systems, working in tandem with electronic dimming ballasts and daylight sensors, can significantly reduce energy use and consequent cost.

A larger space is likely to require several types of lighting fixtures—for example, combining light valances around the perimeter to wash the walls with light, with pendant indirect light in the center of the space. Again depending on the size of the space and the height of the ceiling, that may require multiple pendant indirect light sources. Higher quality, indirect lighting design provides better color and more comfortable and appealing distribution of light while minimizing glare.

Today's light source of choice is fluorescent, with an electronic ballast. Although the initial purchase price of incandescent and halogen fixtures can be relatively inexpensive, they are costly to operate. The heat they produce and the increased energy required to operate them make them inappropriate and real energy hogs. The short life of incandescent lamps also contributes to increased maintenance costs. The initial cost of energy-efficient fluorescent fixtures may be high; however, they are dramatically less expensive to operate. Fluorescent lamp technology today produces

Lighting Terminology Made Simple

Term	Definition
Ambient light	Lighting that produces general illumination throughout an area.
Color rendering index (CRI)	A scale used to measure the effect of a light index source on the color appearance of an object in comparison with the color appearance under a reference light source.
Electronic ballast	An electrical device that uses an electronic (solid state technology) transformer to supply the necessary starting and operating characteristics to a fluorescent tube. The speed at which the electronic ballast operates produces no perceptible flicker.
Footcandle (fc)	A unit of measure for the amount of light reaching a subject.
Fluorescent bulbs or tubes	Light sources last as much as 20 times longer than incandescent and use a fifth to a third as much energy. They are cooler to the touch and, contrary to popular belief, do not cause headaches.
General lighting	The basic lighting that provides a comfortable level of brightness, also called ambient lighting.
Glare	Light in the visual field that is sufficiently greater than the light to which the eyes are adapted that it causes annoyance, discomfort, or loss of visual performance and visibility.
Incandescent bulb	The old standard lightbulb, which uses an electrical current passing through a filament to produce light.
Indirect lighting	Lighting by luminaires distributing 90 to 100 percent of the emitted light upward rather than toward a horizontal plane below.
Light reflectance value (LRV)	The amount of light reflected from a color surface.
Lumens	A unit of measure for the amount of light a bulb produces.
Pendant	Hanging by stems from the ceiling. Depending on the style, a pendant fixture can cast light up toward the ceiling or down.
Task lighting	Lighting directed at a specific surface area that provides more illumination for up-close work.
Watt	A unit of measure for the amount of electricity consumed by a bulb—not its brightness.

color quality very close to natural light and undisputed efficiency. Fluorescent lamps (tubes) last much longer: 20,000 hours, compared to 750 hours for most incandescent lightbulbs, reducing maintenance costs. Utility companies often provide incentives to replace incandescent or older fluorescent lighting with energy-efficient, state-of-the-art, senior-friendly lighting systems.[24]

Sustainability

Mercury reduction is at the forefront of pollution prevention efforts, as evidenced by groups like Hospitals for a Healthy Environment. Although certain lighting manufacturers continue to work to reduce mercury content, all fluorescent lamps require some mercury to operate.

Thanks to advanced technology, we now have energy-efficient, low-mercury fluorescent lighting that performs well. Low-mercury fluorescent lamps are no more expensive than ordinary fluorescent lamps, so they are an easy first step to reducing mercury in the environment. In the 1990s the Mayo Clinic in Rochester, Minnesota, a pioneer in mercury reduction practices, instituted a group re-lamping project to install low-mercury fluorescent lighting.[25]

Another prominent factor affecting designs today—in fact, one of the most prominent is the U.S. Green Buildings Council's LEED (Leadership in Energy and Environmental Design) system for rating sustainable design. In lighting, the LEED system awards points for daylighting, indoor environmental quality, and energy efficiency. As an added incentive, utility companies in New Jersey continue to provide rebates for designs that are better than code. In California, the Savings by Design program provides design assistance and funding to encourage designers and owners to achieve LEED goals.

Lighting is one of the most important design details that continues to support older adults' ability to perform the normal activities of their daily life, particularly those with cognitive difficulties and diminished physical dexterity. Over time, an individual's ability to adapt to less than optimum conditions is greatly diminished, and greater care and planning is needed to maximize abilities and preserve health.

NOTES

Courtesy of the Life Enrichment Center, Kings Mountain, NC. Photographer: Debbie Vaughan

We stand for the most forgetful and the most frail. . . . Whatever it takes!

Hearing Loss
and Sound Solutions

Life is getting louder, in case you haven't noticed. According to the U.S. Census Bureau, in 1999 Americans rated noise—street or traffic noise—as the biggest problem in their neighborhoods, and nearly half considered relocating to escape it.[1] The World Health Organization in 1996 declared noise a "significant threat." *Consumer Reports* magazine increasingly includes a quietness rating in its evaluation of products. Noise from cars, airplanes, the neighbor's leaf blower, even a loud fan can increase anxiety, stress, and high blood pressure. Even low levels of sound are annoying, and more and more we are realizing that sound matters!

Hearing loss is the third most prevalent chronic condition in older Americans, after hypertension and arthritis.[2] It affects almost a third of Americans older than 65 and 80 percent of those older than 85, with an estimated 28 million Americans suffering from some level of hearing loss.[3] Yet only a small percentage will seek help for their hearing problems. The majority of people who seek help are seniors—people in their mid-sixties to mid-seventies—usually suffering from presbycusis or age-related hearing loss in both ears. Persons with presbycusis, the most common type of hearing loss, typically have difficulty understanding speech and filtering background noise, which makes listening especially challenging in common social settings[4] There are two major forms of hearing loss: conductive and sensorineural.

Conductive hearing loss means sounds are not being conducted or getting through to the inner ear where the interpretation of sound occurs. It is usually due to abnormalities in the middle or external ear such as a punctured eardrum, fluid in the middle ear, or an accumulation of cerumen (ear wax) in the ear canal. The treatment for conductive hearing loss may be as simple as removing wax from the ear canal or treating an infection with antibiotics, though surgery is sometimes required.

In *sensorineural hearing loss,* sound makes it all the way through to the inner ear, but once there, the signal is dampened or misinterpreted because of damage to tiny fibers in the inner ear, distorting the sound that reaches the brain. Sensorineural hearing loss accounts for about 90 percent of hearing loss related to aging. It usually occurs gradually in both ears, making it difficult for older adults to understand speech clearly and to filter out background noises. They tend to hear lower-pitched sounds better than higher-pitched sounds. People with this type of loss often feel that others are not speaking clearly. Some have tinnitus, a ringing/buzzing sound that occurs intermittently or constantly, and find this worse than the hearing loss itself. Treatment for sensorineural losses typically begins with hearing aids, which help almost all people with hearing loss, but do not clear up all the distortion that hearing loss creates. Cochlear implants—surgically implanted devices—are recommended for people with specific inner ear problems whose hearing loss is so severe that they cannot benefit from hearing aids.[5] Cochlear implants transmit the vibrations of sound directly to the brain, bypassing the ear.

Everything becomes more difficult when you can't hear. When people let their hearing loss go untreated, the problems they face extend well beyond just their hearing difficulties. They can also experience depression, anxiety, and even social isolation. The diminished ability to hear and to communicate is frustrating in and of itself, but the strong association of hearing loss with depression and functional decline adds further to the burden on individuals who are hearing impaired.[6,7,8] Hearing loss in older persons strongly correlates with depression.[9]

Virtually everyone will lose some hearing with age, and many of us will experience a diminishing ability to hear and to easily understand casual conversation. Hearing clearly in large groups will decline gradually until we, or others, notice it. Simple conversations are a strain. Listening to the radio is out and watching TV is a chore, because you have to constantly adjust the volume. We don't hear doors closing, oven timers dinging, or air conditioners turning off. Those around us now "mumble," and the greatest frustration comes from asking "What?" much to often. Hearing loss isn't just losing volume. In some cases, its gaining volume—but only where you don't want it. Background noise merges with the human voice, and while life gets both louder and fainter, you can always count on it making less sense. Welcome to auditory isolation!

Fortunately, though, the negative consequences of hearing loss are preventable for many people. Using the appropriate new technology in hearing aids and devices to improve function, together with good communication strategies, can enable most people with hearing loss to continue to participate in their social worlds.

Jean Gonick, a writer for the *San Francisco Chronicle,* described in poignant, humorous, and highly accurate detail the struggle to cope with hearing loss.

> The first clue that you're going deaf is deciding you pretty much hate everyone. This is also known as social withdrawal. Tired of saying "What?" all the time, you stay home and watch TV with the volume way up, and if you're alone (which you are to avoid saying "What?"), you don't even know how way up it is. Another clue is increased confusion about life itself, which leads to irritability, which leads once again to social withdrawal—but this time everyone's hating you.
>
> How can you hear what the salesperson is mumbling when he has to compete with the hideous music that for some unexplained reason plays in all stores? Why does every ring of a cell phone startle you into cardiac arrest? Why does no one say, "Excuse me!" before smashing your back with their shopping carts? When did all your favorite restaurants start hurling their cutlery against metal walls, and when did the world become one hostile, cacophonous bowling alley?
>
> Meanwhile, since I kept saying "What?" I did grow mildly curious about how much hearing I'd actually lost, but not enough to remember to ask my doctor to give me a test. In any case she was one of the people I had to "hate" because she spoke both with an accent and incredibly fast and I hardly ever understood what she said.
>
> Hearing loss notwithstanding, some people really do mumble, some actually whisper and expect to be heard. I stopped even trying to understand them. I didn't even care what these people were saying; it was just so relaxing not to have to ask "What?"[10]

Gonick continues the description at some length and then sadly but accurately concludes, "You may be diverted from an ache in your limb, but an ache in your ear takes you over completely because it resides in the same place that you do: inside your actual head."[11]

Hearing impairment, like visual impairment, diminishes the quality of life for older individuals. Uncorrected hearing impairment can lead to social isolation,[12] depression,[13] cognitive decline,[14] and decreased mobility.[15] It has been suggested that sensory loss may compound the problems associated with dementia and represent an environmental factor contributing to problem behaviors.

> *It has been suggested that sensory loss may compound the problems associated with dementia and represent an environmental factor contributing to problem behaviors.*

The behaviors of older people who are hearing impaired (e.g., confusion, disorientation) may appear similar to those associated with dementia.[16] Because of this, hearing disorders sometimes go untreated or get inappropriate treatment because they are mistakenly identified as dementia.

In 1995, one-third of all noninstitutionalized elderly persons 70 years of age and older (about 7 million people) were hearing impaired; that is, they were deaf or had trouble hearing with one or both ears. The prevalence of hearing impairment rises with age, increasing to more than 80 percent in individuals older than 85—part of the same group (those 80 and older) the Census Bureau projects will experience the fastest population growth.[17] Elderly men are more likely than elderly women to be hearing impaired, and sadly only three-quarters of those older adults affected see a doctor about their hearing problems.[18]

As the older population increases, the number of elderly persons with visual and hearing impairments is likely to increase significantly. The impact of hearing loss on society will also increase, not only because the population is aging, but also because the prevalence of age-related hearing loss has increased significantly since the 1960s.[19] Despite the prevalence and burden of hearing loss, hearing impairment in older persons is both underdiagnosed and undertreated

Strategies for Sound Design

Calling noise a nuisance is like calling smog an inconvenience. Noise must be considered a hazard to the health of people everywhere.

W. H. Steward, MD
Former U.S. Surgeon General

We all want to be free of the unwanted sound we call noise. Many residential care settings are now organized in neighborhoods or clusters, creating a distinctly less institutional environment with a more familiar and comfortable feeling of home. Still, as in every healthcare environment, even in these communities noise is a challenge, and one that is especially disorienting for older persons. Their adaptive capacity is lower than it once was, resulting in greater sensitivity to environmental stressors and unnecessary anxiety.

The issue of hearing acuity affects everyone involved on every level of long-term care. While it is often lost among the many other challenges of long-term care, hearing loss nonetheless remains a stigma for the elderly, a frustration for families and spouses, and is ignored as a healthcare risk for providers.[20] Thanks to advances in acoustical research and cognitive psychology, we can now better understand how the residents we design for and serve respond to the acoustical characteristics of a space.

Supporting independence means we must address auditory factors. Designing a supportive acoustical environment for aging adults—many of whom have mild to quite severe hearing loss and some of whom have cognitive loss as well, is a difficult challenge. The problem is made more complex when we factor in that while acoustics is one of the most critical issues

Noise is a challenge, and one that is especially disorienting for older persons.

in designing for older adults and long-term care settings, it is also one of the areas of design least understood by architects and designers. The decline of a person's hearing capacity often contributes to behaviors that cause us to question the person's cognition, coordination, memory, social skills, and, ultimately, independence. Ambient sound can agitate, distract, and disorient persons experiencing hearing loss, affecting their personal well-being. Incorporating furnishings and technologies designed to absorb or muffle unwanted sound can be highly effective, but these measures address only part of the problem.

Planning

People usually don't think about acoustics until it becomes a problem, but leaving the sound environment to chance places quality of life and the quality of the care environment at risk. While sound may seem like the least controllable part of an environment, there are in fact a number of steps that can reduce ambient noise. It is important to develop recommendations or strategies to meet the specific needs of the care setting, the culture of the community, and the activities and objectives designated as most important by the staff.

Plan and plan early. The time to set acoustic goals is early in the design phase—during concept or early schematic design—when the entire design team can influence the outcome. Approaching acoustic design in this way, instead of coming in after construction is under way or completed is more effective and allows greater flexibility in design innovation. Although buildings can be acoustically treated after construction, this is generally more expensive and not as effective as designing the proper acoustics from the start. Windows and doors that have the optimal sound transmission class (STC) ratings make it easier to insulate spaces from outside noise. The ability to diminish ambient noise, however, is only as good as the weakest noise barrier; for example, high STC rated walls are compromised when combined with hollow-core doors and standard windows.

Auditory Assessment

Noise is one of the most invasive aspects of any healthcare environment. The increase in the number of residents, their activity levels, and technological advances in equipment and communication devices have caused overall noise levels to rise steadily in the past 25 years. Susan Mazer, a leading advocate for better sound environments in healthcare settings, suggests an auditory assessment to help identify the factors that may be causing unsatisfactory noise levels. An assessment makes it much easier to develop specific design strategies that will result in a more therapeutic and appropriate auditory environment.[21]

Acoustic Enhancement

Design for Sound Control

Probably the least expensive and most effective way to reach acoustic goals begins with careful space planning and establishing an acceptable level of sound for the continuous volume level. Sound levels vary, and unfortunately there is no single acoustical material or noise-control solution. The recommended average for a residential community is 50 dB (decibels). To support a healthy sound environment, we must begin with the structural and design components that have auditory impact—factors such as flooring, walls, ceiling materials, doors, and windows—and work them all into an effective acoustical design.[22]

Environmental surfaces—floors, walls, ceilings—usually are hard and sound reflecting, not sound absorbing, creating poor acoustic conditions. There are two types of sound affecting the noise level in a building. Airborne sounds are created by sound waves traveling through the air, while impact sound is the noise transmitted when one object hits another. Sound reduction is affected by choices made in floor systems (carpet, wood, or tile), the substrate (plywood or lightweight concrete), the ceiling (gypsum board or acoustic tile), and any insulation in the plenum. Sound transmission, whether it is impact sound or airborne sound, can be limited by selecting the right material for these components and installing them appropriately.

Without adequate acoustical treatment the combination of hard-surface floors and high ceilings creates loud, cavernous spaces. A delightful, bright dining room with a high, open ceiling to a balcony can provide abundant light, plenty of space, and lots of noise as sound reverberates and makes conversation unintelligible.

FLOORS

Even with elevated ceilings, carpeted floors help by tempering the movement of conversational sound from one table to the next when residents are dining. Carpet will absorb footfall and traffic noise up to approximately 3 feet above the floor level, but when cleaning and vacuuming begin, sounds resonate at disturbing levels, which become even more disturbing as they rise upward. Hard-surface floors allow sound to bounce from one hard surface to another, creating a cacophony of noise and distraction. Flooring solutions are discussed in greater detail in Chapter 9.

WALLS

Noise created by conversation, television, and music occurs when vibrations from sound waves strike the wall and reverberate through the space. Reducing the reverberations is the goal. So how can walls be made as

Figure 6.1 Carpet helps to absorb noise at ground level and control conversational noise. *Courtesy of Highland Ridge Senior Campus Assisted Living, Williamsburg, IA. Architect: KKE Architects. Interior Design: Encompass Interiors, St. Paul, MN. Photography: Scott Gilbertson.*

soundproof as possible? Thoughtfully designed acoustic plans can treat television, music, and activity rooms where the most sound is likely to be generated by constructing parallel wall separations with a dead space of at least 2 inches between the two walls of sheetrock. Building sound walls for specific spaces is not costly.

CEILINGS

Ceilings are critical, because they're the largest, most unencumbered surfaces in an environment. Since the ceiling helps to control what and how well the occupants of a space hear, acoustical factors are perhaps the most critical characteristics of ceiling performance. Environmental interventions that have proven particularly effective for reducing noise and improving acoustics include the use of high-performance sound-absorbing ceiling tiles.[23] Although sound waves can travel through ductwork, under doors, and through other cracks in the room, a good acoustically designed ceiling tile will absorb sound waves regardless of which direction they travel.

A recently completed study undertaken at the Karolinska Institute of Medicine in Sweden found that when high-performance, sound-absorbing ceiling tiles were used, the overall average noise levels were less, peaks were reduced, sleeping was better, patient satisfaction with their quality of care was higher, and patients strongly believed that staff were giving them better care. With poor acoustics under noisy conditions, staff experienced more stress and fatigue and considered their work more demanding.[24]

When noise reduction is the goal, it is important to look at the NRC and CAC ratings of acoustic tiles. The noise reduction coefficient (NRC) will tell you how much sound a product absorbs. The NRC ranges from 0 to 1.0, and the higher the number, the more absorptive the tile. A rating of 0.95 means than 95 percent of the sound is absorbed and 5 percent is reflected back into the room. A higher NRC is recommended for settings for older adults. The ceiling attenuation class (CAC), formerly referred to as the sound transmission class (STC), will show how well a particular ceiling tile prevents sounds from passing into the room below. An average product performance rating is 35 to 39; the highest-performing product has a value of 45 to 49.[25]

With the growing use of indirect lighting, manufacturers have improved the light reflectance value (LRV) of acoustical ceiling tiles, resulting in bet-

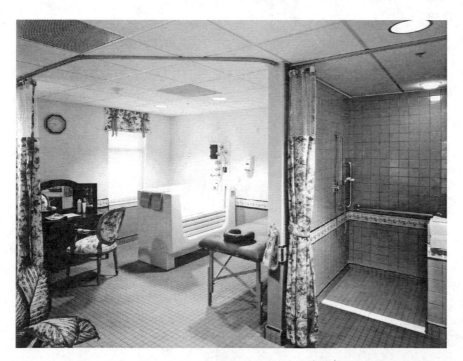

Figure 6.2 Bath Spa at Aldersgate. *Courtesy of Cuthbertson Village at Aldersgate CCRC, Charlotte, NC. Architect: Freeman White Inc., Charlotte, NC. Photographer: Tim Buchman.*

ACOUSTICAL TERMINOLOGY

Acoustics: The science of sound: its production, transmission, and effects.

Acoustical environment: The acoustical characteristics of a space or room influenced by the amount of acoustical absorption, or lack of it, in the space.

Attenuation: A reduction in a sound's energy or sound pressure level (SPL).

Background noise: All ambient noise remaining after considering one sound as a signal (speech). Typically measured as the average sound pressure level (SPL) within different frequency bands and used in calculations of signal-to-noise ratios.

Ceiling attenuation class (CAC): Formerly referred to as sound transmission class, this categorization indicates how well a particular ceiling tile prevents sound from passing into the room below.

Decibel (dB): Sound level in Bels as a logarithmic ratio. Sound intensity is described in decibels.

Hearing impairment: Hearing loss that may be due to any of numerous causes, including illness, disease, or exposure to excessively high noise levels. In general, hearing impairment means mild to severe hearing loss, in contrast to deafness, which is generally defined as the possession of little or no residual hearing ability, with or without the aid of a listening device.

Health Insurance Portability and Accountability Act (HIPAA): A law that requires healthcare providers to take reasonable safeguards to ensure that patients' healthcare information remains private. What's reasonable is not defined and is affected by a number of variables.

Noise: Unwanted sound that is obtrusive or interferes with listening. Noise does not have to be excessively loud to qualify as interference.

Noise reduction coefficient (NRC): A measure of the degree to which the ceiling absorbs key frequencies. An NRC of 0.80 means that the ceiling panel will absorb 80 percent of the sound and reflect 20 percent of the sound back into the space.

Reverberation: The continued reflection of sound from surfaces after its source has ended. Reverberation continues until the sound waves lose energy through absorption and eventually die out.

Sound transmission class (STC): A measure of the effectiveness of the wall or ceiling as a barrier to airborne sound transmission between closed spaces, such as rooms and offices. The higher the number the better the ability to obstruct sound transmission. A minimum of 35 is preferable.

Sound: The sensation felt when the eardrum is acted upon by air vibrations within a limited frequency range (20 Hz to 20 kHz).

Sound masking: The process by which the threshold for hearing one sound is raised due to the presence of another sound. Electronically generated sound sources have been developed to cover disruptive sounds, such as other people's conversation and activity. To be effective the sound masking level should generally be 3 to 5 dB louder than incoming noise levels.

ter light reflectance and greater energy efficiency. In addition, most major manufacturers now carry acoustical ceiling tile products that are made for humid climates. Additional ceiling tile products are designed to inhibit growth of mold and mildew. Focusing on the purpose of the space and the needs of the occupants will definitely help designers make better design and material choices.

Noise can be a significant source of distraction, and because bathing rooms tend to be especially noisy, they often trigger disruptive behavior in individuals with cognitive impairment. Sound quality is an important part of a pleasant bathing experience, especially for persons with Alzheimer's disease, other cognitive impairments, or hearing loss. Significant benefits may be achieved by using attractive, acoustically designed, moisture-, mold-, and mildew-resistant ceiling tile in these spaces.[26]

There are excellent acoustic ceiling tile products on the market today to meet many needs. Halcyon Climaplus (USG Interiors) ceiling panels are fine-textured fiberglass panels with a high resistance to heat and humidity. They offer an NRC of 1.00 and a light reflectance value (LRV) of 0.88. Harmoni (Illbruk) is mold resistant and fire retardant, with a subtle surface pattern and an NRC of 0.90.

Sound and Equipment Standards

One of the most profound changes in acoustical engineering in the last 25 years has been the movement toward sound quality as a method of evaluating products and environments. Encouraging better sound quality doesn't necessarily mean "silencing" products or the environment. Rather, it means applying good acoustic methods in order to quiet noisy and annoying products.[27]

Of course, absorbing, muffling, neutralizing and shutting out unwanted sounds can only get us so far without being matched by a commensurate effort to stop noise from being generated in the first place. The most successful noise reduction strategies combine design and engineering solutions with the human teams operating equipment.[28] People often generate as much or more noise than the equipment.

Sound masking is not an effective strategy for long-term-care settings, where most residents have hearing impairment. Adding sound or noise to cover another sounds only makes it more difficult to hear and to distinguish conversation. It is quite common to discover that ongoing annoyances in otherwise quiet areas are the result of basic mechanical problems that range from squeaky doors and drawers to loud juice, soft drink, and ice machines that "rattle and roll" at a pitch of 85 to 90 dB.[29] Setting acoustical standards in the purchase of new equipment and the maintenance of old equipment is a practical and effective way to control noise in healthcare environments.

The most obvious solutions are often overlooked. An excellent strategy used by hotels is to locate vending machines and ice machines in isolated cubicles to contain the mechanical rumble. An acoustical wall covering product often referred to as wall carpet is available through contract wall covering sources and can be used on the walls of the cubicle housing juice

Sound masking is not an effective strategy for long-term-care settings, where most residents have hearing impairment.

machines. Wall carpet should not be confused with carpet used as a flooring material. Fire safety regulations do not rate carpet for use on vertical surfaces (the walls). The wall covering comes in a variety of colors and can be used as both a decorative and functional insulation for the area around noisy equipment.

Machine noise and bathroom exhaust fans are also major noise culprits. A remote exhaust system is a much quieter solution. Installing separate switches for the light and exhaust fan also provides some noise control. Lubricating squeaky doors, windows, and wheels helps to minimize unnecessary noise. Unfortunately, cellular phones, beepers, computers, carts, televisions, elevators, people, and more people can't be greased to hold down noise pollution. As the number of people in a setting increases, so does the noise level. People will speak 15 decibels or 150 percent louder than the background noise to be understood, and the louder the dialogue, the louder the response.[30] As the noise levels rise, so do the collective voices that rise above the din. Each person has a different level of hearing sensitivity that determines his or her level of tolerance.

Daytime noise levels in many healthcare settings can range from 65 to 95 dB or higher, depending on the time of day; some are as loud as 85 dB in the evening. Both the Environmental Protection Agency (EPA) and the World Health Organization suggest that an evening decibel level be approximately 35 dB.[31] The Occupational Safety and Health Administration (OSHA) has developed guidelines for protection from noise in the work-

DECIBEL LEVELS OF COMMON ENVIRONMENTAL NOISES

Jet engine at takeoff	130–150 dB
Threshold of pain	120–130 dB
Ambulance siren	120 dB
Rock concert	120 dB
Jackhammer, chain saw	110 dB
Leaf blower	95–105 dB
Hand drill	100 dB
Lawn mower	90 dB
Heavy traffic	80 dB
Vacuum cleaner	80 dB
Car noise	70 dB
Normal conversation	60 dB
Quiet office	50 dB
Residential area at night	40 dB
Whisper	30 dB
Rustling leaves	20 dB
Human hearing threshold	0 dB

Bogardus, S., B. Yueh, and P. Shekelle. Screening and Management of Adult Hearing Loss in Primary Care. *Journal of American Medical Association* 289 (2003): 1976–1990.

place and requires protection and short durations of exposure if the average noise level is greater than 85 decibels. Even short blasts of loud noise (greater than 120 dB) can profoundly affect hearing. It's interesting that the workplace environment is protected, but the healthcare settings for residents and patients we refer to as healing environments are not. What's wrong with this picture?

Vacuum cleaners, extractors for cleaning carpets, and floor waxing equipment generate a wash of unnecessary and unwanted noise. Manufacturers seem to have a "deaf ear" when it comes to this problem and have done little to find quieter and better solutions. Too often products and equipment labeled "quiet" are misrepresented. Noise is quite disorienting for older adults, especially those who are hearing impaired. It's disruptive to social activity and takes away the opportunity to converse with each other at mealtimes, when it deprives them of hearing and impairs what little ability they retain to understand language. It is both abusive and a safety hazard. Until we improve the acoustic environment and eliminate disruptive noise that intrudes on the everyday life of frail and elderly adults, we will never be able to describe healthcare setting as healing environments.

Figure 6.3 Residents have a right to expect a quiet home and peaceful surrounding in healthcare settings. *Courtesy of Highland Ridge Senior Campus Assisted Living. Williamsburg, IA. Architect: KKE Architects. Interior Design: Encompass Interiors, St. Paul, MN. Photography: Scott Gilbertson.*

Studies indicate that even noise at low levels increases stress. While healthy individuals react negatively to noise at levels of 45 to 55 dB, their reactions become vigorous at 65 dB. With their diminished tolerance for noise, even at low levels, residents in healthcare settings experience frustration that causes blood pressure to rise as they turn their hearing aids up and down, trying desperately to free themselves of the noise. Quite often the hearing aids are then blamed for their "ineffectiveness."[33]

New equipment purchases should be based on auditory impact, as well as on price. Specify equipment with the proper sound ratings. The decibels for maintenance equipment such as floor buffers, vacuum cleaners, and extractors should be measured and their schedules of use coordinated to minimize disruption. Hold manufacturers and vendors accountable for the auditory impact of their equipment in the same way that other safety and efficiency factors are rated. *Demand more*! In healthcare settings, residents have a right to expect quiet and peaceful surroundings. It is the collective impact of the auditory environment that determines whether a healthcare setting is perceived as therapeutic and supportive or a hostile environment.

> *Even noise at low levels increases stress.*

Assistive Listening Devices

Visual and hearing impairments are directly related to quality of life. The major factor that prevents people with vision and hearing loss from taking part in social situations is conversation. Many more people could benefit from telephone amplifiers than actually use them. Such devices can help people avoid social isolation and other problems associated with hearing difficulties. Studies have shown that correcting sensory impairment can reduce mood disturbances and social functional impairments.[34] Regrettably, in 1995 fewer than 1 percent of the elderly with hearing problems used TTYs (teletyping) or computer links, closed caption TV, or assistive listening devices.[35]

Assistive technology can improve a person's ability to communicate and enhance social interaction. Assistive listening devices are systems that make it easier for hard-of-hearing people to hear and understand spoken communication. Hearing aids make sounds louder and usually help people understand speech, but they do not make speech perfectly clear. They are most effective in quiet environments.

Despite technological advances in hearing aids many older adults choose not to wear them either part or all of the time. Quite often the hearing-impaired individual does not perceive his or her hearing loss to be as much of a problem as family and friends do, and hearing aids don't always live up to expectations. Some persons have trouble inserting hearing aids because of arthritis or visual impairment, and some have difficulty regulating them when the environment changes—for example, when moving from a quiet room to a loud dining room. Even when hearing aids are regularly used by residents in long-term care, their battery life is all too short, and dead batteries are often overlooked by the users and staff. The reality is that most residents need hearing aids, but it is only the exceptional resident who will use a hearing aid consistently and remember to service it.

For one-on-one communication the Pocket Talker Pro, a personal listening (amplifying) device about the size of an iPod, with headphones, has been more successful than a hearing aid for many older adults. The cost is about $150, and while less expensive devices are available through electronic stores, they tend to have lower sound quality.[36]

Group Listening Systems

Technology is rapidly contributing more and better products to the audio market every day that are providing many more choices for group listening systems. Working with a knowledgeable consultant is the best way to find the system best suited to a particular environment. Addressing the issue in the design phase is most cost efficient. Assistive listening systems for large areas must be able to transmit sound effectively to everyone. Systems are designed with an efficient range of 300 to 500 feet, and some of the wide-area infrared systems provide up to 10,000 square feet of coverage, with a 135-foot radius. Installing more complex systems in construction can be less costly than adding them after construction is completed. Wireless systems are also available.

Providing effective listening/hearing environments and devices for the hearing impaired is far more complex than turning up the volume, but there are products and systems available that are making the design job easier. General Technologies and Sound Associates are both listed in the resource section.

A recent wave of new technology has brought hope that we can lower the decibel levels. Some newer car models have "noise cancellation" technology to drown traffic noises. Headphones are available to reduce low-frequency noise such as an airplane's growl, conversation, and music. The best may be yet to come. Hypersonic Sound promises to reduce noise pollution by isolating sound to a single person or source. Imagine being able to shut out annoying cell phone users and their interminable cell phone calls.[37] Why, if we can accomplish this, can we not use the same ingenuity and technology to quiet vacuum cleaners and floor cleaning equipment in home and healthcare environments?

Create the Best Possible Environment

Environmental design is a valuable intervention. Healing environments don't just happen. They are the result of a holistic care and design approach that should reflect the culture of the organization. The design of such spaces should reach far beyond interior design. Designers should seek opportunities to infuse caring into every aspect of the space where care is provided, and where the elders we love and care about are living.

Lighting, Light Sensitivity, and Hearing Loss

Most of us don't think of lighting and light sensitivity in relationship to the ability to hear, but to the hearing impaired, seeing is hearing. Architects and designers who are aware of the importance of light can enable older individuals to communicate better by providing good lighting design and daylight control. Sunlight streaming through the windows to brighten a room is a wonderful way to combat depression when light and glare are controlled, but bright light from windows can obscure the face of individuals seated in front of them.

Too many people who experience hearing loss also become socially isolated when glare and inadequate light increase the difficult struggle for those who rely on speech reading or lip reading to fill in the gaps for what they can't hear. They gather clues by watching a person's lips and facial expressions, combining these with whatever they know about the context of the conversation. Whether hearing-impaired residents are in the dim light of dusk or the glare of the afternoon sun, the result is the same—the struggle to hear is made more difficult by the inability to see.[38]

Don't be afraid to change the seating arrangements or the furniture. Thoughtfully designed seating layouts can help maximize hearing for conversation areas and maintain social connections. When possible, arrange the room so that no one is more than 6 feet apart and everyone is completely visible. In a group, sit closest to those who find it most difficult to

> *Architects and designers who are aware of the importance of light can enable older individuals to hear with good lighting design and daylight control.*

Figure 6.4 Seating arrangements can help maximize hearing for conversation and staying socially connected. *Courtesy of the Life Enrichment Center, Kings Mountain, NC.*

hear. Facing the hard-of-hearing individual directly and on the same level makes communication easier, and sitting in good light so that movements and expressions can be clearly seen maximizes opportunities for good conversation and social interaction.

The sound environment is an essential aspect of quality of life. The environment—by design—can minimize distractions, stress, and discomfort and encourage social interaction.

Seating arrangements should be carefully designed relative to the location of windows, as well as for television viewing and hearing.[39] If residents sit with their backs to the windows, speakers and guest performers can be seen and heard. Conversely, if a speaker or performer is positioned in front of windows, residents are put in the uncomfortable position of looking directly into a bright light source. The glare from incoming light blinds residents, transforms the speaker into a dark faceless form, and creates an impossible situation for hearing-impaired persons who depend or partially depend on lip reading to hear.

The sound environment is an essential aspect of the quality of life. Designers and architects must play a much greater role in shaping sound environments for older adults, rather than allowing them to happen by accident or default. We may not be able to restore hearing, but with greater attention to the concerns of the hearing impaired—noise, the challenges of communication, and the need for visual/hearing support—we can design vastly improved acoustical environments that facilitate better hearing. Instead of promoting fear and anxiety, the environment—by design—can minimize distractions, stress, and discomfort and encourage social interaction.

NOTES

Courtesy of On Lok's 30th Street Senior Services, San Francisco, CA

Physical activity is the key to healthy aging. Walking regularly helps to maintain mobility as you age and often leads to taking a break with a special friend on a sunny bench in the park.

Mobility, Exercise, and Independence

More than ever before, older adults—especially the baby boomers just entering their new "senior" status—are actively seeking ways to delay the physical aspects of aging and to prolong healthy, active lifestyles. By their mid-fifties to early sixties, however, most adults experience some joint or back pain associated with aging, which can temporarily sideline them from their favorite activities. Some simply give up the activity, which unfortunately precludes the opportunity to get sound health advice that could help them stay active and protect them from further injury. When maintaining good health and independence is the issue, lack of activity is certainly *not* the answer. Decreased activity is likely to result in loss of stamina and loss of balance, increasing the risk of falls and injury.

Whether out of vanity, denial, fear, or lack of information, too many older adults fail to take simple preventive measures, often complaining they don't want to "appear old" by using a cane or walking aid. According to the County Commission on Aging in Marin County, California, where I live, of the 911 emergency calls from seniors who have fallen, 85 percent result in emergency room treatment, and these figures are astonishingly similar to nationwide statistics. Falls are the number one cause of emergency room visits and the leading cause of injury deaths among this age group.

While numerous health issues contribute to falls in older adults, there are contributing factors that can be avoided. Without exception, when seniors experience pain that affects walking, or feelings of dizziness or unsteadiness, they should consult their physician. There are many health issues that contribute to balance and gait problems, and often with the treatment of another health issue, the problems with walking dissipate or disappear altogether.

Poor vision, sensitivity to alcohol, medication and medication inter-actions, inadequate nutrition, and inner ear problems can be key factors in gait problems, along with loss of strength, stamina, and motor skills from a wide range of debilitating and prolonged illnesses. Older adults, particularly those recovering from extended illness, are especially vulner-able if they must struggle to get out of chairs, use the toilet, or use steps or stairs.

Falls

As people age, the risk of falling increases, and so do the consequences. One of every three older Americans—about 12 million people—falls every year, and a high proportion of those falls result in broken bones, followed by loss of mobility and independence. Falls are common among older people and put even middle-aged adults at serious risk. Older adults can't bounce back from injury the way younger people can. The impact of a fall can be a dev-astating and potentially life-changing event for an older person.[1]

National figures from Yale University indicate about one-third of people 65 and older fall each year, while half of people 80 and older do. Half of those fall again within six months.[2] About 10 percent of older people who fall suf-fer a serious injury, and what many people don't realize is that people die as a direct result of falls. Most falls happen to women. They occur at home, in the afternoon.[3]

Falls in Care Settings

According to the National Center for Health Statistics, in 1997 three in ten unintentional injury-related deaths among people 65 and older were caused by falls. Six out of ten fatal falls happened to older people at home, three in ten occurred in public places, and the remainder occurred in healthcare institutions.[4] The Centers for Disease Control and Prevention (CDC) research shows that about half of the 1.5 million nursing home residents nationwide fall at least once a year.[5] Of those falls, about 1,800 are fatal. The CDC suggests that elders living in nursing homes are more likely to fall than their peers living in the community, because those in institutional settings tend to be frailer, older, and more cognitively impaired, and they also have greater limitations in their activities of daily living.[6] Nevertheless, the high rate of falls in nursing homes and compa-rable care settings should not be viewed as inevitable, but rather as out-comes that can and must be improved through structured programs. There is strong agreement that getting residents involved in regular phys-ical activity designed to enhance muscle strength, balance, and coordina-tion is potent fall-prevention medicine.[7]

Figure 7.1 Physical activity enhances muscle strength, balance, and coordination and is the key to preventing falls. *Courtesy of the Life Enrichment Center, Shelby, NC.*

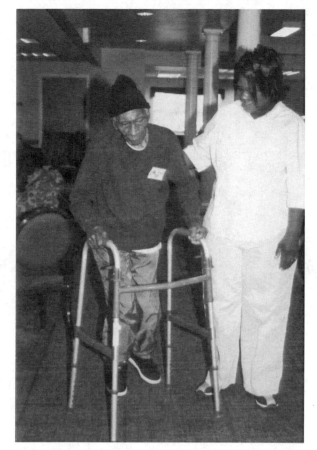

Hip Fractures

Hip fractures have been on the rise since 1990, and more than 90 percent are associated with osteoporosis. Nine out of ten hip fractures in older adults are the result of a fall, making them one of the most serious outcomes associated with falls. About half the older adults who are hospitalized with a hip fracture are unable to return home or live independently again; and of those with a hip fracture up to 20 percent are more likely to die in the first year following the injury than others in the same age group.[8] For those who had lived independently before the hip fracture, between 15 and 25 percent will still be in long-term care settings a year after their fracture.[9]

> *Hip fractures have been on the rise since 1990, and more than 90 percent are associated with osteoporosis. Nine out of ten hip fractures in older adults are the result of a fall.*

Risk Factors

Study results now encourage specifically addressing urinary incontinence, cognitive impairment, use of restraints, depression, and transfer difficulties be addressed as modifiable predisposing risk factors for falls.[10] Typically, falls among the elderly result from a combination of several risk factors.

Age and Fall History. Both advanced age and a record of previous falls are important non-modifiable markers to identify residents at high risk of falls.

RISK FACTORS

- Age
- History of previous fall
- Balance
- Gait disorders
- Cognitive loss
- Medication
- Vision changes
- Incontinence
- Fear of falling
- Weakness/extremity strength loss
- Transferability—upper and lower
- Environmental hazards
- Other medical conditions

Balance and Gait Disorders. When we're young we generally take our balancing skills for granted, but research has shown that balance is not as automatic or reflexive as we originally thought.[11] Numerous studies have shown that balance declines with age. Yet poor balance is not inevitable, nor is loss of balance a natural part of aging. It's caused by any one of numerous conditions—problems with vision or the inner ear, medications, poor posture resulting from arthritis, weakness, osteoporosis, poor diet, or weak back muscles—but the biggest cause is leg muscles weakened by lack of use.

Loss of balance is not a natural part of aging, but it is caused by leg muscles weakened by lack of use.

Cognitive Impairment. Alzheimer's disease affects both judgment and one's ability to react. One of the main symptoms of Alzheimer's is the inability to process information, which as the disease progresses makes even the simplest tasks, such as walking or sitting, difficult and often impossible. Falls often result, and tragically the individual with dementia may no longer know how to react or break their fall, causing greater than normal injury. They may have no idea why there is pain, what caused it, or what to do to relieve it; they may even forget the injury and try to walk, risking increased pain and further injury. The confusion can be further compounded by many other factors on the list, especially medications.

Medication. Medication use is perhaps the most preventable and modifiable risk factor for falling and injuries among older adults. Almost half of all elderly Americans regularly take three or more medications,[12] and according to the U.S. Food and Drug Administration, seniors use about 30 percent of all prescriptions and over the counter medications sold in the United States. The medications prescribed to older adults—

particularly when several are combined—often result in adverse effects, such as hypotension and dizziness, confusion and impaired judgment, delirium, blurred vision, compromised neuromuscular function, and anxiety, that increase the likelihood of falling.

Vision Changes. Investigations have revealed that up to half of all nursing home residents have difficulty navigating around their environment because of vision problems. Residents with dementia and those who have suffered a stroke may also have visio-spatial awareness deficits.[13]

Incontinence. Incontinence has joined the list of serious yet frequently overlooked causes of falls. Bladder problems that send older women rushing to the bathroom at night may also increase their risk of falls and fractures. Those with frequent urinary incontinence were about 25 percent more likely than women without the condition to suffer a fall, and women with what is called urge incontinence are at an even higher risk. People with this condition feel an overwhelming need to empty their bladders, but often cannot make it to the bathroom.[14] Identifying and treating urge incontinence may prove to be an effective intervention for reducing the risk of falls and fractures.

> *Incontinence has joined the list of serious, yet frequently overlooked causes for falls.*

Fear of Falling. Older adults have every reason to be concerned about falls. Injury from a fall can be the beginning of a downward spiral that can result in loss of independence, isolation, and possibly death. Fall-related injuries are the leading cause of death due to unintentional injuries among Americans age 65 and older.[15] The fear of falling can have a significant impact on the emotional health and lifestyle of older adults, often leading them to restrict their activities. Even though bones do not break after every fall, the person who has fallen and broken a bone is almost always fearful of falling again. That fear can diminish a person's sense of well-being, limit mobility, and reduce participation in social and leisure activities, all of which means a poorer quality of life. Many people are so frightened that they all but withdraw from life, prematurely imposing immobility on themselves. As they do less, their physical condition deteriorates, making them more susceptible to falling and dependency.[16] Their inactivity often leads to depression and medication, which can increase the likelihood of a fall, and what they fear most is more likely to become a reality. People need to learn about the trade-off between the risk of immobility and the risk of mobility, and then find the right balance for themselves.

> *People need to learn about the trade-off between the risk of immobility and the risk of mobility, and then find the right balance for themselves.*

The fear of falling even compromises the quality of life of older adults who have not experienced a fall. Between 25 and 50 percent of independently living elders fear falling.[17] The fear may actually increase the risk for falls when individuals restrict movement, which leads to reduced physical conditioning.

"Where's Your Life?"

Of all the nagging worries of old age, none ranks higher than the fear of falling. Everyday life and activities—taking a bath, cleaning the house, shopping for groceries—are frightening. Going up and down stairs and reaching for something overhead involve relatively high levels of fear for older individuals, but the most feared activities are going out when it's slippery and taking a bath. While falls can happen anywhere, most falls happen at home during activities in the kitchen, bedroom, and bathroom, and on stairways. As a result of a fear of falling many older persons cut back on their participation in healthy activities, including walking for exercise.[18] If you go down, what then? A fracture? Or worse still, could this be the big one, the one that sends you to the nursing home without a return ticket?

The worry that most older persons experience was aptly described by one woman in this way: "Yes, you develop an awful fear. You don't know when it's going to happen. It starts affecting you emotionally, mentally, and everything else. Eventually, you get paranoid. You're afraid to do anything. So I'm living with this terrible fear of walking. If you stay home, you go crazy. If you go out, you're in fear. Where's your life?"[19]

As a result of a fear of falling many older persons cut back on their participation in healthy activities, including walking for exercise.[18]

Interventions: What Do We Do About It?

Over the course of the past 20 years researchers have investigated the effectiveness of a number of different strategies designed to reduce the risk factors that contribute to falls, and the actual incidence of falls and fall-related injuries in the older adult population. The three intervention strategies proven to be the most effective in reducing fall incidence rates and fall-related injuries among the older adult population are (1) comprehensive assessment of fall-prone individuals, linked to treatment recommendations and abatement strategies, (2) individualized exercise interventions, and (3) environmental assessment and modifications.[20] A joint United Kingdom–United States evidence-based guideline for fall prevention has recently been developed, which makes recommendations for assessing older adults for multifactorial interventions, exercise, environmental modifications, medication review, assistive devices, and behavioral and educational program interventions.[21]

Exercise

Physical activity is the key to healthy aging. In fact, older people have more to gain than younger people by becoming active, because they are at higher risk of developing problems that regular exercise can prevent.[22] The role of exercise in reducing fall risk and fall incidence rates in the older adult population has been well studied. Many different types of exercise interventions have been used, ranging from single exercise (e.g., resistance exercise, walking, tai chi) to multicomponent exercise programs (e.g., aerobic endurance, flexibility, strength, and balance training). Without question, older adults who have had recurrent falls should be offered long-term exercise and balance training.[23]

There is increasing evidence to show that individualized and group-based exercise can improve balance and reduce falls,[24] and that greater intensity and frequency of exercise are associated with greater reduction in fall risk.[25] Many physically fit older adults practice the same balance recovery strategies as younger adults and as a result are generally better at controlling their balance than their inactive peers. Yoga, tai chi, and qi gong are excellent programs that offer gradual and consistent balance training and build self-confidence. These strategies have proven quite successful in improving flexibility and overall strength. Practicing some type of balance exercises every day helps older adults both to reduce falls and to recover from them.[26]

Exercise is good—combined with balance and strength components, even better. Many simple exercises to help improve balance can be incorporated into general fitness routines, but to be effective, exercise programs must include specific exercises or activities that challenge postural control and address factors that influence balance ability, such as strength, flexibility, pain, and sensory awareness.[27]

Yoga. Yoga is concerned with the health of the individual as a unified whole, and millions of people have come to recognize its benefits. Yoga makes integration of the body, mind, and spirit possible. It stimulates energy

> *Physical activity is the key to healthy aging.*

> *Greater intensity and frequency of exercise are associated with greater reduction in fall risk.*

Figure 7.2 Compelling information about the benefits of exercise and the hazards of inactivity has proved an important incentive toward increasing exercise. *Courtesy of On Lok's 30th Street Senior Services, San Francisco, CA.*

Figure 7.3 Exercise is good—combined with balance and strength components, even better! *Courtesy of On Lok's 30th Street Senior Services; San Francisco, CA.*

and promotes good health through balance and concentration. Yoga exercises are performed in a series of graceful, rhythmic slow movements, with a brief completely motionless "holding" period for certain positions. Strength and balance are improved by concentrating attention on the movements being executed.

Yoga is not competitive, but instead encourages each individual to focus on improving his or her own physical condition with consistency, not by making comparisons with others. This is a program that results in firming, relief of tension and stiffness, improvement in general health, emotional stability, and a positive mental outlook. Perhaps the best news is this seems to be true regardless of age or present physical condition, making it particularly beneficial for frail and elderly persons.

Tai Chi. This martial art has emerged as a viable stand-alone exercise intervention for relatively healthy community-residing older adults. Tai chi programs can be effective with older adults of varying functional levels and ethnic backgrounds, as well as for mildly confused persons[28] who are at risk for falls. Tai chi is a self-defense technique, but it is used in many programs as an exercise for health, fitness, and relaxation. Its flowing forms consist of slow, coordinated movements that result in one continuous motion. It enhances breathing and flexibility and emphasizes proper postural awareness. Tai chi programs for older adults encourage movement and strengthening of muscles while creating a mood of relaxation.

Figure 7.4 What could be better than tai chi in the garden? Tai chi programs for older adults encourage movement and strengthening of muscles. *Courtesy of On Lok's 30th Street Senior Services; San Francisco, CA.*

SENSE OF BALANCE

Three sensory systems play vital roles in giving the body a sense of balance:

- The eyes give the brain information on how you move in relation to the surrounding environment.
- The sensory nerves track the movement and tension of the joints, the muscles, and the body's position with respect to the ground.
- Special cells in the canals in the inner ear detect motion, changes in motion, and body position.

Strength Training. Also referred to as resistance training, strength training enables adults to improve their overall health and fitness by increasing muscular strength, endurance, and bone density and improving their insulin sensitivity and glucose metabolism to reduce the risk of adult-onset diabetes.[30,31] In 2001 the CDC found, however, that the majority of older adults, including those who met the national objective for physical activity, did not engage in strength training. Even physically active older adults are missing opportunities to improve their overall health and fitness through regular strength training.

Both strength training and tai chi have been shown to be very beneficial in preventing falls. In the case of very frail older adults, an early emphasis on resistance and seated balance training may be necessary before balance activities that require weight-bearing ability and aerobic endurance training can be introduced. It is possible to increase muscle mass at any age through systematic strength training; even frail older adults can safely participate. While adults should do endurance exercise such as walking and cycling to enhance cardiovascular function, aerobic activities do little to prevent the gradual deterioration of the musculoskeletal system.

Maria Fiatarone, now part of Harvard University Medical School's division on aging, published a landmark study in 1994 while at Tufts University. Fiatarone truly demonstrated "out of the box" thinking when she studied 100 frail nursing home residents ranging in age from 75 to 98. The average age was 87, and about a third were in their 90s. She also included residents with multiple chronic conditions such as osteoporosis, arthritis, pulmonary disease, hypertension, and cancer. Up to that point, most strength-training studies had been done with younger people and omitted anyone with chronic conditions.[32] The training program was progressive—as strength improved, resistance was gradually increased.

Out of the 100 subjects, 94 percent completed the study, and the results were remarkable. Subjects engaged in strength training increased muscle strength by about 113 percent. They increased gait velocity (walking speed) by 11.8 percent and stair climbing power by about 28 percent. The level of spontaneous physical activity also increased. Such improvement easily translates to an improvement in the ability to perform functional tasks.

Weight training can effectively improve strength, mobility, and ultimately independence for even very old and frail adults. If physical weakness is hampering mobility in the elderly, then weight training may be a good solution. This study suggested that one reason the elderly grow chair-bound is that their muscles are weak from lack of exercise.[33]

Weight training can effectively improve strength, mobility, and ultimately independence for even very old and frail adults.

Culture change is being embraced in long-term care across the country, and it's time for healthcare professionals to take risks and develop innovative approaches that respect individuals' needs to feel productive and prevent decline.[34] Geriatric professionals, physical and occupational therapists, medical professionals, care providers, caregivers and advocates for elders, it's time for change.

Walking. Walking regularly helps people to maintain mobility as they age. With each step comes immediate reward. Walking even a short distance a few times a week can yield dramatic improvements in health. Per-

Figure 7.5 Walking is an excellent form of low impact exercise. *Courtesy of On Lok's 30th Street Senior Services, San Francisco, CA.*

sons who walk regularly receive the most gains. Those who walk less, however, still fare better than nonwalkers. Twenty to 30 minutes of walking most days of the week should maintain functional ability later in life. Walking helps develop stamina, forces oxygen-rich blood into the muscles, and improves circulation—all without trauma to the knees, hips, and ankles.

But the benefits go well beyond the obvious. More than any other activity, walking will jump-start the brain. It sets thoughts in motion and helps us become better thinkers. St. Jerome suggested, "To solve a problem, walk around. The answer will come."[35] Walking also produces increased levels of serotonin, an important brain neurotransmitter that increases feelings of well-being; in fact, walking is often recommended as a treatment for mild depression and anxiety. The most compelling reason to walk, however, is that it's fun, and as an added bonus, it's good for the mind, the soul, and the body. The warmth of the sun, the songs of the birds, and, most of all, the people that we meet along the way bring magic to the day.

It doesn't take a lot of exercise to remain agile into your seventies and beyond. Even among persons aged 90 years and older, physical activity is associated with enhanced quality of life.[36]

Regular physical activity reduces the risk for heart disease, diabetes, and high blood pressure; it helps control weight and maintains muscles, joints, and bone strength. It provides additional benefits for older adults by

Figure 7.6 The most compelling reason to walk is that it's fun. As an added bonus, the warmth of the sun, the songs of the birds, and the people we meet along the way bring magic to the day. *Courtesy of the Life Enrichment Center, Kings Mountain, NC.*

Figure 7.7 Older people have more to gain than younger people by becoming active because they are at higher risk of developing problems that regular exercise can prevent. *Courtesy of On Lok's 30th Street Senior Services, San Francisco, CA.*

increasing coordination and balance, preventing falls, and maintaining independence. Despite the benefits, the prevalence of inactivity increases with age, and approximately one-third of older U.S. adults are not active during their leisure time. Few older adults exercise, and women are particularly likely to be sedentary.[37] Offering compelling information about the benefits of exercise and the hazards of inactivity has proved an important incentive for increasing exercise in this group.[38]

The single biggest problem, illustrated by all the exercise intervention studies conducted with frail older adults, is that the functional gains achieved are lost very quickly once the intervention ends. This means that we must make every effort to design long-term exercise programs and encourage seniors to stick to them.[39] The most effective interventions incorporate exercise and medical treatment of disease with a reduction of medications. Exercise, with simultaneous management of vision impairment and reduction of environmental hazards, is the single most important intervention for reducing falls.[40] While modification of the home environment, advice about fall risk, and staff education are substantially less effective in reducing falls, when coupled with home visits their effectiveness is increased. Dr. Mary Tinetti, a professor of medicine and public health at the Yale University School of Medicine and an expert on falling and the elderly, emphasizes the conditioning of the individual more than modifying the home, though she supports that as well. She promotes exercise that can build or retain muscle strength and stability.[41]

> *We must make every effort to design long-term exercise programs and encourage seniors to stick to them.*

Environmental Modification

Most people still prefer to age in place in familiar surroundings, and there is little doubt that with the explosion of the aging population single-family homes, apartments, and assisted living settings will be the most significant long-term-care homes of the future. As older adults experience age-related physical and social changes, it is a good time to evaluate whether aging in place at home or moving to a new residence is the better course of action. Aging in familiar surroundings certainly provides some security and comfort.[42,43] On the other hand, relocating to a senior community or residential assisted living setting may provide a better physical and social environment and enhance the individual's long-term ability to function effectively.

> *The decision to age in place isn't a one-time event. It's an assumption that is continually challenged by changing needs and circumstances.*

The decision to age in place isn't a one-time event. It's an assumption that is continually challenged by changing needs and circumstances. Most people say they prefer to spend their senior years in their own homes, but many older homes were not built for aging in place. Typically, there are three areas in the home that are barriers to safety and independence: steps and doors leading in and out of the home, stairs inside the home, and the bathroom. Most homes can be modified to make them safer, more comfortable, and easier to move around in when carrying out daily activities—cooking, bathing, and climbing stairs. It should be noted that kitchens and bathrooms are often the most expensive rooms in a house to renovate. Still, it may well be worth it.

Nearly a million older people with health and mobility problems need additional supportive features in their homes in order to age in place and avoid premature institutionalization, according to the U.S. Census Bureau.[44] Two important adaptations to the home are removing environmental hazards to protect residents from injury and introducing environmental modifications to make the home safer and more supportive. Few construction professionals specialize in the safety needs of older individuals, which makes it crucial that design professionals do their homework. Builders and contractors rarely know about the specific safety needs of older adults and people with disabilities.

Injury-proofing the home is important for all ages, but it is particularly crucial for older people experiencing changes in vision, hearing, mobility, and strength. Modifications can be as simple as installing grab bars,[45] handheld showerheads, and lever door handles and improving lighting. More complex modifications may include widening doorways to accommodate wheelchairs and other assistive devices, lowering countertops, or installing ramps and elevators.

Given the growing number of older adults choosing to remain in their homes rather than move into a long-term-care-facility, it would be ideal if

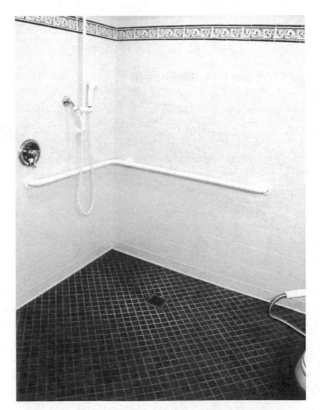

Figure 7.8 Modifications for support can be as simple as installing grab bars in the shower that contrast in color so they are seen and used. *Courtesy of Foulkeways at Gwynedd, Gwynedd, PA. Architect: Reese, Lower, Patrick & Scott, Ltd., Lancaster, PA. Photographer: Larry Lefever Photography.*

identifying environmental hazards within the home or its immediate environs were acknowledged as an effective method of lowering fall incidence rates and fall-related injuries among older adults. Studies, however, have yielded mixed results.[46] Significant reductions in fall rates that required medical attention were only seen when technical and financial assistance was provided to complete the recommended changes. Without this type of assistance, residents were much less likely to implement substantive changes such as the installation of grab bars, stair railings, or additional lighting.

Common sense suggests that environmental modifications are an important component of any fall risk reduction program designed for older adults, whether they reside in the community or a long-term-care setting. Although the types of environmental modifications will differ, the primary goal of this type of intervention is to immediately improve the balance between daily task demands and the older adults' abilities. Once modifications have been made, the next step is to encourage exercise to increase strength and ability within and around the home.[47]

BATHROOM MODIFICATIONS

- Install grab bars in the shower and around the toilet
- Install shower seats or transfer benches
- Place nonskid strips or decals in the tub or shower
- Install a handheld shower head
- Install a floor-to-ceiling safety pole

CHANGES TO IMPROVE ACCESS IN AND OUT OF THE HOME

- Install permanent or portable ramps
- Widen doorways
- Install swing-clear hinges on doors

CHANGES TO EASE MOVEMENT UP AND DOWN STAIRS

- Install handrails on both sides for support
- Attach a glide-a-track mounted seat to one side of the stairs
- Place reflective nonskid rubber strips on edge of steps

OTHER MODIFICATIONS

- Replace doorknobs with lever handles
- Place night-lights in hallways and other high-traffic areas
- Install a single-control faucet in the kitchen[48]

An unsupportive home environment can result in accidents and forced moves to institutional settings. Accessibility problems, for example, can lead older adults to confine themselves to one floor of a two-story home or to venture outside only rarely. Older people with balance problems and limited strength are particularly at risk for hip fractures from bathroom falls, and faced with such dangers, they may forgo bathing.

Poorly illuminated stairs without proper handrails, other instances of poor lighting, clutter, cords, throw rugs, and a lack of grab bars and nonslip mats in the tub or shower are often responsible for falls that result in serious injury among otherwise healthy adults. Small pets are wonderful companions, but underfoot they too can be a serious hazard.

Assessment

During a three-year study of more than 1,000 older adults completed in 2002, researchers found that over half had at least one fall because of a trip or slip. However, they found no consistent association between the falls and such environmental hazards as loose rugs. "Our findings should not be used to condone cluttered living spaces or thwart sensible efforts to promote home safety," the researchers wrote.[49] But their findings do suggest that efforts to reduce falls should target older people themselves, not their homes. Previous research suggests that eliminating hazards in the home can reduce the risk of falling by 10 to 15 percent, while such measures as muscle-strengthening exercises and corrected vision can reduce the risk by 20 to 40 percent.[50] Older adults are more likely to fall as a result of multiple fall risk factors. While identifying and then minimizing all of the risk factors is likely to be the most successful method of preventing falls, the common denominator among most, if not all, intervention strategies should be the inclusion of exercise.

Making sure older individuals are wearing appropriate shoes, correcting vision problems, and monitoring medication will also provide substantial benefit.

The common denominator among most, if not all, intervention strategies should be the inclusion of exercise.

NOTES

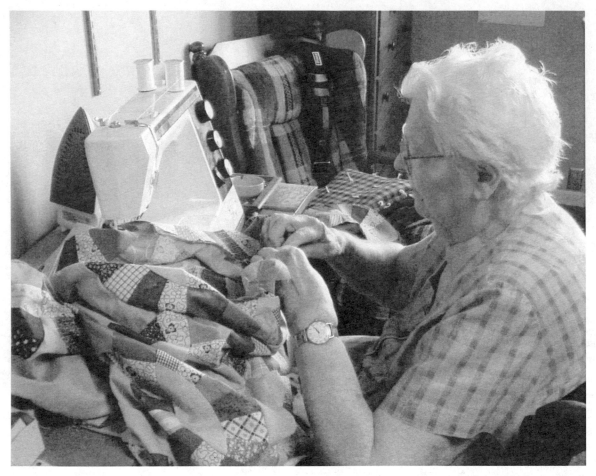

Courtesy of Meadow Lark Hills Retirement Community, Manhattan, KS.

*Busy hands continue to create from a frame of mind that celebrates life
instead of simply letting it go by.*

Color, Finishes, and Fabric

Color is a fundamental element of environmental design. It is linked to psychological, physiological and social reactions of human beings, as well as aesthetic and technical aspects of human-made environments.

Color in Healthcare Environments

There is a growing interest in what is now known as evidenced-based design, or research-based knowledge for the application of color in healthcare design. A recent study commissioned by the Coalition for Health Environments Research reviewed more than 3,000 citations in the existing literature on the relationship between people and color in the environment, with special emphasis on the design of healthcare environments. The authors found "the knowledge base to be fragmented, sporadic, conflicting, anecdotal, and loosely tested."[1]

In an attempt to separate myth from reality and to determine how the literature might contribute to the knowledge of architects, interior designers, researchers, healthcare providers, and users of healthcare environments, this study has literally blown the lid off the large container of generally held beliefs about color. A critical review of the pertinent literature produced no reliable explanatory theories that help to predict how color will influence people in healthcare settings. Regrettably, much of the information about the use of color in healthcare environments is not based on a significant evidence-based body of knowledge.

In spite of this bad news, there are some valuable collective lessons to be learned from the numerous studies reviewed:

1. There are no direct links between particular colors and health outcomes of people. Sufficient evidence does not exist for a causal relationship between settings painted in particular colors and patients' healthcare outcomes.

2. Specifying particular colors for healthcare environments in order to influence emotional states or mental and behavioral activities is simply unsubstantiated by proven results. Spaces do not become relaxing or invigorating simply because of their color.

3. Perceptual impressions of color applications can create impressions that affect experiences and performance. For example, certain colors may evoke a sense of spaciousness in particular settings. However, the perception of spaciousness is attributed to the brightness or darkness of the color rather than its hue.

4. While studies have shown that color-mood association exists, there is no evidence to suggest a one-to-one relationship between a given color and a given emotion. Emotional responses to colors are caused by culturally learned associations and by people's physiological and psychological makeup.

5. The popular press and the design community have promoted the oversimplification of psychological responses to color. Most color guidelines for healthcare design are nothing more than affective value judgments. When applied to architecture and interior design for healthcare settings they seem oddly inconclusive and nonspecific.

6. The study of color in healthcare settings is challenging because it occurs in the context of meaningful settings and situations.[2]

So where does that leave us? If the things we thought were true are not actually supported by evidence, does it mean they have no value? It means that we must learn to pay a great deal more attention to the decisions we make, because as providers and design professionals we affect the well-being of many people in the healthcare environments we design. There are very few things in life that we are able to do with absolute assurance of the outcome. So we're on notice to dig deeper and apply critical thinking in making design decisions about color in the absence of reliable, evidenced-based research.

Designers will need a comprehensive understanding of color, lighting, and aging vision as well as artistic talent to guide them in making responsible decisions about color. Choosing a color palette for specific healthcare settings depends on several complex factors, including geographical location; the characteristics of potential users (their dominant culture, age, etc.); the nature and character of the light source; the size and shape of the space; and the type of activities to be performed in the space. Providers of care, designers, and other practitioners agree that healthcare environments should be friendly, therapeutic, and promote healing to the greatest extent possible.

The body of research regarding color in healthcare environments is minimal, and in many of the reported studies the sample size was small. Rarely was research replicated to validate findings. The Coalition for Health Environments Research study is particularly valuable in that it makes clear that many decisions about color have been based largely on unsupported theories. It further demonstrates:

- Color is complex. The way a color is perceived is influenced by lighting conditions, individual bias, and the perceived suitability of the color to specific use.

- People rate colors in real environments very differently from the way they rate colors in laboratory tests.

- The meaning of the colored object is just as important as the color itself. Since colors carry their own meanings, the question is to what degree one can find a match between the meaning of color and the meaning of an object.[3]

Effective Color Contrast

Fortunately reliable research has been conducted on many of the color issues involved in designing environments for older adults. The Lighthouse Research Institute has contributed a wealth of practical information about color and using color contrast for people with partial sight, low vision, and color deficiencies.

Partial sight, aging vision, and congenital color deficits all produce changes in perception that reduce the visual effectiveness of certain color combinations. Two colors that contrast sharply to someone with normal vision may be far less distinguishable to someone with a visual disorder. For example, if you have normal vision you cannot assume that the lightness you perceive will be the same as the lightness perceived by those with color deficits. They will probably see less contrast between colors. If you lighten the light colors and darken the dark colors you will increase the visual accessibility of the design.

> *Partial sight, aging vision, and congenital color deficits all produce changes in perception that reduce the visual effectiveness of certain color combinations.*

To understand how to make color contrasts that are effective for everyone, we characterize colors by their three most important perceptual attributes:

Hue is the attribute by which we name the basic color and by which it is distinguished from another color.

Lightness, brightness, or *value* is the degree of apparent light intensity. It is the most important attribute in effective contrast between two colors.

Chroma or *saturation* is the purity or intensity of a hue, which is the lightness or darkness of the color.[4]

With color deficits, ability to discriminate colors on the basis of all three attributes is reduced. Designers can help to compensate for these deficits by making colors differ more dramatically in all three ways.

The effects that visual impairments produce on color vision are diverse, ranging from no effect to complete loss of hue discrimination. Typical aging results in a loss of transparency in the lens, reducing the amount of light that reaches the retina. Violet, blue, and blue-green surfaces, which reflect the shorter wavelengths of light, appear darker. In many visual disorders, surfaces and lights that are matched in lightness and hue become more difficult to discriminate. Effective contrast, achieved by increasing the lightness differences between the foreground and background colors, makes objects more visible. Colors of similar lightness or color value to one another should be avoided, even if they differ in chroma or hue. Monochromatic color schemes do not provide effective contrast for those with vision impairment.[5]

Designing effective and understandable environments for those with vision and color vision impairments adds another layer of complexity to the already difficult task of designing healthcare environments for older adults. I highly recommend that anyone designing for adults older than 40 get copies of "Effective Color Contrast: Designing for People with Partial Sight and Color Deficiencies" and a companion brochure entitled "Making Text Legible: Designing for People with Partial Sight." Both brochures can be obtained from Lighthouse International, the leading resource on vision impairment.

"Effective Color Contrast" is an understandable guide, produced in color, effectively illustrating the guidelines for color contrast. The visual examples are worth a thousand words of explanation. The hue circle shows which colors provide the greatest contrast, with guidance in selecting the lighter hues that contrast more effectively with which darker hues.

Color vision deficits vary greatly across eye disorders and among individuals. Using the recommended guiding principles leads to making more effective color choices for the vast majority of partially sighted people. The same principles also produce color contrasts that are effective for most people with congenital color defects, and are equally effective for people with normal color vision.

Color Solutions

Color is an easy way to make a fresh start and create eye-catching improvements that freshen a tired-looking space and brighten the spirit. Paint is often called the easiest and most affordable way to transform a room. Yet paint—that magical makeover in a can—is sometimes the most frustrating part of a project, or at least selecting the color can be. There are no right or wrong colors. There are no bad colors, just bad color combinations. Experimenting with colors, even in small ways, however, can make the living environment genuinely comfortable, and a better reflection of the residents who live within.

THE WONDERFUL WORLD OF PAINT: HOW CONFUSING CAN A
KALEIDOSCOPE OF COLOR CHOICES BE?

Picking colors may be the hardest part of decorating. The overwhelming number of options in textures and finishes is one thing, but the color
choices are something else altogether. Standing before the walls of paint
chips can cause numbing insecurity. Often the actual paint doesn't appear
to match the chip, and when seen on a large scale the color can look very
different. For those of us who may be "color impaired," many paint stores
today have helpful computers capable of showing the color in a simulated
room. The nice thing is that it's impossible to offend the computer as you
look at different color choices. Take the time to study the results. Here are
a few more suggestions:

> *Picking colors may be the hardest part of decorating.*

Selecting Interior Paint Colors

- Collect swatches of fabric, pieces of carpet, and accent colors that
  appeal to you.

- Tape color cards to the wall. Narrow your selection—choose a couple of colors.

- Get a quart of the colors you like best and paint large poster boards
  with these colors. This allows you to place the samples where you
  plan to paint and to move them around. You can put them behind
  furniture, up against drapes, or beside the window. This tells you
  more about how the color looks and works in the room without
  marring the walls.

- If you still can't make up your mind, purchase a quart of each of your
  color choices and paint a large section—at least 2 feet by 2 feet—on
  each wall.

- Colors may look very different under different lighting conditions.
  For that reason, be sure to assess paint colors at various times of the
  day and evening—in both natural light and under artificial lighting.

- Remember that colors appear to intensify and darken when applied
  to large areas, especially when used on several different walls or
  surfaces. To compensate for this, experienced painters know that it
  is better to err on the side of a lighter color value than a darker one.

- After taking time to find the perfect paint colors be sure to use
  durable, top-quality paint on your walls and trim. Paints should go
  on smoothly and evenly, cover well, resist stains, and touch up
  nicely. In short, they should continue to look the way you want
  them to for a long, long time.

- A secret source for accent color is residents' own artwork. Collect
  several pieces; have residents help select some to be framed and
  displayed. Frames and mats are another way to introduce small
  bits of color.

Figure 8.1 A wonderful source for accent color is residents' art work. *Courtesy of Design Concepts Unlimited, Sausalito, CA.*

If choosing paint creates a crisis of confidence, it might be time to consult with a designer with a good sense of color, and especially one who really understands the physical changes in older eyes and is familiar with the special needs of a long-term-care environment. It is difficult to overemphasize these points, for even though this is a residential setting, it is a residential setting with very specific requirements that many well-meaning designers are not familiar with. Making successful color choices for older adult settings involves much more than personal choice and trendy colors.

PAINT FOR HEALTHCARE ENVIRONMENTS

When it comes to paints, a combination of new technologies and new thinking is making it easier to keep healthcare settings clean and looking fresh. Nothing makes a living environment look old and worn and unappealing more than dirty walls. Scuff marks make any setting look run down. Touch-ups are the traditional way of handling the problem, but that rarely leaves a clean, uniform finish. Recent innovations in paint have greatly improved durability, with finishes that better tolerate daily abuse and more routine scrubbing. Water-based products are available with new hard and durable satin finishes, but this is particularly apparent in flat-finish paints with mar resistance.

ScrubTough paint, from the Scuffmaster Architectural Finish line by Wolf Gordon, is an exceptionally scrubbable, cleanable, antimicrobial water-based paint for interior walls. This paint lives up to its name, withstanding far more wear and repeated cleaning than ordinary acrylic latex paints. The antimicrobial additive, Microban, inhibits the growth of odor and stain-causing mold, mildew, bacteria, and other fungal growth on the dried paint surface.

Mold has become a high-profile issue, and buildings with excessive moisture and poor ventilation are particularly vulnerable to mold. Specifying paint products that include antimicrobacterial properties to inhibit growth of mold is a preemptive move in settings that serve older populations. With its durability and superior cleanability, eggshell finish, and enormous range of colors, ScrubTough is particularly well suited for walls in high-traffic environments in healthcare.

An interior paint called Radiance borrows the technology used in energy-efficient windows. A material in this paint forms a barrier that slows heat loss in the winter by reflecting approximately 40 percent of the radiant energy back into a room. In summer the paint reflects back outside heat to help reduce cooling costs.

Have you ever tried painting plastic? Ah, the joy, the puddles, the peeling, the mess! Krylon Fusion is a new spray paint designed especially for plastic. It does not need priming, it covers and adheres to plastic, and the company claims it resists fading and chipping in outdoor environments. Krylon Fusion, available in 16 colors, is also safe for children's toys, flowerpots, mailboxes, yard ornaments—pink flamingos anyone?—milk crates, and more. The paint dries in 15 minutes, so now it's easy to transform all those dirty scuffed plastic chairs in the garden to a veritable rainbow of pretty colors to match the flowers in the raised planters.

The logic of low life cycle costs is all too often overlooked. Good quality paint is the heart of success of any paint job. Buying the cheapest gallon of paint is the biggest mistake you can make. The best way to reduce life cycle costs is to buy high-quality paint. With many of the new paint products it can mean the difference between painting five times or once.

Even when low-grade products are not specified, that is often what ends up on the walls if product specifications are not spelled out. When paint contracts go out for bid, contractors typically base their materials on low-end products so they can better compete, but the fact is that labor is typically the most expensive part of the job. A paint job that costs $2,000 and lasts ten years is a better long-term value than a $1,200 job that lasts two years. To ensure quality performance select paints carrying an ASTM International label, which assures that products perform according to industry standards.

Environmental Responsibility and Good Health

More than ever, we look to the natural environment to get ideas for colors for the built environment. Flora, fauna, sea, mountains, and rain give endless inspiration. Yet the goal today is not merely to mimic nature, but to nourish an underlying sensitivity for the rhythms of life—and to protect it.[6] Environmental responsibility has become an important consideration.

Striking a balance between performance, aesthetic appeal, environmental responsibility, and impact on resident or occupant satisfaction can be challenging when paints that meet performance standards appear to do so at the expense of quality in other areas. In the past environmentally friendly products were a tough sell—frankly many of them didn't work. Yet recent advances in technology now allow us to select environmentally responsible products without sacrificing performance. With the influence of the U.S. Green Building Council's Leadership in Energy and Environmental Design (LEED), new paint formulas have been developed that reduce or eliminate volatile organic compounds (VOCs) without reducing the durability of the product. VOCs in the solvent hold the pigment and paint together when the paint is applied. Some VOCs, such as benzene and formaldehyde, help the paint dry more quickly. As the paint dries, the solvent slowly evaporates along with the VOCs, contributing to the "new paint" smell.

High VOC concentrations can be harmful to some individuals with allergies, nervous disorders, and even cancer. Regulations on VOC exposure vary. California currently has some of the most stringent laws in the nation, and other states are expected to follow suit.

It is only fair to note that low-VOC paints can take longer to dry and cure, since most of the drying agents have been removed. But selecting low- or no-VOC paints can bring major improvement to indoor air quality, and because of the reduction of health-related risks and unpleasant odors, it allows healthcare facilities to maintain normal activities during the painting process.

Selecting high-performance paint can mean the difference between painting once and painting four or five times in 20 years.

One way to evaluate the environmental impact of paint is to select products certified by reputable nonprofit environmental organizations such as Green Seal, which identifies and promotes products that produce less pollution. The Greenguard Certification Program by the Greenguard Environmental Institute (GEI) is similar. Greenguard standards are based on the U.S. Environmental Protection Agency's purchasing standards, Washington State's Indoor Air Quality Program, and Germany's Blue Angel Program. So far, only a few products have achieved this designation.[7]

Green Seal, the organization that classifies and certifies environmentally responsible products, including low-VOC paints, certifies interior flat paints that contain a maximum of 50 grams of VOCs per liter of paint and interior nonflat paints that contain a maximum of 150 grams of VOCs per liter. In addition, paints must meet performance criteria such as scrubbability or abrasion resistance, hiding power, and washability to be eligible for Green Seal certification.[8] Most major paint manufacturers produce at least one high-quality low-VOC line, making several low-VOC options available today. Selecting high-performance paint can mean the difference between painting once and painting four or five times in 20 years.

Wallcovering

Colors, Patterns, and Textures Are Just the Beginning

Senior living environments are visually much more appealing today than they were twenty years ago. Residents, their families, providers, and designers have learned that a living environment can look and feel like home while providing all the essentials of assisted living or skilled nursing and good healthcare. Thankfully, there are fewer debates about whether we can provide attractive housing and healthcare, and more discussion about how we can do so, and how we can make them even better.

Many seniors have lived with wallpaper most of their lives. As they move from private homes into senior living settings, they expect their new living environments to be like their former residences. Well-designed spaces with decorative finishes in colors and patterns similar to those they previously enjoyed often tip the scale in favor of one assisted living community over another.

Painting every room the same color instantly spells "institutional setting." The challenge for residential care environments is finding the best possible color combinations with appropriate designs. Nothing helps to transform an institutional environment faster, and make homes more livable and supportive, than using residentially inspired wallpaper patterns.

Wallcovering adds interest to a room. While it may not be affordable to use wallcovering in every room, one can carefully choose the places that

Figure 8.2 Wallpaper detail makes the interior porch seem like a spring garden. *Courtesy of Allen House at Springhouse, Jamaica Plain, MA. Interior Design: S. Harris Interiors, Boston, MA. Photographer: Sam Drukman, Newton, MA.*

Figure 8.3 Wallcovering can work magic. Both the brick and the flowers are wallcoverings and succeed in transforming this formerly dull room into a lively, often-used back porch. *Courtesy of Allen House at Springhouse, Jamaica Plain, MA. Interior Design: S. Harris Interiors, Boston, MA. Photographer: Sam Drukman, Newton, MA.*

make the most impact. A pretty wall treatment will easily make the dining room, country kitchen, and bathrooms more welcoming. Special coatings have been developed that provide a matte, low-luster finish that reflect less light than many painted finishes. Choose the design carefully, and remember that wall covering with bright, whimsical patterns can also be fun.

Fabric for Healthcare

The trend in healthcare design is toward using color thoughtfully and creating nurturing environments rather than following trendy colors. Color decisions are finally being influenced now by geographical location and resident needs. Designers are trying to convey a sense of emotional security and freedom from worry, resulting in environments with genuine interest and charm that shines like a bright coat of paint.

So where do we find security in an uncertain world? Not in locks on the door. Feelings of security come from the touch of another's hand, from the soft words of a friend, or from comfort foods that remind us of the uncomplicated days of childhood. The beautiful, soft, warm fabrics designed for use in healthcare environments today provide another way to convey warmth, comfort, and security using color, texture, and pattern.

Perhaps, if we're lucky, colors that are gentle on the eye will soothe the soul. Scattered dashes of color around the room can introduce fun and whimsy without creating an overdose of intense color. This is an area where further evidence-based research can benefit design innovation.

Style, Innovation, and Design—Improving on Yesterday

Designers and manufacturers in the healthcare textile market deserve a standing ovation for the contributions they have made to humanizing healthcare environments. Interior designers of healthcare settings must deliver soothing interiors that also accommodate medical procedures and a variety of other demands, a task that is especially tricky when specifying textiles. The difference in just the last ten years in the quality and beauty of fabrics for this market is unmistakable.

Fabrics were once either sophisticated and aesthetically pleasing to the eye and hand, or functional, with stain and soil resistance and antimicrobial properties. Many fabrics today are managing to be both and are very likely to succeed in a healthcare market that increasingly is turning away from the institutional look.

Crypton is one of the best fabric solutions for long-term care settings. We are now seeing styles, patterns, colors, and textures that softly whisper "home and hospitality" rather than screaming "institution and hospital." Crypton Super Fabrics offer an increasing number of options and perfor-

Figure 8.4 Today an overwhelming variety of patterns and fabrics are available for long-term-care settings. *Courtesy of Homestead at Heritage, Framingham, MA. Interior Design: Wdesign, Bolton, MA. Photographer: Stephen Sette Ducati.*

mance features. It's hard to believe that only ten years ago vinyl was the standard in healthcare settings.

Today fabrics for long-term care settings come in a sometimes overwhelming variety of patterns, styles, and textures. Used to having only colored vinyls to choose from, every healthcare designer I know is rejoicing. So, I suspect, are those who live with our designs every day.

Enhanced technology has made it possible to engineer fabrics with high performance that is built in and lasts the life of the fabric. Crypton has superior moisture, stain, and microbial resistance, and it is breathable! This is not a superficial sprayed coating, but a revolutionary upholstery textile that now offers the beauty and richness of a luxury fabric with a practicality once only found with vinyl.

Since the introduction of Crypton, almost four million yards have been used in facilities around the world. Known for its extraordinary durability, it has become the standard for healthcare, restaurants, and hotels. The demands of the hospitality industry are largely responsible for the improved colors, patterns, and textures, now available to healthcare designers.

Crypton is available in many styles, including woven fabrics, suedes, twills, and prints in beautiful patterns and colors. The beautiful and soft chenilles are among my favorites for upholstery. Not only are these fabrics being used in many of the best hotels, but families across the country are finding that peanut-butter-and-jelly-proof colors and patterns fit their lifestyles better than they could have imagined, not to speak of improving their budgets.

Crypton—extraordinary as it is—is not maintenance free. Like any fabric it too requires routine vacuuming, spot cleaning, or deep cleaning. Crypton Upholstery Cleaner, the first cleaner specifically for use on this upholstery fabric, contains two stain removers (one for protein-based stains, one for oil-based stains), a fabric freshener containing germ-killing agents, and an upholstery extraction cleaner. Engineered for Crypton Super Fabrics, the cleaner works on any water-cleanable fabric. (See the Resource listing.)

Beautiful colors and patterns are available as never before for cubicle curtains, draperies, and sheer fabrics that filter sunlight. These fabrics not only meet the demands of a 24-hour environment, but have the texture and appearance of noninstitutional fabrics. As culture change exerts a stronger influence on long-term care the trend toward home-inspired long-term-care settings grows and baby boomers demand more sophisticated residential living environments, products and ideas must also evolve to accommodate a higher level of expectations.

NOTES

Courtesy of the Madlyn and Leonard Abramson Center for Jewish Life, North Wales, PA

No matter what challenges aging or disease may bring, friends still work together, play together, and laugh together often.

Floorcovering

Today, more attention than ever is devoted to the emotional and psychological impact of the interior healthcare environment. As you enter any healthcare setting the ambiance creates a first impression about the quality of the healthcare, and the designer's challenge is to continually reinforce the image throughout the setting. The largest areas of interior finishes are the walls and floors that provide the backdrop for these healing environments. Aesthetically and functionally, nothing has contributed more to improving healthcare environments than the use of soft-surface flooring. It has transformed these institutional settings into more welcoming environments and reduced stress on residents and staff.

Until the early 1980s only hard surfaces were used in healthcare settings, because carpet was believed to be more likely to harbor and spread infectious agents. But in 1982 research by the Centers for Disease Control and Prevention (CDC) concluded that carpet does not influence the spread of illness,[1] and this prompted the floorcovering industry to begin developing better and more appropriate solutions for healthcare use. With the recognition of the many benefits of soft-surface flooring in healthcare settings we are now seeing warmer, more residential environments. Soft-surface flooring can give a soothing quality to areas that might otherwise feel cold and impersonal.

Figure 9.1 Nothing has contributed more to transforming institutional care settings into more welcoming environments than soft-surface flooring. *Courtesy of the Madlyn and Leonard Abramson Center for Jewish Life. Architect: Ewing-Cole, Philadelphia, PA. Photograph: Courtesy of Design Concepts Unlimited, Sausalito, CA.*

Choosing Floorcovering to Support Quality of Life

Floorcovering is the most visible design element in any healthcare setting and one of the most confusing to select. Often decisions are made without understanding the unique nature of long-term care settings, the impact on residents, or how products are likely to perform. While there is a wide range of floorcoverings, not all types of flooring perform equally well in all applications, and poor choices can be costly. The primary categories of flooring used today are carpet and resilient flooring. It's important to understand the advantages and limitations of each. This will help you to formulate questions to clarify the needs of your setting and assist you in making better choices.

Providing older adults with the best possible quality of life requires that we think about therapeutic issues connected with finish selections, particularly flooring. Attention must be paid not only to aesthetics, but also to a flooring's affects on mobility, balance, susceptibility to slips, falls, and resulting hip fractures, glare and noise, indoor air quality, and of course comfort. These issues have not been discussed in the context of quality of life, but without question they directly impact "the quality" and "the life" of residents—especially those with compromised abilities and immune systems in long-term care settings. It's important to recognize the connection and place greater importance on critical selection criteria.

Aesthetics

Design and color provide a wide variety of options for enhancing all living environments, especially healthcare settings striving to deinstitutionalize their look. Flooring is an important design element that can create warm, residential living environments, reducing stress and improving the sense of well-being of residents and staff. Improved design characteristics, style, and color selection mean flooring has the flexibility to meet both functional and aesthetic needs.

COLOR

Many healthcare settings choose color for its value in helping to create the ambiance of a space. Floorcovering, wall color, and lighting not only affect the aesthetic balance of a room but can significantly affect the physical balance of people in the room.

The most overlooked issue in color selection is recognizing that more mature eyes see color quite differently than the younger eyes making the color selection. As the eye matures the lens thickens, takes on a yellowish tint, and becomes less transparent, causing lush lavenders and purples, for example, to turn brown. This is described in greater depth in Chapters 4 and 5. This oversight has made many healthcare settings for older adults quite appealing to younger eyes, but significantly less colorful and exciting—and even dangerous—for older clients.

Color will vary depending both on the type and the amount of light. To be pleasing in natural and artificial light, colors should be selected carefully. It's a good idea to use a large sample to study the floorcovering color in morning, daylight, and evening light. Some colors are wonderful in the morning light but turn bland, dull, or gray in evening light. It is even more critical to make color selections under conditions that duplicate the lighting to be used in the space. It does make a difference!

> *It is critical to make color selections under conditions that duplicate the lighting to be used in the space. It does make a difference!*

PATTERN

Using pattern on the floor can be tricky in any setting for older persons, especially if they have balance and vision problems. Patterns designed to hide dirt, break up large spaces, and offer variety are quite effective for younger, healthier individuals with good vision, balance, and mobility, but they often become safety issues for more frail seniors.

Figure 9.2 We are learning how to use pattern on the floor by controlling color values and contrast. *Courtesy of Collington Episcopal Life Care Community, Mitchellville, MD. Architect: Perkins Eastman. Photographer: Massery Photography.*

With continued research we are learning how to use pattern on the floor by controlling color values and contrast. Optimal flooring for older adults has minimal contrast in pattern and medium hues and color values. Improved product styling has created greater design possibilities, and the availability of new low-contrast patterns inspired by nature has improved flooring performance by reducing problems for those with low vision.[2] Mottled or heathered yarns, rather than solids, are used to hide soil and the wear and tear of traffic.

Recent studies show that bold and intricately designed floor patterns with strong contrast are particularly hazardous to those with vision and balance problems, and further that dark, contrasting borders can create unintended challenges for those with depth perception problems.

A research study completed in 2002 evaluated the significance of floor-covering texture and pattern for mobility and balance in older adults. Significant differences were detected in the amount of time needed to walk a specified distance, depending on the texture and pattern of various floorcoverings. Patterns with large motifs and strong value contrast were found to be most problematic; large floral patterns caused the greatest amount of time to walk and prompted the greatest number of issues related to balance and falls. Patterns that supported the shortest walking times and the lowest number of incidents were those having the smallest pattern motifs and the lowest

> *Bold and intricately designed floor patterns with strong contrast are particularly hazardous to those with vision and balance problems.*

contrast.[3,4] Information from well-designed studies such as this one will be invaluable in the development of color and design patterns that better meet aesthetic preferences and the special needs of older adults.

Mobility and Slip Resistance

Flooring must promote mobility. Reducing the hazard of falling is especially important in all older adult settings. Residents must feel that they can move about with confidence and ease, especially those using canes, walkers, and wheelchairs. The proper flooring can enhance safety and comfort, minimizing the risk of falls. With improved seaming techniques carpet provides a smooth flooring surface that facilitates both foot and wheeled traffic, allowing it to flow smoothly and *quietly*. It absorbs moisture to help prevent slipping, provides a high level of comfort, and to some extent helps cushion falls, a major concern for residents unsteady on their feet.

Another study published in 2002 concluded, "Healthy, older adults do not seem to have great difficulty maintaining static balance while standing on commercial-grade carpet. The results are promising and suggest that with additional testing, this type carpet is a safe floorcovering option in terms of static balance control for healthy, older adults."[5] This is particularly good news since staff is often the most difficult to convince.

Figure 9.3 Patterns with large motifs and strong value contrast are problematic for those with balance and mobility issues. *Courtesy of Mitzi Perritt, PhD, Samuel F. Austin State University, Nacogdoches, Texas.*

Figure 9.4 Glare on flooring and fear of falling often conspire to keep older adults immobile. *Courtesy of Design Concepts Unlimited, Sausalito, CA.*

Glare

A buffed hard-surface floor may once have evoked a sense of exceptional cleanliness, but today it evokes feelings of a cold, unfriendly, institutional environment that causes problems for an aging population. Seniors are often immobilized by their fear of falling and the anxiety and confusion resulting from bright glare and compromised vision. Using appropriate carpet to eliminate painful glare increases safety and should be considered a fall prevention strategy.

Acoustics and Noise Reduction

Acoustical performance must be considered when evaluating flooring. As healthy adults most of us have strong emotional responses to noise, but for the elderly excess noise makes hearing and relaxation especially difficult and can cause irritation and frustration. The best flooring choice will depend on the area where the flooring is being used and the need for sound control.

Residential soft-surface flooring, like carpet, has a greater sound-absorbing quality than hard-surface flooring, which echoes and projects sound. According to the Carpet and Rug Institute, carpet is ten times more efficient than hard surfaces in reducing and absorbing noise.[6] Carpet's sound-absorption qualities contribute to a quieter, calmer, more relaxing environment, helping to reassure residents, improve staff morale, and, most importantly, enhance the ability to hear.

Today the greatest sound-control challenge still lies with the equipment used to maintain floors. Cleaning equipment generates noise levels that are unacceptable in any healthcare setting. The noise and disruption caused by cleaning practices is not only stressful but also a major contributor to confusion and agitation for those with Alzheimer's disease. There is no doubt that the issue of noise reduction will continue to grow in importance. How can we seriously believe that we are designing healing environments and do nothing to reduce the noise associated with required cleaning methods?

Comfort

Carpet increases comfort for residents, visitors, and staff, who spend many hours on their feet. Soft-surface flooring reduces foot and leg fatigue, particularly for residents who find walking on hard-surface floors uncomfortable. Carpet also relieves stress on muscles and joints and coldness at floor level, keeping feet and ankles warmer in winter. This is especially advantageous for elderly residents sensitive to cold temperatures. The floors are physically warmer, which helps to make the total environment seem psychologically warmer.

Indoor Air Quality

Americans, on average, spend 90 percent of their time indoors, where the air can be as much as 100 times as polluted as it is outside, according to the Environmental Protection Agency (EPA).[7] Many residents of long-term care spend 100 percent of their time indoors. This has dramatically raised the importance of indoor air quality. In fact, the EPA lists indoor air quality as one of the top five public health concerns.[8] Healthcare environments, especially older ones, face additional indoor air quality concerns due to HVAC-related problems that can lead to moisture accumulation that encourages microbial growth. Carpet has been shown to have no greater bacterial or fungal growth than hard-surface floors, and moisture-barrier backing and permanently welded seams resist moisture and prevent mold.[9]

AIRBORNE POLLUTANTS

Elderly residents, particularly those in frail health, are vulnerable to volatile organic compounds (VOCs) in their environment. Inadequate ventilation and indoor pollutants such as dust and allergens can lower indoor air quality further, causing breathing problems for asthmatic residents and those who suffer respiratory ailments and allergies.

On hard, smooth surfaces allergens are continually "kicked up" by foot traffic. They remain airborne briefly, falling to the floor only to be disrupted again and again until the floor surface is cleaned. By comparison, soft-surface flooring such as carpet traps allergens within its textile surface until they are removed during scheduled cleaning.[10] EPA studies confirm the effectiveness of carpet in reducing airborne particles,[11] lowering the potential for exposure.

Everyday cleaning solutions, including the stripping compounds and waxes used on resilient floors, contain toxic VOCs that are released into the breathing zone. According to EPA recommendations, maintenance that requires stripping and waxing should be performed only when buildings can remain unoccupied for at least 48 hours; however, this is not practical in most healthcare environments. Soft-surface flooring, installed with a "peel and stick" method rather than using wet glue or adhesives, leaves the air virtually free of VOCs released into the air during installation.[12]

Odor

Undesirable odor is never a good thing, especially in long-term-care settings. Although the goal is to clean all spills immediately, this is not always possible. The most important flooring characteristic for odor prevention is a functional moisture barrier. Impervious backings keep spills on the surface of the carpet and prevent them from passing through to the subfloor, contaminating it forever in the case of urine. This offers the best chance for complete removal when the spot is cleaned, avoiding odor buildup. New advances in carpet, however, do not substitute for a regular maintenance program.

Incontinence and urinary accidents are part of life in care settings. Tea tree oil has been used as an odor-control agent in Australian nursing homes with great results for almost 20 years. The American adaptation of this product, Syon-5, attacks the enzymes that cause off-gassing—the primary source of urine's foul odor—and keeps on working between applications, blocking the return of lingering unpleasant odors common with standard cleaners.[13]

How Do You Choose the Right Floorcovering for a Healthcare Environment?

When asked to choose between a healthcare setting with carpet and one without, invariably people chose the settings with carpet.

Choosing the right floorcovering calls for selecting a product that has visual appeal and appropriate safety characteristics, ensures indoor air quality and ease of maintenance, and contributes to a healthy environment. Inappropriate flooring can create a variety of serious environmental hazards, including off-gassing and an increase in slip/fall accidents. Don't forget to consider the life-cycle cost when choosing floorcovering; it can be even more important than the initial purchase cost.

When asked to choose between a healthcare setting with carpet and one without, invariably people chose the settings with carpet. Both acute

Figure 9.5 The aesthetic of the wood-grain vinyl and functional performance make resilient flooring a good choice for the porch. *Courtesy of the Madlyn and Leonard Abramson Center for Jewish Life. Architect: Ewing-Cole, Philadelphia, PA. Photographer: Jeffrey Totaro.*

and long-term care settings are moving from virtually no use of carpet to installing carpet in main lobbies, corridors, patient and resident rooms, exam rooms, and therapy areas. The Carpet and Rug Institute found that nearly 80 percent of healthcare facility managers are satisfied with the results when they use carpet.[14]

Simplifying the Selection—Complex Decisions

When the clientele is aging residents the complexity increases. Many flooring and carpet companies offer soft and clear colors, natural wood grains, and inviting textures, making it possible to move away from the institutional look, but the large number of choices makes the selection process complex. Step one is to define the functional performance needs and determine how durable the flooring must be and how much maintenance is required for each floor area. In a kitchen, resident bathroom, or beauty shop, for example, resilient flooring is a good choice; in a living room, library, or other social spaces carpet is a better selection, and in a dining area either might be appropriate. Using a floor plan and colored markers to indicate various types of flooring and their location can help you visualize your choices.

Questions to Ask

- Is aesthetic appearance important in one area but not in another? For example, aesthetic appearance is obviously important in living spaces and social spaces enjoyed by residents, their families, and other visitors. It is not important in storage closets, janitorial closets, and select task areas.
- What daily activities take place in each area?
- Are food and drink consumed in the area?
- Do activities include rolling traffic, such as wheelchairs or carts?
- How much traffic does each area see?

High-Performance Carpet

Healthcare environments demand durability and high performance, particularly in the area of floor finishes. While historically decisions about floor-covering have been based primarily on cost and ease of maintenance, technological advances in carpet fiber, textures, moisture barriers in backings, antimicrobial properties, stain resistance, and patterns that hide soil encourage the use of carpet in healthcare settings.

Appearance is an aesthetic choice; appearance retention is a performance issue.

Appearance is an aesthetic choice; appearance retention is a performance issue. While there is a need to balance aesthetics against performance in the specification of many interior products, this need is perhaps most pronounced in the case of healthcare flooring.[15]

Carpet with moisture-barrier backing is recommended for living and social spaces, hallways, and resident bedrooms. Carpet hybrids have a surface constructed of tufted carpet to reduce the chance of falls and absorb glare and noise, while the backing is an impermeable material.[16] In a move to provide carpets that are both sustainable and environmentally responsible, the carpet industry is moving away from the use of vinyl. Many of the new backings are constructed from post–consumer recycled materials such as windshields and safety glass.

Carpet today incorporates high-quality materials, engineered for the most demanding environments, to produce a virtually indestructible loop pile that is designed to ensure resistance to matting and crushing. Nylon (Type 6 and Type 6.6) is the fiber of choice for healthcare settings because of its strength, abrasion resistance, resilience, and aesthetic qualities. New technologies now lock color into fiber, so that it can stand up to anything from aggressive cleaning solutions to intense sunlight without losing its color. The increased range of both soft and vibrant colors helps to enliven long-term care settings. Solution-dyed yarn, while still popular, is no longer the only suitable solution for healthcare flooring.

Carpet performance is associated in part with pile yarn density, which is the amount of pile yarn in a given volume of carpet face. A higher density carpet helps prevent soiling by keeping dirt from penetrating into the carpet. Dense, smooth, lower-pile healthcare carpet provides a flat surface for safer walking and easy rolling and will give the most performance for the cost. Whether the carpet has cut or loop pile, it is the high density that is most important for ease of maintenance.

Resilient Flooring

Resilient flooring materials include vinyl, rubber, and natural-based products, vinyl being the most common. The lowest-cost resilient floor option is vinyl composition tile (VCT), which is typically restricted to spaces where there is little foot traffic. Solid vinyl tile offers better resistance to abrasive wear and impact damage, but because of the large number of seams neither is ideal for long-term care environments with high levels of incontinence.

Resilient flooring has made considerable advances in visual appeal, and the variety of color and patterns in vinyl sheet flooring makes it ideal for wet areas such a bathrooms and bathing/spa areas. Familiar wood-grain patterns that replicate the texture and appearance of natural hardwood flooring provide a durable flooring material with visual appeal, ideal for residential dining, kitchens, and laundry rooms. Vinyl resilient sheet flooring has gained popularity because it reduces the number of seams in the floor, improving both appearance and sanitation. Available in 9, 12, and 15 feet widths, vinyl sheet flooring can be cut to fit. Seams are heat-welded or bonded with liquid vinyl.

Figure 9.6 Familiar wood-grain patterns provide a durable flooring material for this comfortable interior porch. *Courtesy of Friendship Village, Bloomington, MN. Architect: WAI Continuum, St. Paul, MN. Photographer: Saari & Forrai Photography, Blaine, MN.*

Rubber resilient sheet flooring, now available in a broader selection of colors, has only recently become more widely used in areas requiring a non-slip floor.

Linoleum, first introduced in the early 1900s, was replaced by vinyl in the 1960s. A combination of environmental concerns and a new generation of linoleum products may be driving its comeback. Unlike vinyl made with polyvinyl chloride (PVC), linoleum is made from natural materials, including linseed oil, cork or wood flour, limestone, natural pigments, resins, and jute. Linoleum is environmentally friendly and durable, but the disadvantages are that new floors give off a linseed-oil scent, and the linoleum requires an annual coating of acrylic sealer.[17]

Smooth, hard-surface flooring such as wood, ceramic tile, vinyl composite tile (VCT) and sheet vinyl pose a greater risk of falls than soft-surface products such as carpet. Spills and daily wet mopping increase the risk of slips on hard-surface floors, though resilient floors are still the appropriate product for wet areas such as bathrooms, shower rooms, and bath spas. For these spaces select resilient flooring with increased slip-resistance.

Transitions

Transitions between flooring finishes can cause problems. The transition strip required between floor finishes is tough to keep smooth and clean and usually causes a bump. This can, in turn, precipitate a trip or a correspondingly bumpy ride for those in wheelchairs. Low-profile transition strips in a color value similar to the floor color lessens the problem but does not eliminate it.[18] Transitions can be particularly difficult for older adults with vision and depth perception problems. Because a transition strip may alter the flooring color and texture, it can create the illusion of a difference in the height of the floor surface. Using a transition strip of a similar color value to the flooring will help. Seniors may also have difficulty in quickly adjusting their walking to the demands of different floor surfaces when they pass from one surface to another. Using contiguous flooring material to the greatest extent possible minimizes transitions and is less problematic for residents.

Maintenance and Protection

Investigate maintenance costs when choosing flooring. Sometimes the flooring that is initially the cheapest turns out to be the most expensive when you consider the costs that accumulate over the product's life cycle. Carpet is relatively inexpensive to maintain, which helps lower its overall life cycle costs. A Carpax Associates Inc. study found that the cost of carpet ranges from 33 to 78 percent less than that of noncarpeted flooring, making it a cost-effective investment.[19] VCT is the most costly floor to maintain.

Stain resistance and maintenance are increasingly important to cost effectiveness, prolonging the life of a significant investment in high-quality flooring. Cleanliness and proper maintenance affect a floor's performance and lifespan. Today's new carpet products have a built-in moisture barrier that keeps spills from penetrating and are designed so that many stains can be removed with water and a mild detergent alone.

All floorcovering should be maintained according to the manufacturer's recommended cleaning and maintenance methods. Thanks to advancements in technology and fiber engineering, the long-term maintenance of high-performance carpet is less than one-fifth the cost of caring for hard-surface floors. Routine floor cleaning includes daily vacuuming and periodic hot-water extraction cleaning. Carpet in a healthcare setting must be able to withstand not only heavy traffic but many hot-water extractions.

> *The long-term maintenance of high-performance carpet is less than one-fifth the cost of caring for hard-surface floors.*

HEPA

Most healthcare settings vacuum frequently between hot-water extraction cleanings. Advances in vacuum cleaner design, function, and productivity have led to the adoption of high-efficiency particulate air (HEPA) filters. The traditional vacuum can recirculate as much as 30 percent of the dust it takes in; HEPA filters, in contrast, were designed to remove the finest dust particles, pollen, mites, and other microorganisms in hospitals and laboratories.[20] The vacuum cleaner best suited for use in a healthcare setting is one with a HEPA filter that uses water, a natural filter, so that bacteria and airborne particles that are picked up are not blown back into the air.[21] Lightweight and relatively quiet backpack vacuums with HEPA filtration are also available now.

Unfortunately, the one area where improved technology is most needed continues to be ignored. The cleaning equipment used to maintain all flooring products generates unacceptable noise levels. Noise causes stress and agitation, and the most effective way to minimize noise is at the source. We have provided safer, more comfortable, and homelike environments, but at the same time we continue to have wet floors and more noise than a rock concert—a serious problem in a healing environment.

Courtesy of English Rose Suites, Minneapolis, MN

Families are important. Elders need their families,
they need children visiting, and they need laughter.

Sustainability and Green Design

Healthcare environments aren't the first in line to go green, but they should be!

There is a growing interest in "green" or "sustainable" design for long-term care. While the healthcare sector has been slow to take up the cause, providers and sponsors in senior living are showing greater interest. For some the issue is life cycle cost reduction, but for others it reflects the growing interest in environmentally sensitive design.[1]

From the broadest perspective, *sustainability* means meeting the needs of the current generation without compromising the needs of future generations. What does that entail? To begin with, it involves using products manufactured in the most sustainable ways possible and designing buildings and spaces that deliver value for the residents and support the well-being of the occupants.[2] Many of us are struggling to understand the implications of sustainability.

With the world population increasing by 100 million people each year, we are consuming natural resources as though there were an unlimited supply. It's time to quickly manage our natural resources for future generations, and learn to live in harmony with nature. The most prominent issues are solid waste disposal, sustainability, and the protection of biodiversity. The cost of transporting and disposing of waste in landfills is rising rapidly, a problem accelerated because the United States is reducing the number of landfills in which to bury waste. An average of 4 billion pounds of carpet alone is thrown into landfills every year.[3] This is a significant problem, raising the question of how do we minimize the environmental impact by conserving natural resources, reducing emissions, water use and energy use, improving safety and health, and encouraging value recovery?

All the talk about green buildings and products has created some confusion over what makes a product green. It is not the presence or absence of a single item, such as recycled content or volatile organic compounds (VOCs), but a combination of attributes, including the source of the raw materials, the energy used to manufacturer and deliver the product, and the durability of the product. Recycled content ranges in today's green products from much less than half to 100 percent.

> *Whether it is a hospital, an assisted living, nursing home, adult day care, or other healing environment, all settings that serve older adults, particularly those that care for the most frail and vulnerable, should be healthy environments in all respects.*

Whether it is a hospital, an assisted living, nursing home, adult day care, or other healing environment, all settings that serves older adults, particularly those that care for the most frail and vulnerable, should be healthy environments in all respects. What is better than preventive medicine? Sustainability goes beyond natural light and healing gardens to the heart of the design, materials, operations, and maintenance. It involves better and more efficient building design, removing toxic substances from building materials and indoor materials and finishes, removing and replacing toxic cleaning products that contaminate the environment, and promoting conservation.

In senior living environments energy is primarily used in lighting, heating, ventilation, air-conditioning, and water management. The building design and specifications for the environment can impact energy efficiency, facilitate conservation, and assist in reducing associated costs.[4]

Manufacturers are developing greener products and going beyond recycling to find ways to remanufacture the original products for another cycle of use before they are finally recycled. This is particularly true in the carpet industry. Value-added products created from already useful recyclable materials represent the cutting edge of sustainable development today.

A survey conducted by the International Facility Management Association (IFMA) in September 2002 determined that 95 percent of facility professionals view sustainability as an important issue, and most are already taking steps to ensure a greener environment. Their concerns included cost savings, as might be expected, environmental responsibility, product life cycle analysis, and above all (76 percent), improving the health and productivity of those working in and using the building. Of those participating in this study, 58 percent use or plan to add environmental criteria to vendor and product selection. Instead of simply looking at individual characteristics like recycled content, more professionals are analyzing the overall environmental impact of products and processes, including product life cycles.[5]

The Importance of Certification

With the increasing number of environmentally responsible products, manufacturers have flooded the market with environmental claims. These claims can be confusing in today's world of clever marketing, where it's easy for companies to overstate how "environmentally friendly" their products are. Certification provides a reliable way to determine the validity of an environmental claim.

There are varying degrees of certification—first-, second-, and third-party. Third-party certification is considered most reliable. It increases the distance between the manufacturer or service provider and the independent party (with no financial interests) certifying the environmental claims of the manufacturer.[6] Scientific Certification Systems, a U.S. environmental certification claims leader, reviews thousands of products to verify their sustainability claims. It certifies those that meet EPA standards as Environmentally Preferable Products, identifying products and services that are less harmful to human health and the environment than competitors'.[7]

More and more healthcare settings are recognizing that environmentally friendly and responsible design practices can help preserve buildings for future generations. For example, flooring is typically replaced every three to five years. The growing trend is to specify flooring made from recycled components, and manufacturers are in turn producing more products made from recycled materials.

Carpet is also a good example of how evaluating the total environmental impact can help design professionals identify the most sustainable product choice. In addition to life quality and operational attributes, designers selecting carpet should consider environmental guidelines such as the EPA Environmentally Preferable Products purchasing program and the U.S. Green Building Council LEED rating systems.[8] Performance should never be sacrificed for environmental attributes; in the case of carpet fiber, superior performance will extend the service life of the carpet, eliminating the need to replace it prematurely. Proper installation and a dedicated maintenance schedule help retain appearance and performance, improving a carpet's overall sustainability. Keeping carpet in place longer helps conserve resources, including the energy needed to manufacture a new product.[9] It also reduces replacement costs.

When a carpet does reach the end of its useful life, reclamation programs can turn all types of used commercial carpet into other materials. Major renovations of healthcare facilities often cause vast amounts of carpet to be scheduled for landfill burial. Recycling is a more environmentally friendly alternative. When planning renovations, facility planners should contact suppliers about recycling opportunities and consider replacement carpet with recyclable content in the face fiber and backing materials. It is not uncommon for today's major suppliers to use 10 to 50 percent recyclable nylon content.[10]

Ninety-five percent of facility professionals view sustainability as an important issue, and most are already taking steps to ensure a greener environment.

Specifiers make a valuable contribution when they work actively with carpet representatives and write specifications that require the general contractor to make arrangements for separating old carpet from debris and sending it to a recycler instead of the landfill. The DuPont Carpet Reclamation program, in operation since 1991, accepts all types of nylon as well as other fiber types. This program keeps material out of landfills and gives it a new beginning by turning it into products such as resilient flooring, carpet cushion, and automobile parts. It is the only independently certified program for recycling used commercial carpet.[11]

Sustainability is a complex issue. It means incorporating new thinking in the healthcare settings we design, build, and operate. These healing environments should support those who work within their walls and the residents and patients who live in them. What can the design of healthcare facilities do to help the environment? Kaiser Permanente, one of the larger healthcare systems is developing standards nationwide and greening up its specifications. They take sustainability seriously, and so will the people who make its upholstery, flooring, shades, and wallcoverings.[12] That will help the healthcare industry as a whole.

We have to think about the relationship between health and a healthy environment and in a greater sense the global environment. In other words, the issue isn't just indoor air quality, it's also outdoor air quality. Design for healing and healthcare means living in balance and harmony with nature and providing a quality of life consistent with our philosophy on protecting the environment. Specifying sustainable materials brings a great feeling, knowing I'm doing my part to help keep the environment safe and healthy for my family—Mary, Ed, Jason, and Walker—and all future generations.

Culture Change

Creating Home and Community

Courtesy of Meadow Lark Hills Retirement Community, Manhattan, KS

Some people never tire of the challenge of making a good plan come together.

What Is Culture Change?

CHAPTER

11

*C*ulture change is the new buzzword in long-term care. In the world of aging, culture change has been described as everything from new wallpaper and a bird in the lobby to a major social shift in American society. Culture change is the process of moving from a traditional nursing home model, character-ized as a system that is unintentionally designed to foster dependence by keeping residents "well cared for, safe, and powerless,"[1] to a "regenerative" model. This model is also sometimes referred to as "resident-centered" care because it increases the resident's autonomy and sense of control.[2] Culture change embodies an emerging, progressive view of aging and the struggle and determination to find a common thread in the various approaches reformu-lating what it means to grow older in America.

> *C*ulture change is a continuing process of growth.

Nursing home culture change means systemic change throughout a facility from both the individual and the organizational perspective. It is transformation anchored in values and beliefs that returns control to elders and those who work most closely with them. The goal is creating a culture of aging that is life affirming, satisfying, humane, and meaningful. Success-fully implemented, it can transform a facility into a home, a patient into a person, and a schedule into a choice. Culture change is a continuing process of growth with a unique richness. It nurtures hope, encourages growth, and provides opportunities to learn.

Why Change?

Instead of viewing aging as just another step of an incredible personal journey in the second half of life, this country sees aging as a curse. Its long-term care settings aren't necessarily designed as places to live and thrive. But older adults are remaining at home longer, and the number of assisted living settings is growing. This places more pressure on nursing homes to provide living environments that appeal to younger consumers. Baby boomers, described as "well informed, well educated, well traveled, widely accustomed to creature comforts and instant gratification, and historically outspoken," are doing the shopping for parents,[3] and it can safely be assumed that they will not find the traditional nursing home appealing or acceptable. When baby boomers themselves begin requiring care, elder care settings will have to change quickly to accommodate their expectations—expectations for a superlative quality of life for as long as possible.

There are seniors who are bored, helpless, and lonely in facilities all over the country.

While seniors may be physically healthier than ever before, their spirits may not be. There are seniors who are bored, helpless, and lonely in facilities all over the country. This means we urgently need to move beyond the medical model of care and embrace a more social model that focuses on the individual in a meaningful, life-affirming way.

In-depth change requires transformation of both individual and societal attitudes toward aging and elders; transformation of elders' attitudes toward themselves and their aging; changes in attitudes and behavior of caregivers toward those they care for; and changes in governmental policy and regulation.[4] The growing community of those dedicated to transforming attitudes on aging has spawned a national movement: the Pioneer Network, whose mission is to advocate and facilitate deep system change and transformation in the American culture of aging.

The earliest nursing home pioneers began their work in the 1970s as individuals working to rethink long-term care. Their efforts grew into a national grass roots movement focused on transforming nursing homes from a medical to a more holistic care model. As their numbers and experience grew, these kindred spirits knew in their hearts that things could be different for our elders. They believed, as we must believe, that life with meaning is possible in any setting—home, assisted living, or the nursing home. As their focus broadened from nursing homes to include the whole continuum of long-term care, they became known as the Pioneer Network.

We must believe that life with meaning is possible in any setting—home, assisted living, or the nursing home.

Providers, healthcare professionals, regulators, advocates, family members, residents, researchers, educators, policy makers, attorneys, architects and design professionals, people from all disciplines—people like you and me who agree that older adults should be living meaningful lives in a community, in a social model home setting—are driving this change. A founda-

PIONEER VISION, VALUES, AND MISSION

Vision

A culture of aging that is life-affirming, satisfying, humane, and meaningful.

Values

- Know each person.
- Each person can and does make a difference.
- Relationship is the fundamental building block of a transformed culture.
- Respond to spirit as well as mind and body.
- Risk taking is a normal part of life.
- Put person before task.
- All elders are entitled to self-determination wherever they live.
- Community is the antidote to institutionalization.
- Do unto others as you would have them do unto you.
- Promote the growth and development of all.
- Shape and use the potential of the environment in all its aspects: physical, organizational, psycho/social/spiritual.
- Practice self-examination, searching for new creativity and opportunities for doing better.
- Recognize that culture change and transformation are not destinations but a journey, always a work in progress.

Mission

The Pioneer Network advocates and facilitates deep system change in our culture of aging. To achieve this, we:

- Create communication, networking, and learning opportunities.
- Build and support relationships and community.
- Identify and promote transformations in practice, services, public policy, and research.
- Develop and provide access to resources and leadership.

Courtesy of *The Pioneer Network* © 2001, Rochester, NY.

tion of support for transforming environments and practices is being framed through a healthy exchange of ideas and shared experiences.

Finding a Way Back Home

Americans are living longer, and concern about the quality of life in nursing homes and care settings is growing. We fear aging as a time of dependency and loss. Baby boomers are calling for a new paradigm of care, where life continues to have meaning whether one lives independently, in an assisted living community, or in a nursing home. In less than ten years the first baby boomers will turn 65, setting off an explosion in America's elderly population. Their numbers will more than double in the next 50 years, from 34.7 million to 78.9 million in 2050.[5] They, or more accurately we, expect dignity, choice, and self-determination. Unfortunately the conventional policies and practices of nursing homes and assisted living and adult day care programs don't often meet these expectations either for residents or staff.

About 5 percent of all the elderly—1.6 million people—currently live in 16,800 nursing homes across the country. That number will soon soar, reflecting the accelerated growth of the oldest old (those over age 85) and the growing number of working women. Women are typically the caregivers for aged loved ones.[6] Too many seriously ill older adults say they would rather die than to go into a long-term care facility. The problem is not the people; it's the culture. Nursing homes have been modeled after acute hospital care, where routines are inflexible and the focus is on resident dependence. Residents are treated as patients with problems, with conditions rather than strengths. Too often identified by their diseases or conditions rather than their names, they are isolated from the rhythms of everyday life and become disenfranchised as the objects of care services. Staff make daily lifestyle decisions for residents—when to get up, when to eat and what to eat, when to bathe, and when to go to bed. These medical-model nursing homes are nothing like the homes that most residents come from, and all too often they become places of loneliness, depression, and decline. "We supply the necessities of survival, but we deprive them of the necessities for living."[7]

The cornerstone of the Pioneer approach is striking in its simplicity. "Residents first!" The goal is to redesign nursing homes as places for living, with good medical and nursing care supporting rather than dominating daily life. Strongly influenced by the residential nature of assisted living in recent years, the environment is characterized by a "sense of home." Control over daily life is restored to the resident and to those closest to the resident, the Certified Nursing Assistants.[8] A community develops that connects residents, staff, and families to one another. It changes the culture in the care setting to one where residents can continue to grow even in the last years of their lives. The challenge of building a sense of community rests in

*"**W**e supply the necessities of survival, but we deprive them of the necessities for living."*

The goal is to redesign nursing homes as a place for living, with good medical and nursing care supporting rather than dominating daily life.

Figure 11.1 Residential influences are strongly felt in current design for assisted living. *Courtesy of Sumner on Ridgewood, Copley Township, OH. Architect: Dorsky Hodgson + Partners, Cleveland, OH.*

finding ways for residents to participate meaningfully within the community. It is the sense of belonging and having a significant role in the community—where contributions are valued—that promotes joy and aliveness.

Culture change in long-term care must start at the top through governance and the executives, permeating every part of the organization. There is no cookie-cutter approach, and it will never happen if the whole organization is not involved. There are three environments essential for culture change: the organizational environment, the psychosocial/spiritual environment, and the physical environment.[9] Often in the enthusiasm for change the first impulse is to change the physical environment instead of first preparing a strong foundation. The visual impact of a pretty country kitchen won't brighten anyone's life if there is no one in it. A better strategy is to begin by changing attitudes, moving from a medical model to a social model of care, and securing total support from all levels of management. With changes in the first two environments, designing the physical changes to support the psychosocial environment is much easier.

Organizational Change

Culture change must start at the top, with total support and participation from all levels of management. Staff participation in planning and design is essential, for without the involvement of the whole organization culture change will never get off the ground. A flattened organizational hierarchy allows redistribution of authority and responsibility.[11] This approach empowers staff, inspires creativity, and puts more focus where it belongs, on direct care staff, who provide for residents' needs.

Psychosocial/Spiritual Change

The psychosocial/spiritual environment is about relationships—getting to know, being involved with, and often loving the elders we care for. Most people thrive when their basic needs are met: a sense of control over daily life; a sense of identity; meaningful relationships with others; and at least a minimal degree of variety and diversity. The psychosocial/spiritual environment gets to the heart of life and relationships within the community. It's definitely time for a change if the staff rather than the residents are making all the decisions.[10]

Long-term care becomes an environment for meeting resident needs rather than institutional needs.

In all three environments the change that's required is a matter of attitudes and in most cases "serious attitude adjustments." Changing minds, changing the ways we have always worked, the way we were trained, the way things have always been done can be difficult and painful. It can also be exhilarating, fun, and filled with a high level of satisfaction for residents and staff. Change means moving from a task-oriented structure based on efficiency to a person-centered focus in which residents make decisions. Long-term care becomes an environment for meeting resident needs rather than institutional needs.

For example, does it really matter if eight residents got a bath if no one enjoyed it? There is no doubt that we need to put fun and creativity into our work. When we do, residents respond. The care is more satisfying—even enjoyable—for all. This change highlights the need to rethink care-staff evaluations to reflect the new focus and goals.

Activities can be a key place to initiate change. Instead of an activity calendar filled with scheduled events, why not throw out the schedule and give residents a true home experience with all of its spontaneity and opportunity for choices? Gardens and outside spaces encourage walking and exercise. Sleeping late and having lunch in the garden become options and meaningful activities, while providing places for children to play is prompting more families to include children in their visits.

Figure 11.2 Group hugs are the best! *Courtesy of the Life Enrichment Center, Kings Mountain, NC.*

Figure 11.3 Having places for children to play encourages families to visit more often. *Courtesy of Legacy Gardens, Iowa City, IA. Architect: InVision Architecture, Omaha, NE. Interior Design: The Interior Design Firm, Omaha, NE.*

Figure 11.4. Children's outdoor play area. *Courtesy of Village Shalom. Overland Park, KS. Architect: Nelson Tremain Partnership, Minneapolis, MN. Interior Design, Tranin Design, Kansas City, MO. Photographer: Steve Swalwell, Architectural Fotographics.*

Physical Change

Implementing the organizational and psychosocial changes first, provides solid ground work for understanding how the physical environment is expected to function. Modification and change is then made much easier. Design changes can contribute to a social/holistic model of care that accommodates and supports rather than "driving" residents' behavior. The community can be divided into smaller neighborhoods where typically 8 to 12 residents share a living room, dining room, kitchen, and pantry. The reduction in scale helps to create a home that actually looks and feels familiar, like the homes most of us are used to. It's more comfortable and results in residents spending more time together building their community and even looking out for each other.

Meals are a particularly important part of any resident's day. Mealtime is both an opportunity for nutrition and an equally important opportunity to socialize with friends. Person-centered care in smaller, more intimate settings has transformed mealtime by replacing tray service and its task-oriented climate of efficiency to a multicourse family-style meal. Residents decide what and how much they would like to eat. The food is hot, the choice belongs to the residents, appetites improve, and the atmosphere is warm and congenial.

Figure 11.5 The reduction in scale helps to make this a comfortable room to spend time with others. *Courtesy of Minnesota Masonic Home, Bloomington, MN. Interior Design: Encompass Interiors, St. Paul, MN. Photographer: Saari & Forrai Photography,* www.saariphoto.com.

Figure 11.6 The pretty and sunny dining room in the Memory Care center turns out to be where residents and staff choose to spend much of their time. *Courtesy of Presbyterian Homes of South Carolina, Columbia, SC. Architect: James, Durant, Matthews & Shelley, Inc., Sumter, SC. Interior Design: Interior Planning Associates, Greenville, SC. Photographer: Brian Erkens—Studio D Photography.*

Restaurant-style dining has also replaced assembly-line trays and given residents an opportunity to order from menus. With a creative design, Crestview Home (Bethany, MD) added buffet dining as an option. The buffet is structured on two levels to allow ambulatory diners and diners in wheelchairs equal access. Those who are able to walk can access food from one side of the buffet, while people using wheelchairs can easily reach it from the other.

This new culture goes beyond providing excellent medical care. It promotes choice and nurtures the human spirit as it builds an environment that has features of a resident's own home. With the many improvements in care and environments brought about by culture change, elders now have a better opportunity to live their lives in comfortable, satisfying surroundings.[12]

Culture Change Makes a Difference

Culture change is not about nursing homes—it's about transforming a society that's lost its way. In a taped discussion about her ethical will, Mrs. Beatrice Taishoff, a 99-year-old resident of the Jewish Home and Hospital (Bronx, NY), had a hopeful message, "There's a general tendency to see

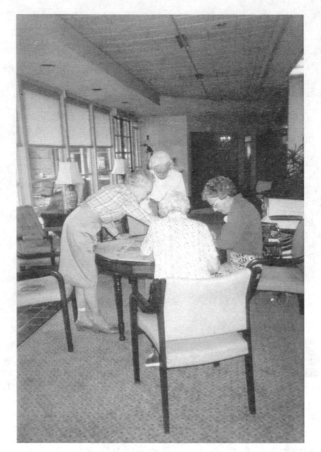

Figure 11.7 There is always something interesting going on when care settings become communities. *Courtesy of Duncaster, a Life Care Retirement Community, Bloomfield, CT and Design Concepts Unlimited, Sausalito, CA.*

elders primarily as having problems and as being frail. I believe that despite those losses, there is something else—that essence is there. We just have to uncover it—go through the layers to find it, and hope to develop this relationship with each person—a partnership—to rediscover meaning in life."[13]

Changing the culture of a nursing home may result in positive mental health changes for residents, including those with dementia. Person-centered care encourages relationships. With improved relationships, the elders we spend time with every day are more responsive and often show improvement in both physical health and well-being. There is more joy and a sense of community. Families are more engaged and more satisfied. Staff retention is enhanced, and perhaps most importantly, elders living in settings affected by culture change have called their experience "a little bit of heaven."

Culture change to be sure is an attempt to deal with yesterday's failings, but it is also an opportunity to deal with tomorrow's challenges. Bill Thomas, MD (of the Eden Alternative) has long predicted the demise of the nursing home for having failed to pay attention to customer needs and preferences. What seniors are looking for is not the right healthcare provider but the right housing environment. It's not hard to understand why settings whose primary purpose is to deal with the frailties and illnesses accompanying aging are not eagerly embraced. The average senior's aversion to them stems more from an unwillingness to confront the realities of aging than from the issue of facility quality.

Older adults want a home that will help them stay healthy or at least as healthy as possible. They recognize but don't want to be confronted with images of their impending frailty. Because housing is their primary focus Continuing Care Retirement Communities (CCRCs) more successfully emphasize housing—not health, with healthcare discreetly in the background.[14] Assisted living and nursing homes using a social model of care must be designed to feel more like home and blend easily into their community or surroundings.

When we transform our long-term care settings into human communities, places for living and growing, then we will ultimately change the very nature of aging in America.[15] Baby boomers are coming along and will drive change as consumers and as residents. Culture change is going to happen. It is the right thing to do.

Culture Changing Outcomes

While research on the outcomes of culture change is still very limited, the information currently available is promising. In 1994 Providence Mount St. Vincent in Seattle became one of the first to institute neighborhoods, areas in the home that serve small groups of up to 15 residents with their own

Figure 11.8 A group gathers in the afternoon for tea and talk. *Courtesy Meadow Lark Hills Retirement Community, Manhattan, KS.*

living and dining rooms and consistent staffing. The evaluation of their culture change program showed an 11 percent reduction in routine medication use, a 19 percent decrease in PRN medication, a 40 percent reduction in the use of medication for bowel management, a 100 percent reduction in the use of anti-anxiety medications, an 87 percent reduction in PRN anti-anxiety medications, a 100 percent reduction in the use of anti-psychotic medications, a 100 percent reduction in sedative hypnotics, a 50 percent increase in resident activity levels, and a more than 100 percent increase in social interaction.[16]

The Institute for Quality Improvement in Long Term Health Care cited a 33 percent reduction in the use of PRN medication for anxiety and depression in nursing homes incorporating the Eden Alternative model. They also recorded a 44 percent decrease in staff absenteeism and a 60 percent reduction of in-house decubitus ulcers. The cumulative rate of bedfast residents decreased by 25 percent; use of restraints decreased by 18 percent.[17]

Long-term care settings adopting Pioneer culture change approaches report positive changes in resident quality of life. Families become more involved in meaningful ways as a sense of community becomes more evident, and staff have seen the "disengaged nursing home look" disappear from residents faces as they become more involved in life. There is an increased level of activity, most notably in specialized care settings for persons with dementia. There is less staff absenteeism, and turnover is reported to be reduced. While this reporting is anecdotal, it is also promising, and additional studies are under way.

I remember how we struggled with Alzheimer's special care units in the early 1980s. There was a strong feeling that the emphasis on special care was necessary to significantly highlight care and the environment changes necessary to better care for residents with dementia and provide a better quality of life. We wanted the emphasis on Alzheimer's disease initially, to focus attention on its special needs, but we also wanted special care for all aging loved ones. It truly warms my heart to know that we are now placing the focus on special needs, special environmental supports, and special care for all older persons without regard to diagnosis. It gives me cause for hope that we can find ways to care for each other humanely and comfortably, as we all hope to be cared for if we need it.

In a three-year study recently completed in New York state, culture change was shown to have substantial beneficial consequences for residents and staff. Resident health and well-being was enhanced, relationship building between staff and residents increased. There was increased social activity, less depression, and a reduction in falls, weight loss, and dehydration.[18,19]

National Models of Culture Change

Person-Centered Care

This philosophy of care supports resident choice. Key components are:

- a philosophical shift from care and protection of the body to helping people achieve lives of personal satisfaction
- the creation of individualized living spaces
- the empowerment of direct support staff as advocates for individuals
- respect of each person's unique lifelong patterns, preferences, and individual needs
- the opportunity for each person to experience personal growth, development, and a sense of contribution
- continued connection to the greater community.

Resident-Directed Care

Developed by Charlene Boyd and Robert Ogden, Providence Mount St. Vincent in Seattle was perhaps the first nursing home to institute dramatic culture change. It has contributed enormously to the knowledge of outcomes associated with these changes by documenting and publishing results. This model is designed to return control and decision making to the resident. Instituting neighborhoods, cross-training staff, committing to consistent staffing, and using registered nurses as experts rather than supervisors resulted in increased interaction time for residents and improvements in medical indicators. The nursing home is made up of small neighborhoods. Each community has its own budget for social work, activities, housekeeping, nursing, personal assistance, and management. Each also has its own laundry and family-style kitchen. With this model,

- Residents have control over their daily activities. Strict schedules for eating, waking, and bathing are eliminated. Residents choose own daily routines; when to get up, when to go to bed.
- Nursing home staff support resident decisions and share responsibility for them. If a resident with a memory problem enjoys making his own tea, the staff makes sure the burner is turned off afterward.
- Facilities have fewer managers and more front-line staff.
- Workers are given extensive cross-training; everyone can make a sandwich or answer a call bell.
- Nurse aides, called resident assistants, are well paid and well respected.

Restraint-Free/Individualized Care

This model of care, developed by Joanne Rader while at the Benedictine Institute of Long-Term Care in Mt. Angel, Oregon, returns residents to familiar and comfortable routines. Individualized care looks for the underlying reasons for inappropriate behavior, depression, or excess disability; for example, the caregiver's own behavior may be the culprit. Bathing experiences are personalized, and physical restraints are eliminated. Problems are solved creatively by viewing life through the resident's eyes. This model is particularly useful with residents who have dementia because it confirms these individuals still have the right to direct their own care. According to this model,

- Staff must be creative and compassionate when addressing behavior and make decisions from the point of view of the resident.
- No physical restraints, and very limited use of anti-psychotic medications; bathing is personalized, based on residents' preferences and comfort levels.
- Staff learns to speak the "language of dementia."

The Regenerative Community

This model was developed by Barry and Debora Barkan of the Live Oak Living Center (El Sobrante, CA). An antidote to institutionalization, it strives to combat the experience of isolation, disconnection, and a life without meaning. It is grounded in the belief that everyone is capable of growth and development, even when ravaged by disease or disability. The Regenerative Community cultivates "communities" led by esteemed elders, including family, volunteers, and staff to provide structure for belonging, a collective voice, and an opportunity to grow and develop and be of service to peers. Community meetings become rituals of shared stories, experiences, and songs. A shared vision connects residents with others and gives meaning to their lives. Hallmarks of the Regenerative Community are:

- Staff members act as community developers, augmenting conventional work responsibilities.
- Regular community meetings are opportunities for residents and staff to socialize and discuss problems. The aim is to build a life of shared experience and concerns.
- Residents are regarded as esteemed elders, regardless of physical or mental disability.

The Eden Alternative

The Eden Alternative was developed by Bill and Judy Thomas when Dr. Thomas became disillusioned with the care provided in nursing home facilities. The Eden Alternative is an educational movement designed to turn institutions into more human habitats by bringing in plants, animals, and children and by training staff to follow its caring philosophy. This model has helped give facilities the sense of a place to grow. Some of the guiding principles behind the philosophy are:

- combating the loneliness, boredom, and sense of helplessness that accounts for so much of the suffering in the typical nursing home
- creating a "human habitat" with plants, pets, and young children
- offering residents opportunities to give as well as receive care
- ensuring residents have continuing contact characterized by variety and spontaneity, and deemphasizing the programmed activity approach
- ensuring direct caregivers and residents are decision makers.

The Green House Project

The Green House Project represents a new, more radical approach also created by Dr. William Thomas. The intent is to design, build, and test small community-based homes for six to eight residents that provide more intimate relationships between residents and caregivers. Green Houses are group homes that use a social model of care. They are designed to feel more like home than today's typical long-term care institution and to blend easily into their community or surroundings. They are caring institutions in a very professional sense, but they look and function like houses. Green Houses have a living room and kitchen where residents and staff gather to eat family-style.

They are staffed by Certified Nursing Assistants who cook, do light cleaning and laundry, give personalized care, and support the care plan and life goals of each elder. Other professionals (nurses, doctors, therapists, and activity and dietary specialists) constitute a clinical support team that visits the Green Houses. The Green House approach to residential long-term care for the elderly is founded on the idea that the physical and social environments in which we deliver long-term care can and should be warm, smart, and green.

The Wellspring Model

The Wellspring Model was created in 1994 in Wisconsin as an alliance of eleven not-for-profit nursing homes. It has now swelled to 57 facilities. Serious problems with quality care persist in many of this country's 17,000 nursing homes. The Wellspring approach recognizes that national policy must move beyond a deficiency correction model to true quality assurance and attempts to improve resident quality of care through both clinical interventions and transformation of organizational culture. Clinical experts train employee teams to achieve high-quality care, establish front-line staff flexibility, monitor quality indicators, and involve top managers in comparing quality performance. It focuses on clinical quality and environ-mental culture simultaneously and in a highly interactive way to:

- develop and implement model practice systems at the provider level
- establish quality assurance systems within nursing homes and strengthen nursing home staff
- improve regulatory standards by developing appropriate outcome measures
- change the Medicare and Medicaid reimbursement systems.

This is a transformational model implemented by:

- the commitment of top managers to making resident care a top priority
- sharing the services of a geriatric nurse practitioner who develops training materials and teaches staff to apply nationally recognized clinical guidelines
- creating interdisciplinary "care resource teams" that receive train-ing and then teach other staff at their respective facilities
- involving all departments in networking to share what works and what doesn't at the practical level
- empowering staff to make decisions that affect the quality of resi-dent care and the work environment
- continuous reviews by CEOs and all staff of data on resident out-comes.

The Planetree Model

Since its founding in 1978 as a nonprofit organization, Planetree continues to be a pioneer in personalizing and demystifying healthcare for patients and families in the hospital setting. Founded by a patient, the Planetree Model is committed to enhancing healthcare from the patient's perspective. It empowers patients and families through information and education and encourages them to form "healing partnerships" with caregivers to support active participation. Through organizational transformation, the Planetree Model creates healing environments in which patients can be active partic-ipants and human caring is integrated with the best scientific medicine and complementary healing traditions.

NOTES

Courtesy of English Rose Suites, Minneapolis, MN

We help to heal the soul by providing warmth, nurturing, caring, and physical and emotional safety in the environments and care we provide.

CHAPTER

12

Hearth and Home

Gathering Spaces

We all want to be at home, no matter where we live, so we're shaping nursing homes into households, neighborhoods, and communities.

Today the development of new and innovative living and care settings that respond to the diverse and changing needs of residents and staff is big business. With it comes the responsibility of providing physical spaces and services, and the challenges of dealing with the issues of long-term personal care. Inherent in the challenge, however, is the opportunity to facilitate the profound process of graceful and dignified aging, up to and through various stages of frailty and even death.

Designers have an awful habit of directing the behavior of a building's occupants, rather than creating spaces that support the users' physical, spiritual, and emotional needs.[1] Understanding resident needs is essential groundwork for any design change, too often facilities simply co-opt an image of "homelike" without understanding the substance, in the mistaken belief that if the setting looks like a home, residents' needs will go away.

Many senior living and nursing home settings initially appear to respond to the older individual's desire for independence; however, in their later years an equally important issue for older adults is the risk of both self and imposed isolation. In nursing homes and assisted living settings isolation is often the result of the building size and the extended distances

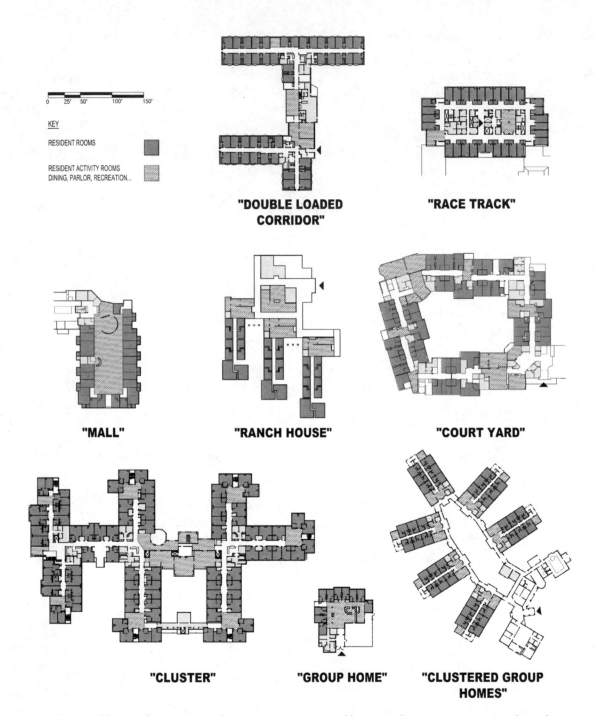

KEY

RESIDENT ROOMS

RESIDENT ACTIVITY ROOMS
DINING, PARLOR, RECREATION...

"DOUBLE LOADED
CORRIDOR"

"RACE TRACK"

"MALL"

"RANCH HOUSE"

"COURT YARD"

"CLUSTER"

"GROUP HOME"

"CLUSTERED GROUP
HOMES"

Figure 12.1 Building configuration typologies. *Diagrams prepared by Quinn deMenna AIA courtesy of Kanalstein Danton Associates, Voorhees, NJ.*

residents who now are less mobile must travel. This unwittingly contributes to seniors living in increasing isolation from the mainstream of community life and emphasizes the urgency for reshaping the physical environment into less imposing, self-contained small neighborhoods that help restore a better balance between independence and community life.

The culture change movement is credited with promoting community as an antidote to institutionalization. While it takes much more than the physical environment to create community or a sense of being at home, architects and interior designers know that the way a space is designed, as well as how it is utilized, directly affects the interactions that takes place within it. Shaping the environment to encourage relationships and community interaction is an important contribution that design professionals can make to eliminate isolation.

Shaping the environment to encourage relationships and community interaction is an important contribution that design professionals can make to eliminate isolation.

Building Configuration

Building configuration is a top design priority because it is the foundation for so much more. Providers, architects, designers, concerned families, and healthcare professionals all want a responsive way to deal with aging. Over the past 50 years building configuration and design has evolved from the traditional medical model, with its long double-loaded corridors, to the racetrack design, a response to the environmental needs of people with dementia at the Weiss Institute, Philadelphia Geriatric Center, followed by the mall configuration.

Innovative Woodside Place, designed in the ranch-house style by Perkins Eastman Architects, PC, was one of the first not-for-profit residential care homes for Alzheimer's special care. The popular courtyard design followed, eventually evolving into the cluster design, widely used today in assisted living and nursing homes. The Green House Project is an example of the group home, designed to accommodate eight to ten residents. Four homes form a small neighborhood that is expected to evolve into a larger group home cluster and eventually a traditional neighborhood as additional homes are completed.

Life and Design Are Changing

Life in eldercare communities across the country is changing. Attempts to make friendlier environments have resulted in modifying and changing building configurations to better support the needs of older residents. Dining rooms designed to serve 60 are being replaced with smaller neighborhood dining rooms for 8 to 12 people. Long double-loaded corridors are disappearing, replaced by smaller cluster configurations with private bedroom rooms and private bathrooms. Nurse stations are being demolished at a record rate. By reducing both the scale and walking distances, residents are nourished and supported in these smaller clustered living environments.

Social living spaces are coming alive. Living rooms and other social spaces where elders enjoy their coffee and newspaper and plan their daily activities are buzzing. Country kitchens invite conversation and encourage residents to eat when, where, and what they want, and people are no longer being moved to one central spot for activities.

Many settings include a "Main Street" or "Town Square" where elders can walk, shop, stop for ice cream with a friend, mingle with children, and share the companionship of a resident dog or cat. Throughout the neighborhoods of these new communities, changed by culture and now by architecture, people are thriving as they continue to enjoy friends and "normal" social activity. Porches, gardens, and outdoor spaces with lovely walking paths encourage exercise and fresh air. Culture change and innovative design are partnering to make certain that daily life is enjoyed each and every day. More care providers are offering adult day care programs, healthcare, activities with children, hospice and home care.

The "Heart of the Home": Living Rooms, Great Rooms, and Dens

Older residents need a sense of control over their lives and environment, the freedom to discover others and enjoy life—especially at a time when decisions are too frequently made for them. Home is usually associated with family, shared memories, and comfortable familiarities. It promises a sense of security, boundaries, and a private place for one's own things within easy reach.

Figure 12.2 The fireplace and warm setting help to create the real "heart of the home," where people naturally congregate. *Courtesy of the Episcopal Church Home, Louisville, KY. Architect: Reese Design Collaborative, Louisville, KY. Photographer: Brian Moberly Photography.*

Figure 12.3 Living room before redesign. *Courtesy of the Hebrew Home of Greater Washington, Washington, DC.*

Figure 12.4 Living room after redesign. A lovely open, see-through design that invites residents to enjoy social time together and see activity going on around them. *Courtesy of the Hebrew Home of Greater Washington, Washington, DC. Architect: Perkins Eastman. Photographer: Massery Photography.*

Figure 12.5 The social living space at Allen House was redesigned to accommodate small group activities and social gatherings. *Courtesy of Allen House at Springhouse, Jamaica Plains, MA. Interior Design: S. Harris Interiors, Boston, MA. Photographer: Sam Drukman, Newton, MA.*

Figure 12.6 The living room provides comfortable private spaces as well as seating for conversation. *Courtesy of Allen House at Springhouse, Jamaica Plains, MA. Interior Design: S. Harris Interiors, Boston, MA. Photographer: Sam Drukman, Newton, MA.*

Figure 12.7 The back porch provides a quiet retreat to watch "the action." *Courtesy of Carlson Boyd Place at Mather Pavilion at Wagner, Evanston, IL. Architect: Mithun, Inc. Seattle, WA. Photographer: Steve Hall © Hendrich Blessing.*

From the design perspective there are three principles—space, light, and order—that give shape and meaning to the experience of home. Somewhere within the generous open space of the kitchen, dining room, and living room is the gathering space, the hearth, the "heart of the house," where people naturally congregate. A fireplace creates a sense of both emotional and physical warmth, especially in cold climates, making a cozy place to share hot chocolate and catch up on the latest stories about the grandchildren.

Sitting areas add to the feeling of togetherness. In addition to gathering for social enjoyment, residents may want to take part in hobbies here. Make sure there is ample illumination for reading, working puzzles, and other

Figure 12.8 Small alcoves and nooks are pleasant places to visit with family and friends. *Courtesy of Duncaster, a Life Care Retirement Community, Bloomfield, CT. Photographer: Design Concepts Unlimited, Sausalito, CA.*

activities. If this is where everyone gathers to watch television or a DVD movie, make sure there are enough electrical outlets to accommodate the stereo, television, DVD or VCR, and that the screen is positioned so that light from the windows doesn't produce glare and interfere with viewing.

Smaller nooks or alcoves along the edge of the gathering space encourage intimate gathering and allow someone to retreat while still remaining connected to the group. These are places where one can be alone but still be visible, or where two people can pursue separate activities yet not feel isolated.

In these smaller neighborhoods, the gathering places, like home, are flexible spaces used for a variety of activities. The kitchen table is not only a place for meals, but a comfortable and familiar place for informal exchanges or discussion groups, classroom meetings, or messy craft projects.

The staff needs a small office space to organize their work and keep records. A clever way to blend a small workspace into the rest of the room is to design the workspace in a large closet that can be closed off when not

Figure 12.9 The table in the Alzheimer's dining room is a comfortable place for many activities and projects, as well as for meals. *Courtesy of Mercy Ridge, Timonium, MD. Architect: CSD Architects and Interior Design, Baltimore, MD. Photographer: Alain Jaramillo.*

in use. This allows overhead shelving or storage cabinets for work-related materials or medications.

Country or Farm Kitchens

The kitchen is a familiar landmark in any home and has become the most popular spot in the house. It's the hub around which much of our life revolves and where family and friends inevitably gravitate. Now more than

Figure 12.11 In addition to the pendant direct/indirect fixtures, overcabinet and undercabinet strip lighting help to raise the overall light levels in the kitchen. *Courtesy of Harbour House, Greendale, WI. Architect: KM Development Corp., Milwaukee, WI. Interior Design: Mithun, Inc., Seattle, WA. Photographer: Skot Weidemann.*

ever the kitchen is an area of constant activity and the design of the open farm or country kitchen has successfully created one of the most active and engaging spaces in many care settings. It's the center of activity. The country kitchen has become a multifunctional space where the family can prepare meals, watch television, work on the computer, design crafts, eat, and visit—making it once again the true heart of the home. The smaller intimate setting of this residential style kitchen is cozier and helps to minimize anxiety and reduce stress.

Instead of moving residents to a large dining room, food prepared in the main kitchen is brought into the country kitchen and served family style. This creates the sense of a more casual family meal. Many of us grew up in three rooms of our homes—the kitchen, the living room and the dining room. The rebirth of the kitchen as the "heart of the home" is reshaping the design into what is known today as the great room.

Good lighting, both direct and indirect, can make this an inviting, pleasant and highly functional space. A great way to brighten this space is to conceal fluorescent or low-voltage strip lights above the cabinets, direct-

Figure 12.12 Mealtime in this dining room is one of the most anticipated opportunities for socializing as well as nourishment. *Courtesy of Sumner on Ridgewood, Copley Township, OH. Architect: Dorsky Hodgson + Partners, Cleveland, OH.*

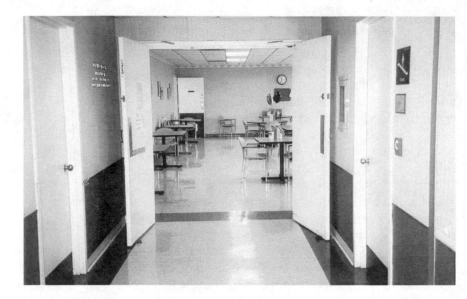

Figure 12.13 Dining before renovation. *Courtesy of the Hebrew Home of Greater Washington, Washington, DC.*

Figure 12.14 What a difference! The greenhouse sun porch infuses the new dining room with light and offers opportunities for various dining experiences. *Courtesy of the Hebrew Home of Greater Washington, Washington, DC. Architect: Perkins Eastman. Photographer: Massery Photography.*

Figure 12.15 Whether at a breakfast bar or at a table, residents should have appropriate seating that allows them to sit close to their food. *Courtesy of Brookestone, Caring Households for Seniors, Omaha, NE. Architect: Vetter Health Services, Inc., Omaha, NE. Photographer: Ervin Photography, Omaha, NE.*

ing them toward the ceiling. A space of at least 12 inches is needed between the top of the kitchen cabinets and the ceiling. This increases the light levels and helps to fill the space with a subtle glow of soft uniform light. A kitchen window adds a familiar touch of home, and windows that overlook a garden or courtyard visually open the space and create comfortable places for socializing and social interaction.

Mealtime, often the most anticipated highlight of the day for residents, offers opportunities for socialization as well as nourishment. It's an opportunity to visit with other residents, to socialize, gossip, and enjoy good food. For convenience, dining spaces and eating areas should be well placed near the kitchen, and for flexibility one of the kitchen counters can be designed to be raised and lowered so that residents in wheelchairs can be involved in food preparation. Whether you use a table and chairs or a breakfast bar/food prep island, consider comfort, the durability of the surface area, and upholstery materials that can withstand heavy use and food stains. Residents should sit in appropriate dining chairs with arms that slide beneath the table surface, allowing them to sit close to the table and focus their attention on eating. Some diners spill because the chair arms don't allow them to get close enough to the table.

Residents, especially those with dementia, are often more comfortable participating in activities and familiar tasks they associate with a residential setting—normal daily activities that occur in any household.[2] The familiarity and comfort of the kitchen, preparing, consuming, and cleaning up after three meals consumes a big part of the day. These kitchen activities are an important part of Life Skills programs for persons with Alzheimer's. This is one therapeutic approach to program development that works very effectively with residents who enjoy household tasks. Residents are encouraged

Figure 12.16 Resident-focused settings have much more flexible breakfast times, allowing residents to sleep later if they choose and have coffee on their own schedules. *Courtesy of Meadow Lark Hills Retirement Community, Manhattan, KS.*

to help with routine, daily life activities such as folding napkins, setting the table, and removing the dishes after the meal. Silverware, napkins, plates, and glasses are stored conveniently in drawers and cabinets, allowing residents to help in setting the table, removing dishes after meals, and putting them away when they are washed. When these activities are carried out in a natural way, residents enjoy the sense that they are making a contribution and gain self-esteem.[3]

Both breakfast and light evening meals are often prepared in the kitchen. In many settings residents are no longer awakened to go to breakfast at a certain time unless they ask to be, but are allowed to sleep until they wake. Breakfast is served within an hour-and-a-half time frame in the morning, and this has resulted in happier, more alert residents during the daytime and better sleep during the night. In resident-focused settings, a baker's rack with snack food, fruit, and other items chosen by the residents is often located in the kitchen. Food is available at all hours for elders in the neighborhood and is replenished daily.[4]

The country kitchen is ideally designed to encourage residents' participation in cooking, for cooking demonstrations by guest chefs, and for educational programs or talks on culinary topics of interest.

Friendship Village Café Bistro. Central Baptist Village, Norridge, IL. *Courtesy Perkins Eastman. Photographer: Hedrick Blessing.*

Resident bathroom. Hebrew Home of Greater Washington, Washington, DC. *Courtesy Perkins Eastman. Photographer: Massery Photography.*

Lounge and library at Willow Towers, New Rochelle, NY. *Courtesy Perkins Eastman. Photographer: Chuck Choi Architectural Photography.*

Isabel and Arthur Meighen Manor/ The Salvation Army, Toronto, Ontario, Canada. *Courtesy Montgomery Sisam Architects, Inc., Toronto, Ontario, Canada. Interior Design: DCA Design, Inc., Toronto, Ontario, Canada. Photographer: Steven Evans.*

Resident apartments maximize access to daylight. Belmont House, Toronto, Ontario, Canada. *Courtesy Montgomery Sisam Architects, Inc., Toronto, Ontario, Canada. Interior Design: DCA Design, Inc., Toronto, Ontario, Canada. Photographer: David Whitaker.*

The library at Geer Village, a senior living community and regional community center, Canaan, CT.
Courtesy of Heym Dowds and Neeman Inc., Boston, MA. Photographer: Warren Jagger Photography, Inc.

Dining on the park at Caleb Hitchcock Health Center at Duncaster, a life care retirement community, Bloomfield, CT. *Courtesy of Ewing Cole, Philadelphia, PA. Photographer: Jeffrey Totaro.*

The European shower at the Health Center at Carleton Willard Village; Bedford, MA. *Courtesy of Wdesign, Bolton, MA. Photographer: Stephen Sette Ducati.*

The front porch entry for the Alzheimer's/Dementia Care assisted living residence at Homestead at Heritage, Framingham, MA. *Courtesy of Wdesign, Bolton, MA. Photographer: Stephen Sette Ducati.*

Color adds amazing warmth to the Alzheimer's/Dementia Care Cape Cod sitting room at Homestead at Heritage, Framingham, MA. *Courtesy of Wdesign, Bolton, MA. Photographer: Stephen Sette Ducati.*

An inviting country kitchen and dining room in the Memory Care residence at Highland Ridge Senior Campus, Williamsburg, IA. *Courtesy of KKE Architects, Minneapolis, MN and Encompass Interiors, St. Paul, MN. Photographer: Scott Gilbertson.*

Main Street at Boutwell's Landing, Stillwater, MN. *Courtesy of JSSH Architects, Minnetonka, MN and Encompass Interiors, St. Paul, MN. Photographer: Saari & Forrai Photography/www.saariphoto.com.*

The library at Boutwell's Landing, Stillwater, MN. *Courtesy of JSSH Architects, Minnetonka, MN and Encompass Interiors, St. Paul, MN. Photographer: Saari & Forrai, Photography/www.saariphoto.com*

A warm and inviting bathing spa at Weils of Bainbridge, Bainbridge, OH. *Courtesy of Dorsky Hodgson + Partners; Cleveland, OH. Photographer: Mort Tucker Photography.*

The beautiful solarium walkway brings an abundance of natural light into the building. St. James Place, Baton Rouge, LA.
Courtesy CSD Architects, Baltimore, MD. Interior Design: Interior Design Associates. Photographer: Chipper Hatter, Hatter Photographics.

A lovely country kitchen for coffee or to share a meal. English Rose Suites, Minneapolis, MN. *Courtesy of English Rose Suites, Minneapolis, MN.*

Sacred spaces are very important to residents. The synagogue at Village Shalom, Overland Park, KS. *Courtesy of Nelson Tremain Partnership, Minneapolis, MN. Interior Design: Tranin Design, Kansas City, MO. Photographer: Steve Swalwell Architectural Fotographics.*

A view to the beautiful gardens at the Avon Foundation Comprehensive Breast Center, San Francisco, CA. *Courtesy of Tsang Architecture. Photographer: Douglas A. Salin/www.Dougsalin.com © 2004.*

A private place for morning coffee under the trellis at the Life Enrichment Adult Day Care Center, Kings Mountain, NC.
Courtesy of DirtWorks, PC, New York, NY. Photographer: David Kamp.

The charm of an interior porch at the Oaklawn Health Care Center, Mankato, MN. *Courtesy of WAI Continuum, St. Paul, MN.*
Photographer: Saari & Forrai Photography/www.saariphoto.com.

Tabletop vignettes can help to recall special people and special memories. Allen House at Springhouse, Jamaica Plains, MA. *Courtesy of S. Harris Interiors; Boston, MA. Photographer: Sam Drukman; Newton, MA.*

Eye-catching design makes finding ones way much easier. Walker Methodist Care Center, Minneapolis, MN. *Courtesy of WAI Continuum, St. Paul, MN. Interior Design: Interiors by Design. Photographer: Saari & Forrai Photography/ www.saariphoto.com.*

NOTES

Courtesy of the Life Enrichment Center, Kings Mountain, NC. Photographer: Debbie Vaughan.

Activities that make up the daily experience provide a sense of usefulness, pleasure, success, and as normal a level of functioning as possible.

Private Spaces

Resident Bedrooms, Bathrooms, and Bathing Environments

The most important thing for each of us to remember—and never forget—is that residents in long-term care settings are the same people who yesterday lived in the community. Their new homes, like the ones they have left behind, should be as humane and normal as we can make them, offering the support, nurturing, and comfort that we all look for and have come to expect from home. While many residents may be different physically or mentally, their expectations are still much the same. Their needs for privacy, social interaction, pets, children, flowers, and coffee or afternoon tea will likely continue.

Clearly, it is possible to design environments that better answer real needs and accommodate different lifestyles. For those accustomed to living at home, one of the greatest affronts often brought by long-term care is lack of privacy. Powell Lawton suggested many years ago that the need for privacy increases with age.[1] With all the talk about supporting dignity, there is nothing more important for preserving dignity than respecting the right to privacy.

> *The most important thing for each of us to remember—and never forget—is that residents in long-term care settings are the same people who yesterday lived in the community.*

Resident Bedrooms

Most research, particularly in the past ten years, has shown that private bedrooms are more successful than shared rooms. While there are exceptions, such as with a husband and wife or longtime friends who prefer to share, there is little doubt that private rooms are the preferred choice of most.

In a shared environment, private rooms provide one space that can be shaped to the individual's personal taste and made uniquely his or her own. They help give residents a sense of control over their environment in a setting where opportunities for this are often limited.

Residents are encouraged to bring their own furniture, but there is often no room for furniture that holds special meaning or large pieces such as a secretary or chest for clothing and other personal items and treasures. It can be difficult adapting to spaces that can only accommodate the smallest items. A small three-drawer chest is rarely adequate for clothing storage, particularly for older persons, who almost always need bulkier items such as sweaters. But where do you put an armoire? A room size of 280 to 345 square feet makes it much more probable that at least a double bed, which is more familiar than a twin bed to most people, will fit. Baby boomers will insist on larger spaces and adequate storage as they become clients in the coming decade.

A ceiling height of at least 9 feet coupled with large windows is a great strategy for making a room seem larger and providing more light. Large windows with low sill heights of 14 to 24 inches above the floor bring natural light into the room and offer a clear view of the garden outside even for those in bed. Sheer curtains or a MechoShade product will filter the light when needed, and post form, molded laminate, or Corian windowsills make an easy to maintain, sunny home for plants.

Many of us crave fresh air, and opening windows comes quite naturally. While there is some justification for having windows that only partially open in dementia resident rooms, opening windows is familiar behavior that means

Figure 13.1 The bedroom is a space that can be made uniquely one's own when it is generous enough to accommodate one's own furniture. *Courtesy of Brookestone, Caring Households for Seniors, Omaha, NE. Architect: Vetter Health Services, Inc., Omaha, NE. Photographer: Ervin Photography, Omaha, NE.*

Figure 13.2 Large windows infuse the room with natural light and provide a connection with outside environment. *Courtesy of Foulkeways at Gwynedd, Gwynedd, PA. Architect: Reese Lower Patrick & Scott, Ltd., Lancaster, PA. Photographer: Larry Lefever Photography.*

Figure 13.3 Window seats provide storage and additional seating or a surface to display photographs and other personal items. *Courtesy of Collington Episcopal Life Care Community, Mitchellville, MD. Architect: Perkins Eastman. Photographer: Massery Photography.*

being at home, and all residents should have the option of opening windows at least to some degree. While a minimum window size is 6 ft. × 6 ft., bigger is better.[2] Large windows will accommodate window seats that can provide additional storage, but won't allow the window to be as low.

A single ceiling-mounted light fixture in the middle of the room has never been sufficient to provide lighting for older eyes, but with a minimum 9 foot ceiling height, it's much easier and less costly to provide indirect lighting. Touch-responsive bedside and table lamps are nice ways to supplement ambient lighting.

There are many ways to personalize a room, beginning with carpet and color that contribute to the ambiance. Color on the walls is an inexpensive and easy way to give residents options. Select perhaps three colors that fit into the overall color scheme of the neighborhood and give residents a choice for their bedroom. Beige and white should not be two of the three choices. However, if the selection is expanded to five, then including these two colors is OK.

With adequate space, a favorite rocking chair or a comfortable chair for reading, covered in a familiar fabric, is a source of comfort and nurturing for some. Treasured books, paintings, and photographs keep persons connected with their previous lives. Small photos are not likely to be as easily distinguished as they once were, though family members, who are often overwhelmed, don't always realize this. Enlarging and framing family photographs can be a good project to do together.

Figure 13.4 A shelf at the entry provides greater opportunity for personalization or a place to set a purse while searching for a key. *Courtesy of Cardinal Ambrozic House of Providence, Toronto, Ontario. Architect: Montgomery Sisam Architects, Inc., Kuwabara Payne McKenna Blumberg Architects/Architects in Joint Venture, Toronto, Ontario. Interior Design: Newcombe Design Associates, Inc., Toronto, Ontario. Photographer: Design Archive.*

Entries

A simple shelf for photographs or flowers helps identify and personalize the entry. Another form of personalization is filling an entry alcove with furniture or artwork. An alcove can be a remarkably beautiful and interesting space, unique to the individual resident. This is just being tried as a strategy for helping residents with failing memory to find their rooms. Furniture and artwork are large enough to be seen, and possibly familiar enough to remain deeply imbedded in remaining memory.

In dementia care settings memory boxes displaying personal memorabilia are systematically used today as strategies for cueing. There is little research or evidence, however, that they work for that purpose. Many are too small, poorly lit, or filled with items that hold no special significance for the resident. Using identical items beside each door diminishes the usefulness of the memory box as a distinctive cue. Many of the identification and cueing strategies we have used have proved much too subtle to be effective. Merely changing the items inside, changing the color of the walls, or using the same wallpaper or wallpaper border in different colors is too

We have learned that subtle cueing strategies do not work.

Figure 13.5 Furniture and artwork personalize many entries at Duncaster. *Courtesy of Duncaster, a Life Care Retirement Community, Bloomfield, CT. Photographer: Design Concepts Unlimited, Sausalito, CA.*

subtle a change to be effective for confused individuals. We have learned that subtle cueing strategies do not work.

Bathrooms

Although it is one of the most important functional areas of any care setting, the design of the bathroom seems to be regularly overlooked in the effort to meet the functional needs of older adults. As we mature, needs change, and to reduce situations that exceed the competence of older adults, design must be flexible. Good design will not only support independence, but it will also accommodate increased need and assistance when necessary.

Older adults have many different needs:

- They may not be full-time wheelchair users or even need to use a wheelchair.
- They may have balance problems that limit stepping over obstacles, for example, the side of the tub.
- They may lack the stamina needed to stand for long periods, as in the shower.
- They may lack the strength to pull themselves out of a wheelchair or transfer (raise and lower) themselves onto a toilet or into a tub or chair, even with the assistance of grab bars and supports.[3]

Toilets

A residential-style flush tank toilet is the preferred type in residential care settings. It's familiar and also provides a stable back support when sitting on the toilet. Although many settings prefer the wall-mount style because it makes cleaning the floor easier, it looks by far the most institutional. The toilet specified most often for use in new long-term care construction is the open-seat, flush-valve style. While the addition of a toilet seat lid makes it a little more palatable, it too is still clearly institutional.

There is some debate about the appropriate height of the toilet seat. The higher seating height of 17 in. to 19 in. required by ADA makes it easier to lower onto and rise from the toilet, unless of course, you are short. This higher toilet height doesn't allow short people to sit comfortably with both feet on the floor. A 15 in. seat height provides flexibility and comfort for many, and a riser can be added if it is needed. It is surprising that a toilet manufacturer hasn't looked at refining the design to better meet the needs of a fast-growing market.

ADA guidelines call for the toilet to be placed 18 in. from the wall to support the independent transfer process. The guidelines were developed more than 20 years ago based on the ability of young wheelchair users, primarily males with good upper body strength, to use grab bars and other

Figure 13.6 A residential-style flush tank toilet is the preferred type in residential care settings. *Courtesy of Foulkeways at Gwynedd, Gwynedd, PA. Architect: Reese Lower Patrick & Scott, Ltd., Lancaster, PA. Photographer: Larry Lefever Photography.*

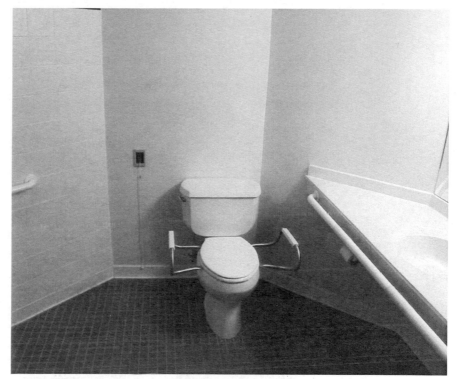

supports for sliding transfers. Independent transfers may no longer be an option for frail elders with limited mobility and reduced strength and stamina. They are at risk of falling and have difficulty transferring even with the assistance of code-compliant grab bars, toilets, and spaces. They need assistance, but the mismatch between the environment (mandated accessible toilets) and function (their physical competence) can create demands that exceed their abilities and result in greater dependence or higher levels of care.[3] Placing the toilet 36 inches from the wall provides the space necessary for personal assistance. Flexible Linido bars (see Figure 13.8) puts further support within easy reach. This configuration does require additional blocking in the wall for support.

Grab Bars

Recommendations in ADA guidelines for placement of grab bars do not recognize the space necessary for assisted toileting or for the lack of upper-body strength characteristic of older adults—particularly older women, making these recommendations inappropriate for aging adults.[4,5] Swing-away Linido grab bars, typically 24 to 30 inches long, with the flexibility (up or down positions) to allow either self-toileting or staff assistance, are more appropriate for an aged population. They have a built-in hold device to maintain the upright position and provide better leverage because they

Figure 13.7 Flexible Linido bars provide appropriate support for older users within easy reach. *Courtesy of Peabody Retirement Community, North Manchester, PA. Architect: Reese Lower Patrick & Scott, Ltd., Lancaster, PA. Interior Design: Carson Design Associates, Carmel, IN.*

come closer to the body.[6] The grab bars should be placed on either side of the toilet, between 1 ft. 4 in. and 1 ft. 6 in. from the centerline and mounted at a height between 30 in. and 34 in.[7] Many older persons will use whatever is available for support. Proper positioning of grab bars encourages their use and reduces the use of a potentially unsteady walker or a poorly secured towel bar for support.

Towel bars are often used as grab bars for support, and for safety a grab bar should be specified for a towel bar. Grab bars are now available in many colors and in several finishes. A matte finish helps to reduce glare, and a softer-textured finish is less slippery and easier to grip, particularly in the shower.

The toilet paper dispenser and other items are often positioned higher and farther away from the toilet for staff use. Some new-styled Linido bars incorporate a toilet paper dispenser at the end of the bar for the convenience of the user.

Showers

The 30 in. × 60 in. roll-in shower provides easy access and is the style most familiar to residents. A fold-down shower seat with no sharp edges is a seating option. However, movable shower chairs or benches provide more

Figure 13.8 Bathroom design floor plans. *Drawings by Andrew Lee Alden Associates, AIA. Reproduced with the permission of DESIGN 2004.*

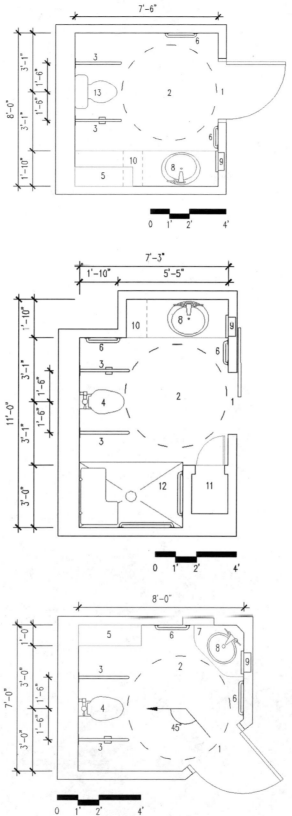

1. Minimum 3′ entry width
2. 5′ minimum turning radius, 6′–7′ preferred
3. Drop-down grab bar with toilet paper holder
4. Flush-valve-style toilet with toilet seat lid
5. Upper cabinet for toiletry supplies
6. Grab bar
7. In-wall cabinet for ADL items
8. Accessible lavatory with "no-drip" edge
9. Recessed towel holder
10. Base cabinet for ADL items
11. Cabinet for linen and toiletry supplies
12. Roll-in shower with folding seat
13. Tank-style toilet with toilet seat lid

room and greater flexibility to accommodate caregiver assistance. Flexibility is the operative word. A height-adjustable, detachable showerhead or handheld shower with an antiscald regulator provides the greatest flexibility of use.

Proper drainage is essential. The best roll-in showers are "lipless" to allow for easy access and safety. The sloped shower floor should extend a few inches beyond the shower into the bathroom to catch any runoff from the shower curtain. The European shower is an innovation in bathroom design where the entire floor of the bathroom is sloped to a drain and the resident sits either on the shower seat, a shower chair or bench, or even on the toilet with a handheld shower nozzle or wand. The European shower essentially makes the entire bathroom a shower, which may present challenges in keeping surfaces dry, but using a 30 in. × 60 in. shower with a floor drain may make some sense. Slip-resistant sheet vinyl is a softer surface than tile on the floor.

Figure 13.9 The European shower is an innovation in bathroom design where the entire floor of the bathroom is sloped to a drain. *Courtesy of the Health Center at Carleton Willard Village, Bedford, MA. Interior Design: Wdesign, Bolton, MA. Photographer: Stephen Sette Ducati.*

Figure 13.10 Grab bars must be visible to be used. *Courtesy of Life Enrichment Center, Kings Mountain, NC. Architect: Holland Hamrick & Patterson Architects, PA. Interior Design: Design Concepts Unlimited, Sausalito, CA.*

Horizontal grab bars and a vertical 24 in. grab bar mounted on the outside edge of the shower should be available for residents entering and exiting the shower.[8] Grab bars must be visible to used. Today there are many colors and textures, including a matte finish, to provide contrast with the background color of the shower and meet if not exceed both safety and the aesthetic needs. A heat lamp for warmth after the shower is one of the touches many residents appreciate.

Lighting

Light in the bathroom is critical. Residents need both quantity and quality. Many older adults have low vision and need high light levels. Indirect light sources can provide both task lighting and general illumination while also addressing sensitivity to glare. The Illuminating Engineering Society of North America recommends at least 30 footcandles for ambient light and 60 footcandles for task lighting. These are minimum—not optimum— requirements, however. By using dimming ballasts and a dimming switch, optimum light levels of 50 fc for ambient light and 100 fc for task lighting

Figure 13.11 Attractive direct/indirect cove fixtures provide higher light levels with a residential ambiance. *Courtesy of Cornice Lighting Systems, Markham, Ontario, Canada.*

can be provided and dimmed as needed. An attractive direct/indirect cove fixture over the vanity can be extended across the wall at minimum expense, to light the toilet as well.

A recessed light in the shower ensures adequate light when the shower curtain is closed, and an amber or red night-light is less disruptive for night visits to the bathroom allowing residents to go back to sleep more easily. To eliminate unnecessary noise put lighting and exhaust fans on separate switches.

Lavatory and Storage

The lavatory countertop should be a maximum height of 2 ft. 10 in. from the floor, with knee clearance under the sink for wheelchair access. Clearance space should begin at 2 ft. 3 in. above the floor with a minimum depth of 1 ft. 5 in. for the first 9 in. above the floor.[9] Residents need ample surface space for personal items, in addition to a small base cabinet with drawers for storing personal hygiene items. The more storage space the better. In

Figure 13.12 The more storage space the better. Residents also need ample surface space. *Courtesy of Peabody Retirement Community, North Manchester, PA. Architect: Reese Lower Patrick & Scott, Ltd., Lancaster, PA. Interior Design: Carson Design Associates, Carmel, IN.*

addition to residents' belongings and staff supplies, bathrooms need storage for extra towels and washcloths, and a lockable drawer or cabinet for treatment supplies. Paper towel, glove, and soap dispensers appear much less institutional when recessed in the wall.

Extending the mirror to the backsplash enhances easy viewing for wheelchair users, and mounting a support rail across the front of the vanity will help many to be able to stand who might otherwise need a chair. Making the basin contrast with the surrounding surface ensures it will be visible to those with low vision. Residential-style faucets with built-in anti-scalding regulators are most attractive. Blade-style handles are easiest to operate for those with arthritis or diminished gripping abilities.

Figure 13.13 Vanity with integral grab bar. *Courtesy of the inventor, Quinn deMenna, AIA.*

The vanity assist is an innovative response designed by architect Quinn Dimenno to meet the needs of older adults. The Corian vanity top with integral handgrips is cantilevered, allowing turning accessibility for persons in wheelchairs. A bank of drawers provides storage for personal items, and the contrasting lavatory bowl makes the basin visible even to those with low vision (Figure 13.13).

When budget is a concern, and when is it not, color is an inexpensive way to make a bathroom both functional and aesthetically pleasing. Effectively contrasting wall and floor colors with a white toilet improves visibility for older eyes. An appropriately patterned vinyl wallcovering can do the same.

White on white may be a very sophisticated color scheme for the young, but not for frail older adults with poor vision. While white porcelain toilets are familiar, too much white can cause situational incontinence. Lack of appropriate contrast keeps the toilet from being visible and contributes to confusion, frustration, and incontinence.

The availability of colored grab bars makes it easier to provide contrast and support tastefully. Colored toilet seats can also be very helpful for persons with compromised vision. Creating *effective* contrast can be tricky in small spaces. Color combinations that maximize visibility for persons with low vision, discussed in an earlier chapter, are likely to be quite different from those selected by someone with young, healthy eyes. With so much riding on the success of this space, the expertise of a color consultant may be worth the investment.

Doors

While door styles may vary, the door's location should allow the resident easy access and a view of the toilet. For residents who must use the bathroom at night and may be confused when they wake, it is particularly important to locate the toilet so it can be seen from the bed.

The door should, at minimum, be at a 45-degree angle to the toilet when the access is on an angle. Hinged doors must open out from the bathroom to avoid blocking access in the event of a resident fall. Pocket doors are an alternative to hinged doors and avoid the problem of overlapping doors, though they are more difficult for some to operate. The popularity of the "barn door" slider, illustrated here, has increased in the last few years. It increases the entry width, is easy to operate, and can slide either on the face of the bedroom wall outside the bathroom, as shown, or on the inside bathroom wall. The panel door is a more traditional style. Even though it slides, this is a large door and can be heavy for frail older adults if not properly specified. Because the door slides rather than swinging open, furniture can be placed on the wall as long as enough room is allowed for the door to slide. This conserves valuable wall space for furniture. Just remember to allow a few inches between the furniture and the door.

A door width of 36 in., with a 5 ft. turning radius for wheelchairs, is considered minimum. A 6 ft. to 7 ft. turning radius is preferred for frail

Figure 13.14 A sliding door increases the size of the entry width. It is also easier to operate and can slide on either the bedroom wall or inside on the bathroom wall. *Courtesy of Design Concepts Unlimited, Sausalito, CA.*

older adults. Some specially equipped motorized wheelchairs are larger and need widths greater than the ADA minimum standards allowance. Again, we must move beyond the practice of relying on minimum standards, since this is not an effective or responsible strategy in designing for older adults.

MORE IDEAS

- Curved shower rods allow more room to shower and eliminate the shower curtain "stick-to-the-body" syndrome.
- Vanities with shelves and drawers provide more space for storage and free up counter space.
- Provide adequate task lighting in the bathroom; poor lighting is annoying and dangerous.
- Tie a small bunch of eucalyptus sprigs with a bit of raffia and put it in a vase or hang it from a press-on hook on the back of the bathroom door. The heat and humidity will release a wonderful natural scent.

Bathe Suites and Bathing Environments

Improving the Bathing Experience

Like eating, bathing is one of the great pleasures in life. Though this has not always been true in long-term care settings, with the intervention of sensitive care professionals and talented designers both bathing and the bathing environment is improving.

In too many long-term care settings, instead of recalling good memories, bathing was transformed into something dreadful. A 1995 bathing survey conducted by Dr. Philip Sloane showed that despite advances only half of nursing directors were satisfied with how bathing was handled, and high rates of resident resistance were attributed to environments and equipment.[10] Dr. Sloane, Joanne Rader, and Ann Louise Barrick, pioneers in the study of bathing in eldercare, have helped care providers and designers understand that bathing is about more than hygiene.[11]

Until recently, bathing environments have been perhaps the least sensitively thought out and most poorly designed spaces in care settings. They have been unpleasant for everyone, residents and staff alike, and particularly unpleasant and fearful for those with dementia. For persons with dementia bathing is substantially more challenging, and bathing environments themselves have made the behavior difficulties consistently faced by caregivers predictable.

Bathing environments too often seem to have been constructed for endurance rather than designed for renewal, revitalization, or pleasure, and there seems to be no limit to the number of ways they have engendered fear in reluctant bathers. Limited lighting and limitless expanses of ceramic tile create noisy environments for aging persons who experience difficulty seeing and hearing. These indignities and being expected to disrobe in a cold room with the overall ambiance of a storage cellar have combined to overwhelm, confuse, and anger unfortunate and unsuspecting residents.

Creating a pleasant bathing environment, particularly for individuals with Alzheimer's disease, requires skill and often necessitates a shift in the philosophy of care—at least around the bathing experience itself. Many providers, care staff, and designers have accepted the challenge and are pooling their skills to substantially improve both the environment and the experience. In an environment where virtually every waking hour is a communal experience, the bath can provide a time for individual attention.

The focus has shifted to creatively exploring ways to make bathing a pleasant experience—something residents can look forward to. As elements of the spa experience are integrated into care, more residents can look forward to this time as a chance to have a warm bath in a lovely setting and enjoy the experience.

Among those with dementia, bathing may generate a host of negative physical and verbal behaviors, from avoidance to combativeness. Analyzing an individual's reaction for clues to its cause can help caregivers develop appropriate interventions, improve the bathing experience for the individual, and make the bath a less grueling task for the care team.

Looking at the environment through the eyes of a person with dementia and seeing the number of possible environmental fear factors can be an eye opener. The shower or bathing room is possibly the noisiest, most disruptive place in many settings. Humidity, inadequate lighting, and glare

Figure 13.15 Residents can look forward to a pleasant bathing experience in a spa environment made special by design. *Courtesy of Foulkeways at Gwynedd, Gwynedd, PA. Architect: Reese Lower Patrick & Scott, Ltd., Lancaster, PA. Photographer: Larry Lefever Photography.*

compound the problem of low vision. Noise generated by running water, exhaust fans, moving furniture, and loud conversation reflects off ceramic tile floors and walls, contributing to environmental stress that triggers fear and the ancient fight or flight survival strategies. Small wonder that bathing is such an unpleasant experience for all.

Light, Space, and Bubbles: Cutting-Edge Bathe Suites

Peacefulness and tranquility are very basic needs and not the descriptive terms normally associated with bathing environments in care settings. While studies have shown the therapeutic effects of water, from detoxifying the body to soothing the mind, this has not been the bathing experience that most residents recall.

The new trend in designing bathe suites is subtlety and simplicity. Spa design has inspired an infusion of natural light, soft finishes, and live plants into this space. Combined with the soothing and calming effects of the water, bathe suites are being transformed into places of sanctuary in a variety of care environments.

Air-jet tubs offering the hydromassage of tiny bubbles are easier on delicate skin than a whirlpool. Warm air is forced through tiny holes strategically placed in the tub walls and floor, delivering a gentle massage that is less forceful than the whirlpool. Reconnecting the user with the calming properties of water without calling attention to the pipes often means placing greater attention on the design and use of material and colors. On a practical note, air-jet tubs are easy to maintain because the channels are blown dry after the water has drained.

Enriching the Environment

Designing a warm, intimate bathe suite is the key to a positive experience for residents. The ideal layout generously accommodates both a whirlpool tub and a shower, providing residents with a choice. Privacy is essential, and attractive dressing and grooming areas and a private toilet room allow residents to maintain their personal dignity.

Better lighting means less agitation. Reducing noise and increasing light levels are essential to reducing fear and creating a setting that encourages an enjoyable bathing experience. Windows and skylights are familiar features that provide welcome sources of daylight and warmth from the sun. Indirect cove lighting or pendant indirect fixtures with dimming options are much easier and more relaxing on older eyes than direct light sources. Both relieve glare and provide a flexible, energy-efficient lighting solution. Light levels can be increased or dimmed as necessary. A light fixture that supplies sufficient light in the shower is also a must.

The profusion of hard surfaces typically found in many care settings magnifies noise. One of the most effective interventions is the intelligent manipulation of the noise and stimulation to which bathers are exposed. Slip-resistant sheet vinyl flooring in wet areas, combined with moisture-

Figure 13.16 A warm, intimate bathe suite is the key to a positive experience for residents. *Courtesy of The Sylvestry at Vinson Hall, McLean, VA. Architect: Reese Lower Patrick & Scott, Ltd., Lancaster, PA. Photographer: Larry Lefever Photography.*

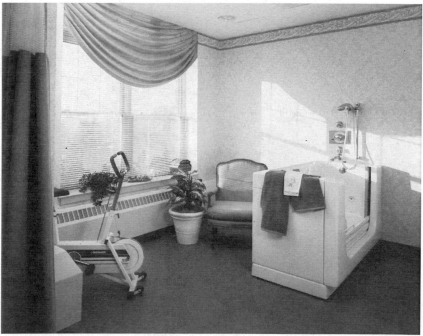

Figure 13.17 Reduced noise levels, more natural light, and better lighting create a setting that encourages enjoyable bathing. *Courtesy of Asbury Villas, Mt. Lebanon, PA. Architect: Perkins Eastman. Photographer: Massery Photography.*

barrier carpet in the dressing and grooming areas, reduces the amount of hard-surface ceramic tile. Many individuals with dementia are unable to consciously tune out distracting sounds, and the noise levels in traditional bathing rooms are exacerbated by hard surfaces, contributing to fear and combativeness.

Quiet, relaxing environments contribute to more pleasant experiences and calm, relaxed residents. Moisture-resistant acoustical ceiling tiles specifically designed for humid conditions can help control noise. In addition to improving the acoustics in the bathing environment, these tiles are also mold, mildew, and bacteria resistant. Window treatments, shower curtains, towels, and other soft items add color and life to the space and absorb noise.

European-style showers are being used with greater frequency to eliminate the trip hazard of a lip on the shower and to allow a shower chair to be rolled in easily. A bench is also a seating option. Seating in a contrasting color is more visible for those with low vision; for example, a white seat against the white background of the shower cannot be seen and likely will not be used. Similarly, grab bars in a contrasting color are highly visible. Handheld showerheads can be used for either standing or seated showers. They are easy to control and produce less anxiety in persons with dementia. A hook placed outside the shower puts towels or a robe within easy reach.

Pretty patterns in vinyl wall covering can be used or combined with painted surfaces to make bathe suites more inviting. For splash protection around the tub, nonslip resilient flooring or tile are appropriate, but con-

Figure 13.18 Pretty wallpaper patterns can make the bathe suite more inviting. *Courtesy of Covenant Village, Gastonia, NC. Architect: FreemanWhite, Inc., Charlotte, NC. Photographer: Billy Simcox.*

sider using a moisture-barrier backed carpet of the same color for the dressing and grooming areas. The softer surface helps control the acoustics and makes a more intimate, less institutional space.

Special Touches

Special touches can make the bathing experience pleasant, nourishing, and even memorable. Separate HVAC controls in the bathe suite allow care staff to adjust the room temperature and ensure the room is warm and comfortable when a resident arrives for a bath or shower.

A small painted chest or table next to the tub provides a convenient surface to place items such as shampoo, soap, lotion, or even a bouquet of flowers. An armoire is ideal for storing a supply of large towels in delicious colors—raspberry, lemon, peach, and lime—that look pretty when the armoire is open. Washcloths, personal soaps, shampoo, lotions, and aromatherapy products, tins of cookies or candies for handy distractions, and a CD player and CDs or audiotapes for music fit right in.

A warm bath sheet can be wrapped around a bather as an alternative to a robe after a bath. Terry-cloth bath mitts may be easier for some to use than a washcloth or provide a distraction for someone with dementia.

Figure 13.19 Good planning and thoughtful design put the things you need within arm's reach. *Courtesy of Carlson Boyd Place at Mather Pavilion at Wagner, Evanston, IL. Architect: Mithun, Inc., Seattle, WA. Photographer: Steve Hall © Hendrich Blessing.*

Figure 13.20 Attractive vanity areas can be the focal point of the bath and provide a lovely grooming area. *Courtesy of Harbour House, Greendale, WI. Architect: KM Development Corp., Milwaukee, WI. Interior Design: Mithun, Inc., Seattle, WI. Photographer: Skot Weidemann.*

Bathing and grooming are rituals for many women. An attractive vanity with a mirror and comfortable seating can be the focal point of the bath. A comfortable moisture-resistant wicker chair with pretty cushions makes this room a comfortable place to sit and dry off, relax, and regain strength after a warming bath. Color, detail, living plants, and other special touches can transform a bathing environment into a treat. When the bathing experience goes smoothly, it's a nurturing exchange and a richer, more fulfilling experience.

Fragrance can enrich the most ordinary occasion—especially the bath. We shower, bathe, and shampoo in it. Scented soap, potpourri, or the refreshing sent of a vase of lavender can be an unexpected treat, and the fresh scent of lemons is always delightful. Use your imagination and creativity to stimulate the sense of touch, sight, sound, and good smells.

The more we realize how seemingly insignificant items can make a significant difference, the easier it is to design a welcoming, highly personalized bathing environment where the expectation is for nurturing, increased personal attention, even pampering and sensitivity in attending to personal care needs. We then communicate an entirely different message through a visually and emotionally supportive space and acknowledge both the need for good hygiene and the equally important emotional needs of the individual to feel safe and cared for.

NOTES

Courtesy of the George G. Glenner Alzheimer's Day Care Centers, San Diego, CA.

"I hope you'll dance. When you get the chance to sit it out or dance—I hope you'll dance."
Written by Tia Sellers and Mark Sanders.

Social Living Spaces

Loneliness kills! Experts say social connectedness is one of the most important predictors of health and independence in later years. A major public health study involving more than 116,000 people found that those with strong relationships had less mental decline and lived more active, pain-free lives without physical limitations.[1] Other studies support these findings, including research that indicates people with good social networks live longer and are physically healthier than people who are socially isolated.

Older people may be more likely to lead solitary lives, especially if family and friends have moved away or died. Many experts believe that social isolation may create a chronically stressful condition that accelerates aging. Combating loneliness requires effort, both in establishing new relationships and in deepening existing ones.

Combating loneliness requires effort.

Social Activity

The social and behavioral aspects of life for older adults can make a difference in health and well-being. A fulfilling life for older adults is characterized by social interaction—life with people. Men and women both benefit from social activity at older ages. Interactions with friends and family members can provide emotional and practical support, and those who continue to interact with others tend to be healthier, both physically and mentally, than those who become socially isolated. The most frequent social activities include going out to church or temple for services and activities with family.[2]

Figure 14.1 Encouraging social activity and connectedness is more effective when residents feel they are members of a community that cares—one that encourages opportunities to feel useful. *Courtesy of the Madlyn and Leonard Abramson Center for Jewish Life, North Wales, PA. Architect: Ewing Cole, Philadelphia, PA.*

Older adults consider social interaction an important aspect of their daily life. Both cognitively impaired and intact nursing home residents report often feeling lonely and needing more opportunities for socialization.[3] Encouraging social activity is more effective when residents feel they are members of a community that cares—one that nurtures friendships for the lonely and encourages opportunities to feel useful. Above all it's important to keep in mind the very basic human need for inclusion and stimulate purposeful engagement within the community setting.[4]

Our goal should be to create a home and community with a rich, stimulating environment full of opportunities for involvement, which residents are free to accept or reject at any time. One of the best reasons for activity programs in older adult settings is to encourage regular social contact. Throughout the community elders can continue to grow socially and spiritually and enjoy interacting with friends and family. The social activities and interaction considered especially valuable for older persons are those that:

- *Engender and support opportunities for continued growth.* People who share common interests, such as gardening, cooking, or environmental issues, can explore ways to share and expand their interests; for example, by baking cookies, planning and preparing a special dinner meal with shared recipes, or inviting a guest chef for a lecture or to prepare a meal.

  Many community garden clubs will give lectures, lead garden craft projects, or design projects to involve residents in preparing garden ornaments, painting birdhouses, or other interesting, productive, and fun activities.

Walking and fitness clubs improve health and while people walk they get to know their neighbors. At Woodside Place residents often walk with another resident, a family member, or care staff. Pairs are often seen walking arm in arm; in fact the pattern is so prevalent that it has been named "social walking."[5] And don't overlook animal companionship; furry or feathered friends can bring great joy and purpose into our lives.

- *Enable continued productive contributions to the community.* Volunteering time for a cause creates opportunities to learn more about other residents in the care community, as well as the opportunity to meet persons with common interests from the greater community. Residents can also serve as tutors or call latchkey kids when they're home alone.[6] This type of activity is a wonderful way to give to others and raise self-esteem. Often these connections turn into lasting friendships. Environmental groups can always use help, and there is no end to the chance to join political discussion groups or opportunities for speakers.

Figure 14.2 The Potting Shed provides a place for people with common interests in gardening to explore ways to share their interests. *Courtesy of Cuthbertson Village at Aldersgate CCRC, Charlotte, NC. Architect: FreemanWhite, Inc., Charlotte, NC. Photographer: Tim Buchman.*

- *Encourage meaningful connections with family and the community.*
  Visiting is often difficult for family members, and they are always
  appreciative when ways are found to make them feel more comfortable. Inviting them to a variety of joint activities with other
  residents and families or recruiting them to help prepare a special
  "theme" meal once a month for the small resident group allows
  families to feel both a sense of contribution and less like outsiders.

Wagging Tails Have Healing Power

The philosophy of the Eden Alternative is to eliminate the three plagues of
long-term care—loneliness, helplessness, and boredom—and to make
nursing homes and care environments habitats for human beings rather
than institutions for the frail and elderly. Since gardens are known to provide social, spiritual, and dietary benefits, founder Bill Thomas, MD, created a Garden of Eden.

Incorporating animals, plants, and children in the culture of a nursing
home helps to create nurturing environments that reflect the elements of
normal life and enhances the quality of life for elders. The Eden Alternative's mission is to show how a spontaneous environment and the opportunity to care for other living things can succeed where medications fail.
Helping to care for animals gives residents a sense of purpose. One resident
feeds the fish and lets the cat out in the morning, while another walks the
dog. It gives residents an opportunity to balance the care they receive with
ways they can give care. It's an opportunity to "give back" to someone or
something, fulfilling the human need to be needed.

People with Alzheimer's benefit most from this environment because
they don't need their memories or communication skills to have relationships with others. Canine comfort provides companionship and warmth
and contributes to a spontaneous and fun-filled atmosphere. Dogs don't
really ask anything of you. They don't ask any questions or give any
advice—they're just there. They accept how humans are and heal with
unconditional love.

In the effort to combat loneliness and effect social and cultural change
in long-term-care settings, fuzzy critters capture public attention. It's tough
to measure reductions in feelings of loneliness and hopelessness, but there
are other indicators of success that show a 71 percent reduction in the daily
drug cost per resident and a 26 percent cut in the turnover of nurse
aides.

Design

The growing trend of smaller cluster environments or neighborhoods has
succeeded in eliminating long corridors and made it much easier to create
smaller gathering spaces reminiscent of an extended family. The great room
and other spaces that are more intimate and private come alive with elders

planning their activities for the day. Residents also have the added comfort and security of knowing they are not far from their rooms.

HANDRAILS

All long-term-care settings, in fact any environment for older adults, should be designed to support mobility and independence. Well-designed handrails do not detract from the image; to the contrary, they enhance balance, encourage movement, and help to allay fear of falling, conveying a message of support. Handrails such as the one shown have a distinctly residential appeal and can easily be adapted for residential use.

The loss of grip strength, more limited range of movement, and diminished energy levels that characterize many elderly residents can make small round handrails difficult to use. They can be especially difficult to grip for residents with arthritic hands. A broader oval-shaped handrail, flat on top and bullnosed on each side, is easier to use for support. The most important feature of this design is that it enhances mobility by allowing a resident to grasp the rail or to use it as a leaning rail. Leaning on the forearm, one can glide along the rail.

Handrails should be provided on both sides of a corridor. A mounting height of 33 in. to 36 in. from the floor to the top of the handrail is recommended, although the height may vary according to need. Wooden

Figure 14.5 Well-designed handrails offer support, encourage movement, enhance balance, and help to allay fear of falling. *Courtesy of Duncaster, a Life Care Retirement Community. Bloomfield, CT. Photograph courtesy of Design Concepts Unlimited, Sausalito, CA*

Figure 14.6 Town Square, infused with natural light, is bordered by a variety of places for residents and families to go and things to do. *Courtesy of Cuthbertson Village at Aldersgate CCRC, Charlotte, NC. Architect: FreemanWhite, Inc., Charlotte, NC. Photographer: Tim Buchman.*

Figure 14.7 The interior Memory Care "Main Street" activity area is an interesting space with a variety of opportunities for activity. *Courtesy of The Village at Waveny Care Center, New Canaan, CT. Architect: Reese Lower Patrick & Scott, Ltd., Lancaster, PA. Photographer: Larry Lefever Photography.*

handrails offer a warm finish and residential look. The broader handrail is now available in a variety of powder-coated finishes to provide color, texture, and a hard finish.

Innovative and interesting new building designs are helping to broaden the types of experiences available. Life in many new communities is now centered around a town square, a large open space infused with natural light and bordered by movie theaters, beauty shops, libraries, cafes, ice cream parlors, gift shops, chapels, synagogues and other places of worship, and much more to be enjoyed by residents, family, and friends—all with the added benefit of being easily accessible and no parking problems.

These large spaces offer opportunities to develop many activities appropriate for indoors or outdoors. Trees, colorful umbrella tables, and park benches can create a park and lovely spaces to paint as part of a "Memories in the Making" art program developed by the Alzheimer's Association. Interior park spaces, porches, and gardens are making it possible to enjoy animals, children, gardening, and walking both inside and outside.

If successful aging is defined as an optimal state of overall functioning and well-being, only a happy few meet the criteria. However, many elderly persons view successful aging as a process of adaptation, and using this perspective, many more persons can be considered to be successfully aging.[7]

Sacred Spaces: Religion and Spirituality

Spirituality has to do with how individuals make meaning of what happens to them, affecting how they feel and even act when confronted by conflicts

Figure 14.8 Studies have shown that individuals who pray regularly and attend religious services stay healthier and live longer. *Courtesy of Garvey Manor, Hollidaysburg, PA. Architect: Reese Lower Patrick & Scott, Ltd., Lancaster, PA. Photographer: Larry Lefever Photography.*

Figure 14.9 The beautiful entry doors to the Mary's Woods at Marylhurst Chapel were saved from the original convent to be used in the new location. The glass was created by a local artisan. *Courtesy of Mary's Woods at Marylhurst, Lake Oswego, OR. Architect: Mithun, Inc., Seattle, WA. Interior Design: Stanzione Associates, Sarasota, FL. Photographer. Eckert and Eckert.*

or barriers. Spirituality influences whether people see a disability as an insurmountable mountain or a new challenge.[8]

At one time, physical health and spirituality seemed worlds apart, but their differences are diminishing. Many physicians today have come to believe that medical interventions may be more effective when teamed with their patients' spiritual activities, and dozens of studies have shown that individuals who pray regularly and attend religious services stay healthier and live longer than those who rarely or never do—even when age, health, habits, and other factors are considered. A six-year study by Duke University of 4,000 men and women of various faiths, all over 64 years of age, found that the relative risk of dying was 46 percent lower for those who frequently attended religious services.[9]

Dr. Harold Koenig, director of Duke University's Center for the Study of Religion/Spirituality and Health believes that prayer affects the quality, if not the quantity of life. "It boosts morale, lowers agitation, loneliness and life dissatisfaction and enhances the ability to cope in men, women, the elderly, the young, the healthy and the sick." In the same group of 4,000 people over 64, studies found that those who prayed regularly had significantly lower blood pressure than the less religious; and those who attended religious services had healthier immune systems than those who did not.

How does prayer help? Nobody knows and science may never prove that prayer can heal. It would be difficult to shape a study to prove it, but according to Dr. Koenig, we now know enough, based on solid research, to say that prayer, much like exercise and diet, has a connection with better health.[10]

These studies also show faith and religious practices can have a positive impact on physical and mental health in relation to chronic illnesses, suggesting not only that spirituality is a resource in maintaining well-being, but that the use of this resource is more significant on individuals with greater levels of frailty. Spirituality and religion have been found to play an important part in many older people's lives, and religious and spiritual beliefs are thought to play a protective role with physical health,[11] mental health, and well-being. They lower the likelihood of hypertension and they lower mortality levels. Women and older adults consistently hold the strongest spiritual and religious beliefs.[12] This seems to indicate that providing a dedicated space for religious and spiritual activities would add significant value to the health and lives of many residents.

Religious and spiritual beliefs can still be maintained and benefit both people with Alzheimer's disease and their caregivers. Both research and anecdotal reports indicate that even those with advanced Alzheimer's often respond to familiar hymns, prayers, and liturgies as well as to the visual cues of collars and crucifixes.

One of the most welcomed additions in religious gerontology is the growing research that seems to demonstrate "scientifically" the effectiveness of religious beliefs and behaviors for health in general and healthy aging in particular. Stephen Sapp, PhD, chair of the Department of Reli-

Figure 14.10 Many individuals embrace formal religious beliefs and practices for their spiritual connection. *Courtesy of Mary Queen of Angels Assisted Living Community, Nashville, TN.*

Figure 14.11 Attending worship services is an activity that can be accomplished whether living at home or in a care community setting. *Courtesy of The Evergreens, Moorestown, NJ. Architect: Nelson Bauzenberger. Photographer: Joel Schwartz.*

gious Studies at the University of Miami, provides and apt description: "Modern science can offer us the means to live longer and healthier lives, but for all its successes and contributions, it is utterly powerless to offer us any meaning to live for. The central teachings of the great religious traditions about the inherent value of every human being, whatever the person's condition, can serve as an important counterbalance."[13]

It is our quest for meaning, place, and purpose that defines us as human beings. Many individuals embrace formal religious beliefs and practices for their spiritual connection. Virginia Bell and David Troxel refer to Tom Kitwood's description of our role as caregivers as "physicians of the human spirit." They go on to say it is important to open opportunities for spiritual needs to be met, with the goal of creating a spiritual space or spiritual moments for them.

Many older adults have been members of a religious tradition since early childhood. They have attended religious services, sung in choirs, visited the sick as representatives of their faith community, and even been religious leaders in their communities. This connection to others and to their God has given meaning and purpose to their lives, and they should be encouraged to continue these activities. Attending worship services, participating in the choir, visiting and delivering meals to shut-ins with a friend are all activities that can be accomplished whether living at home or in an assisted-care setting.[14]

My mother was a longtime active member of the Presbyterian church and spent much of her life visiting and delivering countless home-cooked

Figure 14.12 A small chapel in a care setting can play a large role in the lives of residents. *Courtesy Highland Ridge Senior Camps, Williamsburg, IA. Architect: KKE Architects, Minneapolis, MN. Interior Design: Encompass Interiors: St. Paul, MN. Photographer: Scott Gilbertson.*

The more understandable the architecture, the less time that will be spent on additional cueing and wayfinding strategies.

meals from her kitchen to shut-ins, particularly older members of the community. With all the things that she forgot as Alzheimer's disease stole her mind, she still dressed for church every Sunday. As time went by and she became more confused she sometimes dressed up on Wednesdays or Tuesdays or Fridays, thinking it was Sunday. She wanted to go to church. It brought her great comfort. While reading from a book of devotions or singing a hymn satisfied her often, I always wished that a small chapel had been available in the nursing home where she lived. It would have meant so much to her and probably to others to have a place to visit and to practice her faith. Somehow, as well meaning as it is, rolling out a cart on Saturday or Sunday with the appropriate religious symbols just isn't quite the same.

In faith-based care settings, chapels, synagogues, and other special settings play a large role in the lives of the residents. We need to make a greater effort to find spaces for religious celebration and do more to make this a reality. If these special places can make people's souls feel better, help to settle them when they're distressed, and help to comfort them, it's time to make the design of sacred spaces a priority.

Figure 14.13 Memory boxes filled with interesting items and used in select locations can and do stimulate conversation. *Courtesy of Garvey Manor, Hollidaysburg, PA. Architect: Reese Lower Patrick & Scott, Ltd., Lancaster, PA. Photographer: Larry Lefever Photography.*

Wayfinding

Minimizing Confusion

To many, wayfinding means the addition of signage. In actuality, it means much more. Wayfinding is the cognitive process that allows a person to navigate to a particular place and back again. Design that allows people to find their way begins with a holistic concern. Architects, planners, and designers must challenge the traditional forms in circulation, spatial design, color, and lighting. Circulation patterns for older adults, especially those with dementia, who are easily confused, should reduce conventional arrangements of corridors, elevators, and stairs and introduce dedicated paths, walkways, atriums, and gardens. Sequences of public spaces carefully connected to walking spaces can nurture a sense of inclusion.

Homelike settings that are small in scale are less of a challenge to older adults. The cluster or neighborhood concept eliminates the confusion of long corridors. Rather than relying on traditional signage, the aroma of coffee or spiced apples from the kitchen or the warmth of a fireplace is unquestionably more effective than arrows or signs. The more understandable the architecture, the less time that will be spent on additional cueing and wayfinding strategies.

Though memory boxes may not have proved as effective as we hoped for helping individuals identify their rooms, when they are used in select locations and filled with interesting and visible items, they can and do stimulate conversation.

Large, well-lighted display boxes that offer changeable displays can be used as wayfinding cues. For example, a collection of fine china—replicas of beautiful Russian china patterns used by the czars—located outside the dining room is consistent with the dining location. It would likely draw interest, stimulate comments and conversation, and for some might signal they are, indeed, in the right place.

Finding My Way

My views about cueing radically changed two years ago when I experienced an aggressive treatment of simultaneous radiation and chemotherapy for colon cancer. It was painful, disorienting, and enlightening, and not an experience I want to repeat. The treatment was, thankfully, successful, and I learned more than I ever really wanted to know about memory loss—the difficulty of trying to live each day with no current memory and the difficult, labored search for recall of past memories. I remembered what breakfast was, but I couldn't remember what I had for breakfast, because I couldn't remember eating breakfast. More importantly, I couldn't remember to take critical medications, or when asked, whether I had taken them. Friends were frantic trying to devise something that would remind me. Eventually when all else failed, they set up a schedule to either bring the required medication to me or call every four hours and wait on the phone to ensure that I took it.

I experienced what is known to many cancer survivors as "chemo brain." It was either one of the things that slipped through the cracks, or I simply did not remember being told of the possibility of losing my memory, although it seems impossible or at least improbable, with my long personal history with Alzheimer's disease, that I wouldn't have remembered being told that one of the side effects might be memory loss.

I have never been so frightened in my life—to the point that I almost discontinued treatment. Several almost simultaneous events convinced me that I had Alzheimer's, just as my mother had. It's one thing to talk about memory loss. It is another stunningly and unbelievably frightening experience to try to find your way. I couldn't retain anything in my mind longer than three seconds. I suddenly understood the fear I had seen in my mother's eyes so many times when her ability to remember or retrieve information failed her. Sometimes I was aware that the information was stored somewhere, but most times I just felt lost, like being in a vast place of blankness or nothingness.

After my treatment one day, I was asked to wait to see the nurse. I said OK, walked through the door, and went home. The following day a very kind radiology technician made the same request, then thought better of it, took my hand, and walked me through the waiting room and around the corner. He placed my hand into the nurse's hand and, laughing, said, "hang on to her or she'll be out the door." That confirmed what I feared. How often had I shared that same concern for so many others. I was sure that I had Alzheimer's disease and burst into tears. It made no sense to me to continue treatment—to get well, only to have to cope with Alzheimer's. It took several doctors the better part of three days to convince me that my "head problems" were a result of the very powerful chemotherapy drugs and would eventually dissipate.

The point of sharing this experience is that it has given me a new perspective on helping people with memory impairment to find their way. I know that finding good solutions won't be as easy as I once thought. I'm more skeptical; I've been there. I experienced severe memory loss and confusion for months, and I know that arrows on the floor—or a line of psychedelic hippopotamuses in a riot of color marching down the corridor wall—could not have helped me remember or find my way. I couldn't hold on to anything—any information. It was literally as though there was only air in

> *The thing that works best is the kindness of human touch. The strongest and most important message—because I care, you haven't lost your way.*

my head, so that when information went in one ear, it was a straight shot out the other ear, with nothing but air between. The only thing that was clear to me was thinking, this must be what it's like not to be able to remember, not to have a clue. It was devastating!

On another occasion returning home from treatment I was stopped for a traffic infraction and the police officer asked, "Don't you know when a traffic light is out, you must treat it as a four-way stop?" I was so confused and frustrated trying to figure out what and if I remembered that I never answered. With the painkillers in my system I would have been in serious trouble if I had been tested for drugs; I quit driving that day. Two years later, my memory is much better but not completely restored.

I understand confusion and memory loss. Experience is a powerful teacher. I don't think we should stop trying to find better solutions, but until we find a better way to solve this problem or to reinstate memory, the thing that works best is the kindness of human touch. Walking arm in arm, or the simple act of taking a person's hand and walking with them, conveys the strongest and most important message—because I care, you haven't lost your way. What worked for me was the kindness of those around me who took my hand, or took my arm and stopped asking questions that I obviously struggled to answer.

Entry alcoves personalized with furniture or artwork can be remarkably interesting spaces, unique to the individual resident. Familiar furniture and artwork large enough to be seen become a larger adaptation of how we use memory boxes. Whether such spaces are actually components of a wayfinding strategy or not, they add interest and variety to settings. Incorporating spaces of this nature into the design and testing them over time would be worthwhile and might prove more beneficial that we suspect.

Figure 14.14 Personalizing an entry alcove with furniture or artwork unique to the resident creates an interesting space and may help the resident recognize his or her room. *Courtesy of Duncaster, a Life Care Retirement Community, Bloomfield, CT and Design Concepts Unlimited, Sausalito, CA.*

Building design has improved dramatically in the past few years. Generous spatial design, augmented by natural light, is fundamental to creating healthy, nurturing, and satisfying environments. Yet as needs continue to change, the culture change movement is pushing designers to take another look at design for care settings and to stretch their imagination in spatial planning.

The image of the ideal care setting today is one that nurtures physical, social, and creative activity, incorporating arts such as music, dance, and painting as beneficial agents for sustaining health. *As the focus shifts yet again, to the design of caring, intimate, and enriching experiences to meet special needs, we may just find that we are building care settings that are spatially generous and congenial, and offer services that motivate activity, companionship, and a will to enjoy.*

SECTION

IV

Innovative
Care Models

Courtesy of The Green House® Project, New York, NY

Friendship is ageless, and good friends are our most treasured gifts.

The Green House

Elders are like the rest of us, flawed . . . broken . . . lacking insight in many ways, but they have one virtue you and I don't have—the experience of a life lived. What they have to teach us is how to live like human beings.

Dr. William Thomas, MD

The most common reasons for admission to nursing homes are related to functional losses, especially cognitive impairment, incontinence, and decreases in the ability to manage ADLs (activities of daily living) and IADLs (independent activities of daily living). A 1995 study revealed that nursing home residents needed help with an average of 4.4 ADLs.[1] Astoundingly, a typical resident in a nursing home receives only 70 minutes of care per day, five minutes from licensed nursing personnel[2] and the remainder from the certified nursing assistant, primarily in the form of assistance with activities of daily living. The entire focus of the nursing home model is skewed toward a very small piece of the elder's total existence, and it seems clear that we must change the way we think about, regulate, and deliver services to people who are frail, disabled, or elderly.

The philosophical foundation of the Green House® Project is drawn from the work of Dr. William Thomas, MD. It is a movement toward humanized care, with a new conceptual model for care of the frail elderly and chronically ill—a radically new approach to long-term care that redefines and redesigns how care is delivered to elders.

Figure 15.1 The Green House replaces the institutional skilled nursing home with a residence where the primary focus is on the elder's quality of life. *Courtesy of The Green Houses of Traceway Retirement Community, Tupelo, MS, and The Green House® Project, New York, NY. Architect: The McCarthy Company, Tupelo, MS.*

The Green House replaces the institutional skilled nursing model with a residence, operationally connected to a larger organization. A group home for elders, the Green House places the primary focus on the elder's quality of life. It draws a strong distinction between care and treatment, with treatment defined as the provision of competent, comprehensive therapeutic services, and care as helping another to achieve the highest quality of life given his or her condition and impairments. The goal of this new model is to provide frail elders with an environment that promotes independence, dignity, privacy, and choice.

The Green House is staffed by a universal worker called the elder assistant, who is responsible for the care of the elders and their environment and assists with the delivery of some of the therapeutic activities that are part of the treatment plan for the elders. Clinical treatment is designed and delivered by the clinical support team (CST), made up of the physician, registered nurse and licensed practical nurse, occupational therapist, physical therapist, recreational therapist, social worker, dietician, speech therapist, and any other professionals needed by the elder. This team assesses and designs a plan to meet the clinical treatment needs in cooperation with the elder assistant. These professionals are not located in the Green House, but visit based on the clinical assessment and treatment needs of the elder, and in compliance with regulations. An emergency alert system will summon designated CST members to the Green House when needed. When they come to the Green House, they come as guests, invited into a private home.

Structured more like a home than an institution, the Green House is built to a residential scale that situates necessary clinical care within a habilitative, social model[3] and meets regulatory requirements for skilled nursing, assisted living, and adult homes.

By emphasizing competence and participation in daily activities in the household, the Green House is attempting to reverse the loss of control too many elders experience.[4] Research has consistently linked personal control to positive psychological well-being.[5] Too many medical-model nursing homes promote dependency by encouraging helplessness and inducing disability.[6] The more things are done for the resident and the less residents do for themselves, the less they are able to do, which leads to loss of function and often depression. In contrast, elder assistants in the Green House encourage the use of adaptive devices to maximize the elders' independence [7]

The Green House environment respects resident choices by placing decisions back in their hands as often as possible. The household does not operate on a fixed schedule. Elders are encouraged to have meals, receive personal care, sleep, rest, and engage in activities at the times they choose, and they are encouraged to participate in household activities, including

Figure 15.2 Elders are encouraged to engage in activities when they choose and to participate in household activities. *Courtesy of The Green Houses of Traceway Retirement Community, Tupelo, MS, and The Green House® Project, New York, NY.*

meal preparation, gardening, caring for the household pets, cleaning, laundry, and meal planning. Household decisions are made jointly around the large dining table at the house meetings.

Long-term care is failing elders and their caregivers today, according to Dr. Thomas, because its very concept is deeply flawed. It approaches old age in an unabashedly negative way.[8] Elders are seen as broken and needing repair, with the emphasis on medical technology to alleviate their physical and mental decline. The focus is in the wrong place. Rather than focusing on what *is* working, it's focused instead on what isn't. Spiritual and social needs are ignored. Dr. Thomas explains, "The Green House proceeds from the view of old age as a distinctive, healthful, vibrant phase in the human development life cycle. It is dedicated to enlarging upon and enriching the native goodness of old age."[9]

A pioneering project, the Green Houses of Traceway Retirement Community in Tupelo, Mississippi, opened the initial phase of four Green Houses in 2003. When fully developed there will be twelve homes blending architecturally with neighboring homes in a residential neighborhood. The homes are connected by driveways and winding roads rather than parking lots, just as the homes are replacing traditional large nursing facilities.

The architectural design of the typical nursing home is based on the operation and tasks commonly performed in a medical setting.[10] While this design successfully facilitates the provision of clinical treatments, it unfortunately does not attempt to accommodate for the holistic needs of frail elders. Long corridors are unnecessarily challenging for the frail elderly. Rather than attempting to address their mobility needs with design solutions, such homes are forcing many elders prematurely into wheelchairs. Massive dining rooms clearly do not encourage a pleasant dining experience for older adults; typically, the lighting is poor and the acoustics are worse, making hearing and conversation difficult. Under these conditions dining can hardly be described as an inviting, social experience. Shared bedrooms and bathrooms provide little opportunity for privacy. The use of similar or identical furnishings, floorcoverings, and window treatments throughout creates an unmistakably institutional environment. With little or no access to the outdoors or healthy fresh air and sunshine, it's difficult to see how this environment contributes to a better quality of life.

The Green House, in contrast, is a residence—not an institution—where frail elders can receive assistance and support with activities of daily living and clinical care, without the assistance and care becoming the focus of their existence. The focus of the Green House is clearly on the quality of life experience.[11]

The architectural model relies on the design concepts expressed by Christopher Alexander in *A Pattern Language*.[12] Alexander presents a group of design concepts or patterns that focus on the experience of being in a home. For example, the presence of light as a pattern is explored through the use of interior sunlight and street windows; the relationship between

The focus of the Green House is clearly on the quality of life experience.

TRADITIONAL NURSING HOME VS. THE GREEN HOUSE

	TRADITIONAL NURSING HOME	GREEN HOUSE
SIZE	Usually 120+ beds divided into 20–40 bed units	8–10 elders
PHILOSOPHY	Medical model—provide services to frail patients	Social habilitative model, an intentional community where primacy is given to quality of life
ORGANIZATION	Steep bureaucracy, nurses control all unit activity	Flattened bureaucracy, empowerment of direct care staff; nurses visit the house to provide skilled services
DECISION MAKING	Decisions made by the organization	Decisions placed as close to the elder as possible; house councils plan menus, activities, house routines
ACCESS	Space belongs to the institution; elders have access to their room and public areas, many spaces off-limits	Space belongs to the elders, who have access to all areas of the house
OUTDOOR SPACE	Often challenging to access, particularly without assistance	Easy to access, fenced, shaded, and in full view of the hearth and kitchen, allowing observation by staff
LIVING AREAS	Commonly double bedrooms and shared baths; lounges and dining rooms usually at the end of long corridors	Private rooms with private baths, and a central hearth with an adjacent open kitchen and dining area; short halls with access to the hearth
KITCHEN	Off-limits to elders and visitors	Elders and visitors have access and may participate in cooking activities
NURSES' STATION	In the center of most units	None; medication and supply cabinets in each room; nurses visit rooms and administer medications
DINING	Large dining rooms with many elders	One long dining table that acts as a focal point for a convivium—an enjoyable community meal
STAFFING	Departmental, with segmented tasks	Elder assistant (Shahbaz) is a universal worker, providing direct care, laundry, housekeeping, and cooking.
VISITORS	Limited ability to participate	May participate in meals and other activities, may prepare snacks in the kitchen, or hold family celebrations in the Green House

Figure 15.3 The Hearth, the heart of the home, is complete with a fireplace, an open farmhouse kitchen, and a large family-style dining table where residents and staff gather to eat. *Courtesy of The Green Houses of Traceway Retirement Community, Tupelo, MS, and The Green House® Project, New York, NY. Architect: The McCarthy Company, Tupelo, MS.*

inside and outside is developed through positive outdoor space, the garden walk, and living courtyards.

The Green House is a residential house built to comfortably accommodate six to ten elders. The front door is for family and friends, and the home's residents admit guests just as they would in a family home. The floor plan is designed with ten private rooms with private baths surrounding a generous gathering space called the Hearth. Elders bring their own furniture from home and pick the color, window treatments, and other environmental choices for their own rooms.

The Hearth has a fireplace, an open farmhouse kitchen, and a large family-style dining table that seats 12 people, where residents and staff gather to eat. The interiors are inviting, expressing the warmth of home, with short passages rather than long hallways. In addition, the spa room encourages pleasant bathing experiences, with dressing and grooming areas and an adjoining beauty salon.

Green House plans isolate service areas, with service access accommodated through a side door. There is no nurses' station; instead medical data and medicines are securely stored throughout the house and out of sight. A small work area for cross-trained, on-site staff—the Shahbazim—consists of a residential-style desk with a computer.

Skilled nursing is delivered much like home healthcare, by a clinical support team located off-site in the nearby Traceway Retirement Community. When nurses visit the Green House they ring the doorbell as they would when visiting someone's home. This is an environment designed with the clear intention to revolve around the elders rather than around healthcare.[13]

Warm, Smart, and Green

Drawing on the Eden Alternative, the Green House was founded on the idea that the physical and social environments in which we deliver long-term care can and should be warm, smart, and green. The Green House is a social model of care, emphasizing home and the warmth of the environment.

Smarter Care Delivery

What makes the Green House possible now is the information technology revolution, which has made it easy to move information and expertise and to distribute care. We have always known technology ought to serve older people at least as well as younger people, but we just haven't had the options before. Introducing high-level technology into a nineteenth-century nursing home structure is difficult and expensive, if not impossible. Now is the time to change our social structure so the technology can work for us.[14]

Building technology at the Green House includes traditional and wireless nurse-call systems; ceiling mounted patient lift systems; and high-speed Internet access, with large-screen monitors for Web-based activities, telemedicine, communicating with family and friends, and webcam viewing of on-site animals and woodlands.[15]

With the help of the latest wireless and computer technologies the highest quality of life is available for residents. Cell phones with preprogrammed directories for quick contact with emergency services or clinical support makes necessary staff immediately accessible, and wireless laptops and Palm Pilots for collecting and transmitting medical data reduce time-consuming paper shuffling. Emergency call systems and computers are wired from each house into the campus network, and on-site workers transmit data to the clinical support team. These technologies already work in other professions but are not widely used in nursing homes today. The Green House is providing a much needed model of how technology, wisely used, frees staff to spend more time with residents. A minimum of 36 hours of care per day, or six hours per resident, is anticipated in the new Green House model.

Green and Connected

To create interesting views from the homes and from the secured walking garden just beyond the hearth, the Green House site will remain in a natural state. The Green House defines "green" as the connection to the outside world, with courtyards for gardening and other outdoor activities, the laughter of children, and if the elders choose, plants and animals.

> *Probably the most important function of life in a Green House is to help the elder understand that old age is a significant time of life, and there is still meaningful work to do.*

This is a home where elders pursue the most positive experience possible within the context of their age. Probably the most important function of life in a Green House is to help the elder understand that old age is a significant time of life, and there is still meaningful work to do.

Many providers feel such planning, design, and caregiving innovations will help free elders from the cycle of loneliness, helplessness, and boredom that is thought to contribute to mental, physical, and spiritual decline. The

Figure 15.4 In the Green House home residents share a growing appreciation for the rich opportunities of late life. *Courtesy of The Green Houses of Traceway Retirement Community, Tupelo, MS, and The Green House® Project, New York, NY.*

Green House Project director, Judith Rabig, reports, "We are beginning to see some evidence of expected outcomes, including less wheelchair dependency, encouraging weight gains, increased appetites, and lots of happy laughter. The Shahbazim have been working successfully in self-managed work teams, and they are collaborating with the clinical support team very effectively."

Dr. Thomas makes the case that older adults deserve access to ways of living in late life that do not force them to become residents of a nursing home. It is possible to correct our mistakes, to take people out of large institutions and give them Green House homes in a neighborhood—a small, intentional community for older people who come together to pursue the most positive elderhood possible, a place where they can find respect, dignity, and quality of life much more easily than they can in a nursing home. There is growing appreciation that late life offers some delectable surprises, and the future is going to be rich with opportunities to create intentional communities that support us as we age.[16] The current baby boomer generation is extremely unlikely to accept institutionalization as an option for their old age. They are, however, more likely to increasingly embrace elderhood in an intentional community as a distinctive way of living.

The Green House Project is an attempt to design, build, and test a radically new approach to residential long-term care for the elderly. It is a model that strives to put personal caring back into care and is truly making long-term care about "life worth living" for today's elders and for many of us tomorrow. Planning is currently under way for two sites in Michigan and Nebraska, with other sites under consideration in New York, Florida, Georgia, North Carolina, Arizona, and Kansas. The movement toward more humanized long-term care has already won the approval of the American Healthcare Association and the American Association of Homes and Services for the Aging.

Courtesy of the Life Enrichment Center, Kings Mountain, NC. Photographer: Debbie Vaughan.

The doll-making business allows participants to create some amazing and treasured gifts and experience the opportunity of giving back by contributing to community service projects.

Adult Day Care

With Americans living longer—and often healthier and better than ever before—aging and retirement have become a chance to savor life's pleasures, sometimes for the very first time. But for at least one in five older people, the golden years are not all that they had dreamed of. About 20 percent of older Americans need help getting out of bed and bathing. Overwhelmingly, it is their families who provide that help. And in less than 35 years, older adults in this country will actually outnumber children.[1]

For frail adults and their caregivers, continuing to live independently at home can be a daily struggle. The challenge becomes even greater when a health crisis occurs, such as a stroke or injury—compounded by social and emotional problems. Adult day care brings together therapeutic medical care and the services elders and their families need to help them get through a health crisis or to manage a chronic problem. Just as importantly, adult day care provides a safe, enjoyable place for people to go during the day while their caregivers work or rest, and this can make all the difference in helping to keep the individual at home.

With the growing number of persons turning 65 and older, more and more people are finding themselves in the role of caring for parents, and for most caregivers, providing care for an older member of the family is only one aspect of an already hectic life. Many also have children to care for, as well as personal, social, and work commitments; in fact, more than 60 percent of caregivers are employed outside the household. The demand for assistance in handling these tremendous responsibilities will only increase.

Between 1988 and 1996 the number of households providing care for elderly relatives tripled, from 7 million to 21 million. Adult day care helps to alleviate the tremendous responsibilities placed on primary caregivers. Adult day care activities can give adults with disabilities and older adults a renewed interest in life while providing their caregivers with emotional support and the opportunity to continue working or otherwise remain active outside the home.

Adult day care helps enrich the lives of older adults who need assistance with daily tasks, as well as providing their caregivers the necessary time to run errands and complete everyday tasks. Perhaps most importantly, adult day care allows caregivers the time to maintain their own personal health while continuing to care for their loved ones. Relief from full-time caregiving can mean the difference between keeping a loved one at home or moving him or her into a nursing home.

> *Adult day care allows caregivers the time to maintain their own personal health while continuing to care for their loved ones.*

Despite the tremendous number of families who could benefit from the adult day care experience, many families don't know these services and centers exist. There are many times when an adult day center is the perfect alternative to nursing home placement for older people and families who want their loved one to stay at home. There is no question that the role of the adult day care center as an effective community-based solution to long-term care should be expanded, instead of, as in many parts of the country, quietly remaining such a secret.

What Is Adult Day Care?

Adult day care centers are community-based programs designed to meet the needs of functionally and/or cognitively impaired adults through an individual plan of care.[2] These structured, comprehensive programs provide a variety of health, social, and other related support services in a protective setting during any part of a day, but do not provide 24-hour care. Adult day care centers generally operate during hours that best serve caregiver needs. Some programs offer services in the evenings and on weekends.

> *There is no question that the role of the adult day care center as an effective community based solution to long-term care should be expanded.*

Adult day care for older adults serves those who can't stay home by themselves during the day. Day care centers provide health care, a variety of engaging activities, physical and mental exercise, and opportunities to socialize in a safe and caring environment.

While adult day programs are often stereotyped as serving only frail elders, they in fact do much more. They provide appropriate programs in community-based care settings for frail elders, as well as persons of all ages with multiple and special needs associated with conditions such as Alzheimer's disease, developmental disabilities, and vision and hearing impairments. They provide the supervision and structure for older adults to socialize in the comfort of a familiar environment with friends who care.

Figure 16.1 Rehabilitative care is often pro-
vided in a well-designed
and -equipped physical
therapy room. *Courtesy
of Minnesota Masonic
Home, Bloomington, MN.
Interior Design: Encom-
pass Interiors, St. Paul,
MN. Photographer: Saari
& Forrai Photography/
saariphoto.com.*

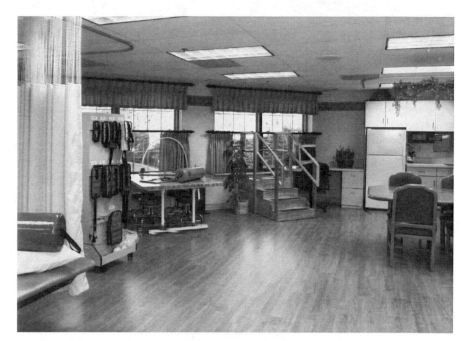

Adult day care provides an affordable alternative to at-home or nursing
home care. It allows both younger adults with disabilities and older adults
to socialize, participate in recreational activities, and receive medical supervision and personal care assistance. Services may also include rehabilitative
activities such as physical and speech therapy, and even various forms of
respite care.

While activities are often undervalued in traditional nursing homes,
they are the lifeblood of most adult day programs. Activities in adult day
care can provide diversions or be therapeutic; but activity programming for
an adult day care can be truly successful only when therapeutic activities
are thoughtfully planned and creatively conducted. The Life Enrichment
Center, the Friendship Center, and the George G. Glenner Alzheimer's
Family Centers are adult day care centers that I have been privileged to
work with, but more importantly, they represent many innovative programs
across the county.

The Life Enrichment Centers in Shelby and Kings Mountain, North
Carolina, are two of the many extraordinary adult day centers. They open
their doors at 5:30 A.M. because many of the families they serve must be at
work at 6:00 or 6:30 A.M. Participants gather around the kitchen table as
they arrive, for morning coffee or to help the staff prepare breakfast. Inclusion is inherent in this program. Everyone has jobs—for some beginning
with breakfast preparation, for others during the course of the day—and
everyone helps each other.

> *While activities are
> often undervalued
> in traditional
> nursing homes, they
> are the lifeblood
> of most adult day
> programs.*

Figure 16.2 Participants at the Life Enrichment Center revitalize their doll-making business every Christmas as a community service project. *Courtesy of the Life Enrichment Center, Kings Mountain, NC.*

The programming at the Life Enrichment Centers is unusually varied and rich, allowing participants a wide choice of interesting activities and projects. Community service projects allow participants opportunities to remain connected with the community and to continue to experience giving back. To ensure that less fortunate children in the community are not forgotten at Christmas, participants revitalize their "doll-making" business. Surprisingly, many of the men get just as much enjoyment as the women, participating in stuffing and outfitting the dolls and creating some amazing and treasured gifts. The greatest gift, however, is the smiles on the faces of these older adults. Just as you and I feel good about ourselves when we give, these seniors gain self-esteem and pride from their ability to continue making meaningful contributions. They are valuable and they can and do make valuable contributions.

Many family members find it difficult or may be too frail themselves to provide bathing and personal hygiene for frail relatives. There is a great deal of comfort in being able to rely on this adult day care centers to provide these services. The Life Enrichment Centers have two beautiful new whirlpool bathing rooms, and a beauty salon takes care of bad hair days. Physical or occupational therapy and rehabilitation services are also available for participants who need them.

Parties are one of the favorite activities. It seems that on every occasion I have been there, "there's been a party going on." And what variety—from beach parties, to birthday parties, to Valentine's Day, and the Fourth of July. If there's no special occasion, they make one up. The back porch, patio, and garden offer a variety of places to have multiple activities happening simultaneously, including visits from a Clydesdale horse who lives nearby.

Figure 16.3 Being able to rely on the beauty salon at the adult day care center provides comfort and support to many families. *Courtesy of the Life Enrichment Center, Kings Mountain, NC.*

The Many Benefits of Adult Day Care

Adult day care is much more than respite. It is an effective treatment for people with Alzheimer's and other cognitive impairments. Good programs tailored to the needs of individuals with dementia can reduce agitation, mood disturbance, and other behavioral problems. They can also help prevent additional disability, health problems, and functional decline. Adult day care plays an important role in the continuum of care, with the potential not only to delay nursing home placement but also to reduce hospitalization and other acute health care costs.

You're never too old to make new friends. Like many others, Armando welcomes the love and attention he gets and the friends he's made at the Friendship Center in Santa Barbara, California, and prefers to spend most of his day socializing with his buddies at the popular domino table. Other participants spend part of the day enjoying activities in the community and then have lunch outside socializing with friends.

There is never a shortage of fun things to do. Many participants enjoy the Cooking Sensations class on Tuesdays. Manicures are on Wednesdays,

Figure 16.4 Playing a friendly game of checkers is part of the daily routine for some participants. *Courtesy of the Life Enrichment Center, Kings Mountain, NC.*

Figure 16.5 Dolly, the friendly llama delights residents who visit on their daily walks. *Courtesy of the George G. Glenner Alzheimer's Day Care Centers, Inc., San Diego, CA.*

Figure 16.6 Dogs in adult day care centers are furry friends who provide companionship. *Courtesy of the George G. Glenner Alzheimer's Day Care Centers, Inc., San Diego, CA.*

and the Elder Flower Garden Club meets on Fridays, when members assist in creating lovely garden crafts and help to keep the Sweet Pea Patio and courtyard looking beautiful.

A large variety of activities involve participants in music, arts and crafts, bingo (with great prizes), exercise, discussion groups, games, singing, humor, history, entertainment, walks to the nearby ocean, field trips, intergenerational programs and activities with children and young adults, and adult education classes through City College's OMEGA program.

At the Friendship Center the goal is to support and enhance members' lives by focusing on their abilities, strengths, experiences, and knowledge. Special programs are designed and recommended based on the needs and appropriate skill levels of the individual. At the end of the day, it's a happy and contented group who look forward to returning another day.[3]

The George G. Glenner Alzheimer's Day Care Centers in southern California express great cultural diversity in their programming for clients with Alzheimer's—some of it with an "only in California" flavor. Volunteers from the U.S. Border Patrol visit weekly to lend a hand with exercise classes and walks, and where else does the Drug Enforcement Administration hand out ice cream?[4] At the Encinitas Center, which is shared with the Silverado Senior Living Community, there is a weekly Drumming Circle complete with sound shapers. This is also the home of Dolly Llama, whom participants visit on walks every day to see how he is doing. The South Bay Center is home to two wonderful golden retrievers—Simon and Jagger. Both of these furry brothers are certified with Create-a-Smile, a program of trained therapy dogs, and they consistently bring smiles to the faces of enthusiastic participants.

Adult day care programs provide elderly members with psychological benefits and respite,[5] and they give families a break from constant caregiving. Adult day centers such as these also give families, especially those caring for someone with Alzheimer's disease, peace of mind, with the knowledge that their loved one is in good hands.

Intergenerational Programs

An innovation among centers providing community-based social interaction for older persons limited in mobility, health status, or cognitive ability involves intergenerational programs that combine adults and children in a common day care setting.[6] Programs that bring children and older adults together have proliferated in communities across the United States, with varied goals of intergenerational contact. Some hope to improve children's learning, provide mentoring, or reduce substance abuse, while others aspire to transform ageist attitudes, decrease isolation, and build generational interdependence. These programs have spread from school-based programs to adult day care centers, assisted living and to nursing homes.

While intergenerational programs in aging services and adult day care centers show promise of very positive benefits for both generations, theory development and evaluation research to determine the success or failure of these programs is lacking[7] and should be pursued.

Figure 16.7 Intergenerational programs in adult day care bring adults and children together in joint activities. *Courtesy of the Life Enrichment Center, Kings Mountain, NC.*

The Physical Day Care Setting

Research is beginning to focus on quality of life outcomes in older adult environments, particularly in environments for people with dementia. The role of the physical setting in therapeutic environments for people with dementia is generally receiving more attention, but regrettably, this type of inquiry is quite absent from the adult day service literature.[8] In this new era of evidence-based design, very little empirical research has been conducted that considers to any significant degree the role the physical environment plays in adult day care. Powell Lawton does suggest that individuals with lower competence levels are more susceptible to the impact of the environment than those with higher degrees of competence;[9] he states, "a small improvement in environmental quality could make all the difference in the world to a person with major limitations on his [*sic*] competence."[10]

Design recommendations developed for residential settings providing dementia care "facilitated a tremendous shift in the design from a medical/institutional model to a residential/social model," but these recommenda-

Figure 16.8 We are now beginning to see adult day care center environments designed to reflect a more residential, social setting. *Courtesy of the Life Enrichment Center, Kings Mountain, NC. Architect: Holland, Hamrick & Patterson Architects, PA, Shelby, NC. Interior Design: Design Concepts Unlimited, Sausalito, CA.*

tions, until recently, have had an almost negligible impact on the design of adult day care centers.[11] This is particularly interesting since "the majority of adult day service programs serve individuals with cognitive impairments."[12] Most adult day care centers today are structured on the social day care model, and we are now beginning to see environments designed to reflect a more residential, social setting, as the previous examples demonstrate.

Most research on design and dementia has occurred in the last ten years, but it has been primarily related to residential care environments. Attributes determined to be most important for the physical settings are:

- atmosphere
- sensory stimulation
- safety, orientation
- spatial organization

Research on physical environments for adult day care has so far been limited mainly to studies concerning types of furniture and the number

Figure 16.9 With changes in furniture, finishes, and furniture arrangements, living room and dining room spaces were easily separated without using physical barriers. *Courtesy of the Life Enrichment Center, Kings Mountain, NC. Architect: Holland, Hamrick & Patterson Architects, PA, Shelby, NC. Interior Design: Design Concepts Unlimited, Sausalito, CA.*

and type of toilets. It seems that we're overdue for meaningful research, particularly research that explores physical settings that successfully support participants with special needs, including those with dementia. It seems equally important to explore how the physical design supports staff. Their performance and how well they are able to meet the needs of these very special clients is directly impacted by the design. There are far too few postoccupancy evaluations, and this often leads us to repeat mistakes.

There is no question that sensory stimulation is an important consideration in environments serving individuals with dementia. Large open spaces are usually created to maximize flexibility and staff observation opportunities. Conversely, however, stimulation is more difficult to control in a large open space. Creative designers often develop furniture and seating layouts that create multiple arrangements of cozy nooks and small groupings that produce intimate settings within a large space.

At the Life Enrichment Center we did just that. We divided a large space into a dining room and a living room. This was accomplished with changes in furniture, finishes, and furniture arrangement, without using a wall or any physical barriers. The dining room furniture was distinctive, as was the

Figure 16.10 The furniture arrangements in the living room create multiple seating groups and opportunities for activities. Seating can easily be rearranged to meet participants' needs. *Courtesy of the Life Enrichment Center, Kings Mountain, NC. Architect: Holland, Hamrick & Patterson Architects, PA, Shelby, NC. Interior Design: Design Concepts Unlimited, Sausalito, CA.*

furniture in the living room. Dining chairs remained in the dining room and chairs in the living room remained there. A variety of seating options were placed in the living area—upholstered loveseats, club chairs, and residential recliners. A variety of patterns and color were used in the upholstery fabrics.

The furniture arrangements in the living room create multiple seating groups and opportunities for activities, including tables for checkers. We found that clients and staff can easily rearrange the seating for larger group activities, which happen frequently, and that participants rearrange the furniture to meet their needs. Perhaps because participants are free to move about and go outside, and their entire day is not spent in a large group activity, they enjoy being together in a group.

These spaces are enhanced by the quantity of light available. Natural light pours through six large skylights in the living room and dining room, and is balanced by large, lovely palladian windows across one side of the living room. There is immediate access from this room to a large porch and garden providing higher levels of daylight.

The following are additional recommendations based on case study research:[13]

- Provide environmental options, including settings such as living rooms, dining rooms, and "away places."
- Design settings to accommodate small groups, whether for one small group (as in a living area for eight people or an "away space" for two to four people) or multiple small groups (as in a dining area with tables that accommodate four to six people).
- Keep visual access between areas, allowing participants to preview activities and settings and facilitating unobtrusive staff surveillance.
- Choreograph the program to encourage natural movement and transition between environmental options.
- Empower staff members to redirect participants not only in terms of behavior but in terms of setting.

The populations that adult day care centers serve are wide-ranging and highly variable, and programs are still controversially discussed in terms of medical versus social orientation. As adult day care services expand it will be interesting to evaluate the differences in settings and to explore the strength of the physical environment in encouraging social interaction and activity engagement.

While adult day programs are located in many settings that range from the proverbial church basement to remodeled residences, assisted living centers, nursing homes, and now purpose-built settings, it will be interesting to evaluate how successful our well-thought-out and designed purpose-built settings are in meeting the challenges of older adults with special needs.

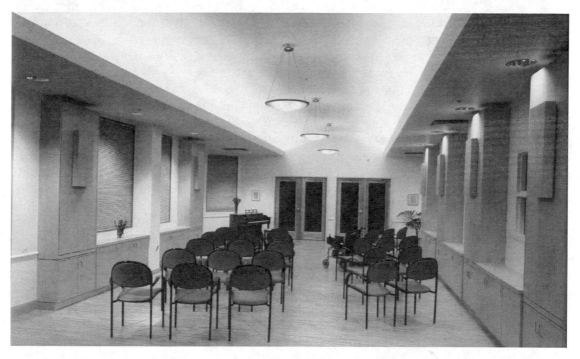

Figures 16.11 and 16.12 The highly innovative design of this space increases the flexibility of use and allows for multiple types of activity. With the tables recessed into the wall, this room easily converts to a more formal setting and accommodates increased seating. *Courtesy of On Lok's 30th Street Senior Health Services, San Francisco, CA. Architect: Tsang Architecture, San Francisco, CA. Photographer: Douglas Salin/www.DouglasSalin.com.*

Large open spaces are usually created to maximize flexibility and staff surveillance opportunities, but that comes at a therapeutic cost.[14] The concept of a large space in which different activities take place encourages assembling large groups of participants together within the same space and can significantly impair intimate and personal interactions—the types of social interactions that are of greatest therapeutic benefit.[15] The arrangement at the Life Enrichment Center may be a way of "having your cake and eating it too" for some adult day care programs. Observation is maximized, and there are opportunities for both large and small group activity. In spite of the overall size of the space and perhaps due to the number of soft surfaces and the arrangement, noise and overstimulation has not been a significant problem. It should be noted as well that organization within the space—especially storage—puts things that staff need in close proximity. The organization and abundance of storage has contributed enormously to the success of this design.

Flexibility, orientation, and stimulation are all important and interrelated factors that should be treated as a whole, rather than thought of separately. The spaces people are to use must cue them to some degree as to what is expected to occur there. For people with dementia, that level of cueing should be enhanced. Stimulation is also more difficult to control in a large open space, but with careful planning large spaces, as shown, can be arranged to provide smaller group settings, with the flexibility to easily convert for larger group activities.

Activity programs for adult day care are frequently tied to an organization's mission and are often crafted prior to the design, renovation, or selection of a physical setting. Careful planning is necessary to ensure the physical environment supports the activity program, the staff, and most importantly, the participants. It is highly likely that if the design fully supports the staff and the program, participant needs will be met more easily.

Caring for our aging seniors is a challenge already faced by more than 22 million Americans. The time for reflection is past; we must seriously examine the situation facing today's families and provide solutions for them. The intrinsic ability of adult day care to provide cost-efficient care has led to their proliferation in the United States. The National Adult Day Services Association has documented that adult day centers are doubling in number roughly every decade. In 2001 there were an estimated 4,000 day care centers across the country, with at least 10,000 required to meet our national needs.[16] Meeting the challenge of caring for a growing population of older adults requires the talents and commitment of active older people and a range of groups and organizations. Those seniors who are most vulnerable are also most likely to live alone and have limited incomes. For many, nursing homes are the most familiar eldercare option, especially for those suffering from a severe physical or mental impairment. What we really need are more nursing home alternatives.

While it seems strange to think of adult day care services as an alternative healthcare option, most families are faced with two choices when it comes to care for older adults. They can access services individually from their own homes in the form of day care, or they can receive full-scale nursing home care. Adult day centers can be a way to meet the changing demands of today's families. Many families are able to avoid institutionalization because of the services—nutrition, transportation, healthcare, and personal care services provided by adult day care facilities. The goal is to improve the quality of life while helping individuals maintain their independence and dignity. Adult day care services are designed to help people stay in their homes and to help family members care for them as long as possible.

Courtesy of the Life Enrichment Center; Kings Mountain, NC. Photographer: Debbie Vaughan.

*"Friends are quiet angels who lift us to our feet when our wings
have trouble remembering how to fly." —Anonymous.*

The Planetree Model

Planetree is clearly one of the best kept secrets in healthcare today. Whether providing patient-centered (acute) care or person-centered (long-term) care, it is a healthcare model that has been extraordinarily diligent in using architecture to support its mission and philosophy. Those of us who have struggled to achieve similar results can appreciate and learn from their story.

More than 50 percent of hospital patients today are over 65, and only 1 percent of nurses are certified in gerontology. Hospitals are designed and well trained to respond to emergency and acute healthcare needs, but not necessarily well trained to respond to those needs in older patients. Many patients today are older persons who are easily disoriented in a hospital setting, particularly those who have dementia. This adds an additional layer of complexity to an already complex situation. One of the greatest difficulties in treating individuals with Alzheimer's in an acute setting is the fear and disorientation that can cause these patients to become disturbed, loud, and sometimes combative. Most hospitals are not trained or staffed to work with persons with dementia and as a consequence, and to their lasting detriment, these patients are quickly sedated. Having a family member or familiar caregiver close by can alleviate some of the problems, but most hospitals are not set up to accommodate dementia on a round-the-clock basis.

Planetree is a particularly valuable model for addressing care challenges with older adults because it already offers many of the essentials of best

> *More than 50 percent of hospital patients today are over 65, and only 1 percent of nurses are certified in gerontology.*

practice in long-term care, including person-centered care, a strong emphasis on family inclusion, and a more familiar environment. Over the next three years the American Journal of Nursing is partnering with the Gerontological Society of America to promote best practices and deliver cutting-edge research information on the care of older adults to nurses across clinical practices.[1] Combined with a "friendlier" care environment, this could prove to be a giant step forward in eldercare. The Planetree model, already accepted in many hospitals, is a model that could prove adaptable and ease the challenges of delivering care to older adults with Alzheimer's disease and dementia in acute settings.

Planetree was founded in 1978 by Angelica Thieriot. Her experiences as a patient during several traumatic hospitalizations for a rare virus left her with mixed emotions. The high-tech environment was commendable, she acknowledged, but the lack of personalized care during her stay was appalling, causing her to describe her hospital stay as cold and dehumanizing.

Planetree, named for the sycamore, or planetree, under which Hippocrates taught medicine in ancient Greece, determined to reclaim the patient-centered focus of early medicine. The approach is holistic, focusing on a patient's mental, emotional, spiritual, social, and physical needs. "Healing partnerships" are created among patients, families, and caregivers, and conventional medicine is integrated with complementary therapies. The importance architecture and interior design play in the healing process where nature and art are incorporated is reflected in the patient's environment.[2]

One of the cornerstones of the Planetree concept is patient involvement in their own care. That involvement includes having a patient care conference at the bedside after admission and giving patients access to their own charts. Physicians, patients, their families, and nurses all talk about why the patient is in the hospital and what's going to happen. With an inbred philosophy of nurturing, caring, and compassion, the nursing staff is openly willing to demystify nursing care. All this takes place in a healing environment that is patient, not staff centered, and one that looks at the entire patient—body, mind and spirit.

Planetree recognizes the importance of architecture and design as a "complementary therapy." Because its innovative architecture and interior design are highly visible, many people mistakenly think that creating a healing environment is Planetree's primary goal, while in fact the physical design is only one of the ten components of the Planetree Model.[3] Planetree recognized early on that while its patients came for medical care, nursing care, and health care, they also came for *caring*.[4] Susan Frampton poignantly described a condition understood far too well by anyone who has had contact with the conventional healthcare system, whether in a hospital or in long-term care. "They come to us when they are most vulnerable, looking for support, comfort, and hope. They come to be heard, to be helped, and we make them wait too long in our emergency rooms, seated in uncomfortable, ugly furniture. We isolate them from their loved ones, treat them like children, and withhold information. . . . We spend too little time listening and answering questions, and we spend too much time on documentation and filing insurance forms."[5]

A growing body of scientific data indicates the built environment can contribute to improved patient outcomes and satisfaction. Studies show that patients who feel comfortable, respected, and nurtured are empowered to participate in their own process of healing, and that secure, familiar, nonthreatening surroundings help foster those feelings. Barrier-free design principles and homelike comfort support patient dignity while also encouraging family participation in care.

Planetree uses architecture to bring together the design concepts of the healing environment with a patient-centered approach to delivering care. In doing so it has made remarkably successful and sometimes startling

Figure 17.1 Physical barriers between patients and staff are removed by replacing traditional nurses' stations with open work spaces. *Courtesy of Planetree, Derby, CT, and San Jose Medical Center, San Jose, CA. Architect: Kaplan McLauglin Diaz, San Francisco, CA. Photographer: © Donna Kempner Architectural Photography.*

Figure 17.2 Family lounges and activity rooms are close to patient rooms. *Courtesy of Beth Israel Medical Center, New York, NY. Architect: Larsen Associates, New York, NY. Photographer: Miller Photography, Ltd.*

changes in the operation and design of patient care settings. Physical barriers between patients and staff have been removed by replacing traditional nurses' stations with open, airy work spaces.

Because of the unusual degree of family involvement and 24-hour visitation policies, many patient rooms in Planetree health centers include a Murphy bed or a chair designed to transform into bed, allowing a family member to remain nearby. Family lounges and activity rooms are close to patient rooms, and kitchens can be used as social gathering places or to make a family meal. By offering rooms—such as a kitchen that draw people together, Planetree enables patients and families to support each other and share information about coping and caregiving.[6]

While design is important, its greatest power lies in its ability to shape the context for patient-centered care. The Planetree design concepts were developed in the 1970s at the University of California at Berkeley, whose program in the "Social and Behavioral Aspects of Design" has been emulated by many other schools of architecture. The architectural principles of the Planetree Model were developed by the late Roslyn Lindheim, a professor of architecture at UC Berkeley, working with colleagues S. Leonard Syme, PhD, an epidemiologist from Berkeley's School of Public Health, and architect Christopher Alexander, author of *A Pattern Language: Towns, Buildings, Construction.*

The Planetree design theory they developed is a synthesis of social-science research findings and information gathered from Lindheim's cross-cultural travels and later from patient focus groups. Lindheim described the healing environment as one that encompassed the patient's entire experience of healthcare. She stressed the importance of meaningful social connections, participation and control, a sense of being valued, and connection to nature.[7,8]

Her design concepts have become vital to the Planetree model, not simply for their architectural and aesthetic qualities but because they have been shown to influence behaviors, interactions, and emotional responses. As the Planetree Model evolved, it also focused on comfort, stress reduction, personal growth, and a sense of order.[9]

The first Planetree Health Resource Center opened at Pacific Presbyterian Medical Center (now California Pacific Medical Center) in San Francisco in June 1981, followed in June 1985 by the first Planetree Model hospital project. This original Planetree unit was structured as a three-year demonstration project, and as part of the pilot, the University of Washington agreed to evaluate the impact of the unit on the patient experience, the level of satisfaction among nurses and doctors, its effect on the quality of patient care, and its cost effectiveness. The study showed such positive outcomes as increased patient satisfaction with the environment, the technical quality of the care provided,

Figure 17.3 Nurses use smaller workstations just outside patient rooms. *Courtesy of Planetree, Derby, CT. Architect: Roslyn Lindheim, AIA.*

and the education provided, as well as a decrease in return visits to the emergency room. The study described the project as a "successful example of patient-centered hospital care."[10] Data from other Planetree Model sites have shown decreased length of stay, fewer medication errors, lower infection rates, increased staff retention, and little significant difference in cost. More recently, Griffin hospital in Derby, Connecticut, found patient satisfaction increased from 83 to 97 percent during the four-year period in which it fully implemented the Planetree Model throughout the hospital. Between 1999 and 2002 the inpatient volume increased by 27.5 percent compared with a 7.7 percent average statewide increase, while staff-to-patient ratios and operating expenses remained the same.[11]

The design focus of Planetree hospitals is on the physical aspects of healing patients and supporting patient-centered care. At some Planetree sites a patient, when admitted, is assigned a specific nurse who oversees the patient's care throughout the stay, and even if he or she is readmitted later. This patient focus rather than a team concept makes it easier to develop a bond. Janet Heffernan, clinical director for critical care and telemetry at Griffin Hospital, says, "We try to have very low nurse-patient ratios—a 1–4 ratio whenever possible."[12] Primary nurses utilize a smaller workstation just outside the patient room rather than a centralized nurses' station, another unique feature.

Nurses involved in Planetree speak highly of its success as a work ethic that supports and nurtures healing on all levels: mental, emotional, spiritual, social, and physical. It is what nurses trained for and the kind of environment that encourages them to continue in the profession. Lorie Pierce, the clinical director of two med/surg units at Griffin Hospital described it this way: "Nurses do what they feel from the heart, and there isn't a day that goes by that a family member doesn't say 'you are treating the patient like your own family.' "[13] Even the most resistant physicians often become passionate about Planetree after its implementation. Physicians ultimately discover they need the philosophy behind Planetree for their own renewal and survival nearly as much as the patients do.[14]

Ten Elements of Patient-Centered Care

Human Interaction

Planetree is about "people caring for people." This involves not only providing nurturing, compassionate, personalized care to patients and families, but also encouraging staff to care for themselves and each other, and ensuring organizations create cultures that support and nurture their staff. Healing partnerships between patients, family members, and caregivers are encouraged by a model that enables patients to be active participants in their healthcare.

Healing Partnerships: The Importance of Family, Friends, and Social Support

Social support is accepted now as vital to good health, and an increasing number of medical and social researchers are finding that promoting a sense of love, connection, and community can be healing. Planetree supports and encourages the involvement of family and significant others whenever possible. Families find being involved easier with unrestricted visiting hours and sleeping accommodations available when needed. Murphy beds are often incorporated in patient rooms.

Empowering Through Information and Patient Education

Planetree emphasizes patient and family education. A variety of educational materials are made available to the patient, the family, and the community through consumer-friendly health resource centers. Customized information packets are provided for patients, and collaborative care conferences are held after admission.

Satellite libraries are located in many Planetree units, and books, videotapes, audiotapes, and computers are available near patient rooms to provide information about their health and medical care. Someone is always avail-

Figure 17.4 Satellite libraries are located in many Planetree units, with books, audiotapes and videotapes, and computers available to provide information about patients' health and medical care. *Courtesy of Beth Israel Medical Center, New York, NY. Architect: Larsen Associates, New York, NY. Photographer: Miller Photography Ltd.*

able to help, talk, and answer questions. One of the most valuable resources available is the patient's own medical chart. The open chart policy encourages patients to read their chart daily and write in their medical records. This is not a mistake—patients have open access to their medical records.

Nutrition: The Nurturing Aspects of Food

Nutrition is recognized as an integral part of health and healing, essential not only for good health but for pleasure, comfort, and familiarity. Kitchens on the patient floor encourage families to prepare favorite foods or meals for their loved ones. They also serve as gathering places, much as they do in our homes. They help create spontaneous support groups. At Planetree centers, volunteer bakers bake breads, muffins, and cookies to provide "aromatherapy" and to create a nurturing environment.

Figure 17.5 Kitchens on the patient floor serve as gathering places, create spontaneous support groups, and encourage families to prepare favorite foods for patients. *Courtesy of Griffin Hospital, Derby, CT. Architect: The S/L/A/M Collaborative, Glastonbury, CT. Photographer: Woodruff/Brown Architectural Photography, Simsbury, CT.*

Spirituality: Inner Resources for Healing

Spirituality plays a vital role in healing the whole person; patient care by its very nature is spiritual. Supporting patients, families, and staff as they connect with their own inner resources contributes to a healing environment. How these spiritual needs are addressed may differ, but being sensitive to traditions, cultures, and religious and spiritual practices is essential. The purpose of spiritual care is to honor the whole person and all that his or her life reflects. Chapels, meditation rooms, gardens, and labyrinths provide opportunities for reflection and prayer. Chaplains are vital members of the healthcare team.[15]

Human Touch: Communicating Caring Through Massage

Massage is a powerful way to communicate caring, and it was once an essential element of good nursing care. It offers a profound means of balancing the intimidating environment of a hospital with the gentleness of human touch. One of the first hospital-based massage and training programs began at a Planetree Model hospital in California. Though not often a revenue-generating service, the sense of connection it provides between caregiver and patient, coupled with its healing influence, makes massage priceless.[16] Therapeutic touch, reiki, and hand-holding programs, manicures, pedicures, facials, hair dressing, and cosmetics are among a host of homelike healing practices that have evolved at Planetree sites.

Figure 17.6 Labyrinths are becoming increasingly popular opportunities for reflection and prayer. *Courtesy of Mid-Columbia Medical Center, The Dalles, OR. Photographer: Mount Burns.*

Healing Arts: Nutrition for the Soul

Entertainment, music, and arts programs are part of the Planetree Model, making flexible spaces for music, concerts, and spaces for artwork an essential part of architectural design. Often on loan from local art museums, artwork is incorporated in patient rooms and in various ways to ease wayfinding.

Careful selection of artwork is crucial. Patients experience stress and feelings of fear, anxiety, anger, and sadness, and many suffer acute emotional distress. Artwork for anyone under stress must emphasize unambiguously positive subjects that resist negative interpretations.[17] A clear-cut conclusion supported by well over a hundred published preference studies on real visual environments—such as building facades, room environments, and forests—is that populations across the world evidence a strong preference for nature scenes over urban or built environments, especially when the latter lack nature content such as foliage and water.[18,19]

Complementary Therapies

Aromatherapy, acupuncture, meditation tapes, yoga, healing gardens, and pet visitation are now commonplace in many Planetree settings. The message is simple—the patient comes first. The best achievable outcomes in healthcare will be realized when expert guidance to a continuous spectrum of treatment options is routinely available.

Aromatherapy, acupuncture, meditation tapes, yoga, healing gardens, and pet visitation are now commonplace in many Planetree settings. The message is simple—the patient comes first.

Figure 17.7 Arts programs are part of the Planetree Model, making flexible spaces for artwork an essential part of the architectural design. *Courtesy of Design Concepts Unlimited, Sausalito, CA.*

Architectural Design Conducive to Health and Healing

Design is only one of the critical components that can change a frightening institution into a supportive and nurturing environment.

Architecturally, softer lighting and carpet make a space a more welcoming environment. Redesign of traditional nursing stations to locate nurses closer to their patients and improved patient room design with views to the outside and greater privacy are among the features that make Planetree hospital settings less threatening. This is an environment designed to encourage individuals to be out of bed, where kitchens with fresh baked bread contribute a sense of the familiar and afford a gathering place for social interaction.

Figure 17.8 The Planetree Model environment provides gathering places for social interaction and is designed to encourage individuals to be out of bed. *Courtesy of Planetree, Derby, CT, and San Jose Medical Center, San Jose, CA. Architect: Kaplan McLauglin Diaz, San Francisco, CA. Photographer: © Donna Kempner Architectural Photography.*

Healthy Communities: Expanding the Boundaries of Healthcare

Hospitals are redefining their relationship with the community and working with schools, senior centers, churches, and other community partners to expand their commitment to health and wellness. Design for health today emphasizes gardens and outside spaces, walking clubs, and exercise. Transforming the focus of hospitals from illness to wellness also means choosing environmentally friendly cleaning products.

The Planetree Alliance

There are more than 90 Planetree affiliate sites in the United States and Europe, in a variety of healthcare settings, with individual adaptations incorporated by each site to meet its unique needs. Adaptations vary, but sites always include most of the ten basic elements. They range from small rural hospitals to large urban medical centers and include acute and critical care, emergency departments, long-term care, and outpatient services, as well as ambulatory care and community health centers.

AARP's *Modern Maturity* magazine recently recognized 13 hospitals across the country as "Hospitals with Heart." Eight of those 15 were Planetree Alliance hospitals. The four main principles used to make the designation are:

- Treat everyone with dignity.
- Share unbiased information with patients and their families.
- Strengthen the patient's sense of control.
- Collaborate with patients, families, and the broader community in deciding how the hospital looks and functions.

A fifth principle might be added that sums up the Planetree philosophy: "Most important is the way people are treated—with kindness." By combining homelike surroundings and patient education with the latest medical technology, Planetree gives patients some of the answers, choices, and control they have requested for years. This is what makes the Planetree Model.

Working with very ill people and older adults, especially those with dementia, can be challenging, but with 50 percent of patients in acute care settings now over 65 years old, we will have to be creative in finding better ways to meet that challenge. Planetree is an example of a working model that is well adapted and quite adaptable to meeting special needs. In the words of Laura Gilpin and Marc Schweitzer,

> Planetree was created to challenge each of us, whatever our role in healthcare, to rethink what healthcare facilities can, and should, be in supporting patient-centered care and promoting health and healing. Every time we design a hospital, clinic, physician's office, or long-term facility, we have an opportunity to shape the future of healthcare.[21]

NOTES

Courtesy of the George G. Glenner Alzheimer's Day Care Centers, San Diego, CA

Happiness in the moment alleviates many of the problems we deal with.

CHAPTER

Hospice

18

End-of-Life Care

We are just culturally waking up to the ability to talk about dying.

Daniel Tobin, MD
Director of the Life Institute/
Veterans Administration Healthcare Network

Most people are healthy most of their lives, but rarely is anyone healthy to the end. Advanced age is associated with poorer health, and age-related disease and its varied treatments produce stark differences in the quality of life in its final stages.[1] Frail individuals who die lingering, expected deaths such as those from old age show consistent patterns of functional decline and are more than eight times more likely to be ADL dependent at the end of life.[2] Until the beginning of the twentieth century, most people died at home, surrounded by loved ones.

Today, however, despite the growth and success of the hospice movement over the past century, nursing homes have increasingly become the place of death. An estimated 85 percent of Americans currently die in institutional settings—60 percent in hospitals and 25 percent in other healthcare facilities, most often nursing homes.[3] They often suffer unnecessarily in a depersonalized and medically prolonged process of dying.

Many people dying in these institutional settings have unmet needs ranging from pain relief and emotional support to being treated with respect. Family members of deceased individuals who received care at home with hospice services are more likely to report a favorable dying experience. Adequate pain medication was 1.6 times more likely to be a concern when the dying patient was in a nursing home than at home receiving hospice care.[4]

What Is Hospice?

Hospice offers compassionate care and comfort to people with life-limiting illnesses. The philosophy is comfort care for end of life—physically, emotionally, and spiritually—for the patient and the family. The concept of hospice, which was popularized in this country by Elizabeth Kubler-Ross, author of *On Death and Dying,* is to allow one to die comfortably, and often at home, surrounded by loved ones.

Though many people think a hospice is a place to go to die, hospice is actually a program of flexible services that provides compassionate medical care wherever the patient chooses to live. In most cases, hospice care enables people to die at home, without pain, surrounded by the people they love. Ninety percent of all hospice patients die at home.

Still, the choice for hospice care does not always come easily. Fear is perhaps the biggest reason one may delay making the decision to contact a hospice program. Some are afraid that beginning hospice means giving up hope—that "I will die tomorrow."[5] With hospice support the focus is realigned from quantity of life to quality of life—from cure to comfort.

Figure 18.1 Fear is perhaps the biggest reason one may delay making the decision to contact hospice. The chapel at Midland Hospice is a place of great comfort for many patients and families. *Courtesy of Hospice House at Midland Hospice, Topeka, KS. Architect: GLPM Architects, Inc., Lawrence, KS. Photographer: © Mike Sinclair Photographer.*

Care and Comfort

The hospice model of care characterizes a good death this way: The patient is living the final months, weeks, or days in a manner that is consistent with his or her wishes. Most patients opt for comfort care rather than curative care, and many choose to remain at home, surrounded by the people and things they love. Others wish to die somewhere other than home. For some, becoming at peace with spiritual questions characterizes a good death. For others the opportunity to make amends, or to accept amends, creates life closure. A good death means different things to different people.[6]

Coping with terminal illness presents many challenges—physical and emotional—to both patient and family. Studies show that most people are afraid of dying alone, dying in pain, or becoming a burden to their families. Hospice offers choice. It gives patients permission to set the terms of their own dying process and to maintain dignity and respect. Hospice ensures that no one, regardless of illness, has to die in pain or alone.

How Hospice Works

Home is wherever the patient lives, be it a family home, an assisted living center, a skilled nursing or long-term care facility, or a hospice setting. Hospice provides services designed to ease pain and alleviate symptoms experienced with terminal illness, as well as practical, emotional, and spiritual support for the patient and family. Nine out of ten Americans say they would prefer to be cared for and die at home. Hospice allows this choice and makes the most of living while dying.

The most benefit is derived from hospice when the choice is made as soon as possible after learning of a terminal diagnosis, instead of waiting. Hospice helps people to feel comfortable, giving them control of decision making. The hospice team is there to support the patient and family and help them maintain dignity. In the hospital, by contrast, the patient and family are part of someone else's schedule. While hospice stays vary, the average is about 65 days; unfortunately, one-third of hospice patients die within seven days or less. Hospice is an option everyone should know about before they need it.

Alzheimer's End-of-Life Care

The care of persons with dementia offers many challenges to the hospice model of care. There are barriers that make it difficult for hospices to respond effectively to the needs of patients with dementia. The difficulty of predicting the course of the disease and the nearness of death, as well as pain management, may be difficult. Nursing home residents dying with advanced dementia are not perceived as having a terminal condition, and most do not receive optimal palliative care. Management and educational strategies to improve end-of-life care in advanced dementia are needed and long overdue.[7]

While supporting the autonomy of persons with Alzheimer's disease may not be practical, the hospice model of palliative and family-centered care still offers much to individuals with dementia and their families.[8] There is value in encouraging innovative hospice programs for persons with dementia.

One frustration for families caring for someone with Alzheimer's is determining if the patient is at the end stage of the disease. The end stage of the disease is characterized by a loss of virtually all cognitive and functional capabilities. What so often confuses people is that it can vary, depending upon the person. An individual with end-stage Alzheimer's is now distinguished from an individual with an acute condition.

Figure 18.2 Lovely gardens designed with private spaces are places of quiet comfort for patients and for families. *Courtesy of Alive Hospice, Nashville, TN. Architect: Hnedak-Bobo Architects, Memphis, TN. Landscape Architects: Hawkins Partners, Inc., Nashville, TN. Photographer: Bob White.*

Hospice care can be invaluable, whether patients are at home, in an assisted living residence, or in a nursing home. In 1982, when it was recognized that hospice care in nursing homes was not a duplication of end-stage care, but a valuable supplement, Medicare created a hospice nursing home benefit. The principles of hospice—the determination to provide comfort and reassurance to dying patients and support for families during a time of grief and bereavement—can be applied to all during the final stages of disease.

> *Hospice care can provide support for both patients and families and help to preserve their comfort and dignity of loved ones as they reach the end of their "long goodbye."*

At the end, Alzheimer's disease is hardest on family members, who so badly want their loved one to come back, remember them, and be the person he or she once was. With all of the support that exists, people shouldn't have to go through this time alone. Hospice care during the final stages of Alzheimer's disease can provide support for both patients and families and help to preserve their comfort and dignity of loved ones as they reach the end of their "long goodbye."

Palliative Care—A Better End of Life

Some residents who are suffering from terminal illnesses are no longer seeking cures and do not want heroic measures used in the course of their care. Rather, they are looking for a way to have the highest quality of life possible during their last days. The word *palliative* is helpful, because it doesn't imply a cure; rather, it implies caring—the physical, emotional, and spiritual aspects of caring.

A relatively new branch of medicine, palliative care seeks to aid people at the end of life. It's designed to help lessen pain, control symptoms, and give patients as much time as possible with family and friends. Although the specifics may vary from person to person, the goal stays the same—to try to achieve as high a quality of life as possible during the time that remains.

> *Palliative implies caring—the physical, emotional, and spiritual aspects of caring.*

Modern palliative care grew out of the hospice movement and shares its focus on maintaining dignity and increasing comfort at the end of life. Hospice care, by definition, is for people with six months or less to live. Palliative care seeks to extend this approach to the last year of life or longer. It often precedes hospice care but may include it when the time comes. In practice the two forms of care are quite similar.[9]

Residents remain in their familiar living quarters, with their familiar daily routine of bathing, dressing, and medication, and with their regular care team. In accepting death as a part of life, we can make each day as meaningful as possible. Being a source of support is the key, and if getting outside once a day is what nurtures a person's spirit, then caregivers will find a way to do that.

Palliative care should start early for those who need it, and should involve health and social services adjusted to fit the anticipated patterns of illness and death. When it comes to providing quality palliative care, a one-size-fits-all model doesn't work well.

Hospice—End-of-Life Care

Hospice care is the sole health service devoted exclusively to end-of-life care. Receiving hospice care substantially increases the chance of dying at home for people of all ages.

The limited use of hospice resources by older adults still living at home is influenced by the same factors that generally influence hospice use over all: lack of familiarity with the hospice benefit, failure of providers to make a hospice referral, the unwillingness of the patient to agree to the clinical requirements for accessing hospice benefits, and lack of availability of services.[10]

Older adults in the United States die in a variety of settings. Despite their expressed preference to die at home, only 19 percent of older adults actually do so;[11] most die in hospitals. Because the setting at the time of death (home, hospital, assisted living center, or nursing home) affects the philosophy of care, as well as the types and intensity of services that can be delivered, it also inevitability influences the quality of death. Though transitions to hospice care have a profound impact on the quality of dying for older adults, only 7 percent of older people who die, a remarkably small number, transition to hospice care in their place of residence, a hospital, or an inpatient hospice.[12]

Assisted living is the fastest growing housing sector for frail older adults, with slightly more than 30,000 assisted living communities in the United States, with slightly less than 800,000 residents and a mortality rate estimated to be approximately 28 percent annually.[13,14] There is growing concern about the quality of end-of-life care and the quality of dying for assisted living residents. Virtually all states now permit, indeed encourage, assisted living settings to offer end-of-life care provided by a certified hospice agency, but there is no reliable data about the number of older people receiving hospice-managed terminal care in these settings.

Approximately 20 percent of deaths in the United States occur in nursing homes, with the mortality rate estimated to be 25 percent annually.[15] When integrated into nursing home care, hospice care is associated with less hospitalization for Medicare hospice patients. Additionally, possibly through diffusion of palliative care philosophy and practices, nonhospice residents who died in nursing homes with a hospice presence had lower rates of end-of-life hospitalizations.[16]

Between 50 and 60 percent of all deaths in nursing homes are residents who have a diagnosis of dementia.[17] End-of-life care and quality of dying for nursing home residents who have dementia raises special concerns, because many persons with dementia are unable to report their symptoms or make their wishes known. Consequently, their symptoms are generally underreported and, unfortunately, too often undertreated.

The Physical Environment for End-of-Life Care

Surrounded by family, those who love and care for them, and the warmth of a familiar environment, the support of a hospice program brings immeasurable satisfaction to someone who is dying. Any need for changes to the environment seems more than worth the effort to accommodate people who choose to die at home in a familiar environment.

While culture change is affecting end-of-life care in some care settings, the less than favorable comments heard from families who have coped with the end of the life of a loved one in institutional settings have been consistent. The physical environment was not conducive to end-of-life care. The rooms were crowded, there was little privacy, and the facilities were noisy. In one survey, a resident complained she felt isolated because there was no telephone jack in the room, and she could not call her family and friends.[18] Learning to use a cell phone at this stage in her life seemed overwhelming. It's interesting to note that almost none of the problems identified in this study were things that could not be changed easily with thoughtful, well-planned design.

Small, crowded rooms with inadequate space scream, "You're in the way." This is a particularly sensitive and emotionally difficult time for families, and cramped rooms are not an acceptable way to express the value of a dying resident or for his or her family and friends.

Florence Nightingale, in her book *Notes on Nursing,* discussed the importance of the environment when providing nursing care. In 1859, she wrote:

> In watching disease, both in private houses and in public hospitals, the thing which strikes the experienced observer most forcibly is this, that the symptoms or the suffering generally considered to be inevitable and incident to the disease are very often not a symptoms of the disease at all, but of something quite different—of the want of fresh air or of light, or of warmth, or of quiet, or of cleanliness, of each or of all of these.[19]

Design of the physical environment is particularly important in the care of older people. We are now seeing private rooms with private baths in assisted living settings, and many nursing homes are also moving in that direction. We are also seeing a trend toward more generously sized bedrooms. A larger private room not only allows a more comfortable and more personalized room setting, but it can be better adapted to accommodate hospice and end-of-life care without moving the resident. Providing spacious rooms with well-designed, good-quality indirect lighting and large windows to the outside improves the physical environment.

The living setting is transformed into a warm room filled with sunlight, views to the outside, and room for family and friends. The more generous room allows the resident to remain in a familiar environment, while accommodating for a family member who may want to remain close by at this time. A chair that converts to a bed can be brought in, contributing to an

Figure 18.3 A generously sized room allows the resident to remain in a familiar environment, while also accommodating a family member who may want to remain close by at this time. *Courtesy of Hospice of Lancaster County, Lancaster, PA. Architect: Reese Lower Patrick & Scott, Ltd., Lancaster, PA. Interior Design: Interior Planning Group, Lancaster, PA. Photographer: Larry Lefever Photography.*

invaluable sense of inclusion, as well as providing sleeping accommodations in close proximity to the resident.

Indirect, dimmable lighting allows light levels to be adjusted easily, and French doors to the outside allow access to fresh air and sunlight. With French doors, the bed can actually be rolled outside so the patient can experience fresh air and the warmth of the sun. Once again, designing assisted living and nursing home settings well initially allows greater flexibility for care and the humane inclusion of families at times that matter most.

The Residence at Alive Hospice (Nashville, TN) was built so that hospice patients who could no longer remain in their own homes might have a comfortable environment in which to spend the remainder of their lives. As with Alive Hospice's homecare program, the Residence provides a full range of care, from symptom control and pain management to bereavement services and education for families. Registered nurses with expertise in the care of the terminally ill are on duty around the clock, as are "Care Partners," who assist with personal care. Social workers, chaplains, and trained volunteers offer companionship and assist hospice. Pet therapy and music enrichment programs are offered for residents' enjoyment.

Resident rooms are generous, and while the rooms are furnished, families are encouraged to bring in furniture from home and to decorate the room in any way they like. All of the rooms have a view to the outside and easy access to the beautiful garden, which residents and families use often.

Lounges are available for resident and family use, with tea, coffee, hot chocolate, soft drinks and snacks available. Families can make favorite foods in the kitchen or relax in a comfortable family room. Family members come and go and are greeted by staff just as though the Residence were their home.

Figure 18.4 A residential design and homelike atmosphere is essential. Lounges are available for resident and family use, with tea, coffee, hot chocolate, soft drinks, and snacks available. *Courtesy of Hospice House at Midland Hospice, Topeka, KS. Architect: GLPM Architects, Inc., Lawrence, KS. Photographer: © Mike Sinclair Photographer.*

Despite the large body of research on the effects of the environment on older people, to the best of my knowledge, there has been no research on how the environment influences the care of terminally ill nursing home residents.

A Celebration of Life

In the arms of the angels—may you find some comfort here . . .
Sarah McLachlan

More and more facilities are recognizing death as part of life, an event deserving of as much attention, preparation, and participation by friends, family, and caregivers. New traditions are emerging that help to facilitate bereavement for family, staff, and surviving residents.

In assisted living and nursing homes, residents often become as important to each other as relatives, and losing a beloved member of a community can be especially difficult. Fairport Baptist Homes holds a "neighborhood" or "household" memorial service within about two days of a resident's passing. The neighborhood service is "a time of remembrance." It provides an opportunity for residents and their caregivers to exchange special memories of a resident who has passed on, by sharing favorite stories about the deceased, singing favorite songs, telling jokes, and celebrating the life of one

Figure 18.5 The chapel offers comfort as well as providing a lovely place for remembrance and celebrating the life of ones no longer in our midst. *Courtesy of Alive Hospice, Nashville, TN. Architect: Hnedak-Bobo Architects, Memphis, TN. Interior Design: Anderson Interior Design, Nashville, TN. Photographer: Bob White.*

no longer in their midst.[20] This celebration provides a much needed opportunity for all to mourn before moving on.

Grateful families often share their appreciation for touching celebrations of a passing life, similar to Rose Marie Fagan's touching description:

> My mother died in a nursing home that is on the path to culture change. When she died, they let us stay with her, and after a time, they rang a chime over the intercom three times and said her name. Within 10 to 15 minutes staff and residents from all over the house gathered in my mother's room, and we had a memorial bedside service, right at the time of death.
>
> The staff and the residents shared stories about my mother, and we as a family thanked the staff for their excellent care and for accepting us and having us be part of the team and the community. Then the staff and the residents went up to my mother and said goodbye to her, just like you would at a funeral home. I couldn't help but think how important that is to the residents, especially from older generations, who don't get to go out to calling hours at funeral homes anymore. It's very important; it brings closure. Then they put a beautiful shroud over her, and we had a procession of staff, residents, and family from my mother's room out to the side door.[21]

Culture change and hospice services are bringing a much needed humanizing influence to dying and the end of life.

This is very different from what most people experience when their loved one dies in a nursing home. Culture change and hospice services are bringing a much needed humanizing influence to dying and the end of life.

Gardens and
Outdoor Spaces

Courtesy of the Portland Memory Garden and the Center of Design for an Aging Society, Portland, OR

Gardens are wondrous, inspired, and inspiringly beautiful, fragrant places where friendships grow.

Creating Gardens and Outside Environments

. . . the ultimate innovation in low technology

Until recently there has been little focus on the outside environment or the need to encourage older adults to spend time in the fresh air and sunshine so necessary for well-being and for the enjoyment of life itself. Today, however, there is a growing appreciation for gardens as a vital component of comprehensive therapeutic programs and a fresh realization that the outside environment can provide a high level of pleasure for older users. Outdoor settings provide many opportunities for socialization, sensory stimulation, and meaningful, fun activities that encourage a sense of well-being and are effective therapy for residents in long-term-care settings.

As they age, people become more dependent on their environment to compensate for increasing frailty and sensory loss. Studies have shown that well-designed physical environments have a particularly strong behavioral influence on persons with Alzheimer's disease and can enhance the ability to function and improve quality of life. Mildly to moderately impaired people— those whose quality of life can be most improved—are made particularly vulnerable by environments that inhibit movement, stimulation, and a sense of personal safety. However, careful planning and design can help reduce confusion, agitation, and other challenging behaviors. Gardens and other outdoor spaces are a wonderful way to encourage the movement and activity so necessary for good health.

Too often, these essential outside spaces are not included in the overall space design or the care program. Instead, they are added as decorative afterthoughts, without any serious consideration of their value in enhancing quality of life. Spending time outside in safe, secure settings provides many benefits, including opportunities to walk and exercise, which increases physical strength, and to enjoy fresh air and light exposure, which increases emotional well-being and contributes to better sleep.[1] Even the need for privacy can be fulfilled in the garden. Appetite, physical condition, self-confidence, and general good health all quite often increase as a result of time spent outdoors, and loneliness and anxiety are often relieved. Increased efforts must be made to ensure the design of these beneficial outside spaces is included in the overall plan.

To be old—at least to be over 80—often means needing some help. Designing environments for older adults challenges each of us to skillfully address the complex needs of physically and often cognitively challenged seniors. Designing safe, secure outdoor spaces to promote healthy independence and movement requires understanding the typical needs of an older adult population, whose difficulties may include arthritis; balance, coordination, and mobility problems; vision impairment; hearing loss; and Alzheimer's disease. These conditions are discussed in depth in previous chapters.

Human concern coupled with the knowledge of skilled designers can transform outside spaces into imaginative gardens appropriately designed for a variety of activities. Good design has the greatest impact on quality of life when it enhances the ability to move about in greater comfort and alleviates the fear of falling. As providers and staff, architects and designers, we

Figure 19.1 Many pleasant days are spent by residents in the garden. *Courtesy of Pleasant Bay Nursing and Rehabilitation Center, Brewster, MA. Landscape Architect: Dirt-Works PC, New York, NY.*

hold the key to enabling older adults and improving their quality of life with the environments we design.

Restorative gardens focus on the needs of elderly residents, accommodating varying levels of strength and stamina, sunlight sensitivity, sensory ability, awareness, orientation, interaction, privacy, and independence. This is a tall order, but we are seeing wonderful examples of gardens that are drawing older adults outside, providing beneficial exposure to increased natural light levels and encouraging walking and other forms of exercise. These gardens truly support the value of nature as a complement to traditional medical and social programs.

Designing Gardens

Gardens and outdoor activity spaces conceptualized early in the design process can provide for a wide range of activities and opportunities for socialization to help maintain connections with the natural environment. By contrast, when outside areas are left to chance in leftover space, they rarely fulfill the needs of residents, especially those with dementia. Successful gardens and outdoor settings depend on the strong interdependence of people, place, and program.

Successful gardens and outdoor settings depend on the strong interdependence of people, place, and program.

Activity programs are essential to the success of the garden and should be planned early—before beginning the design for the garden. Spaces programmed and designed to accommodate specified activities as part of an overall plan are much more likely to provide meaningful experiences. Flexibility in the design allows people and activities to change over time.

Designing gardens specifically to enrich the lives of older participants has been an overlooked opportunity to encourage exercise and good health and to create meaningful places that are rich in association and responsive to the magic of the changing seasons.[2] Gardens infused with cultural traditions and fond memories are valuable for people of any age, especially for the cognitively impaired. They often bring smiles, if only for a moment.

The layout of the garden must be easily understood and minimize confusion to encourage its use. Ideally, a professional landscape architect should be included in the design team from the start. This team member will see the possibilities of the garden well before others do and has the skills to transform concepts of orientation, function, and ambiance into a colorful, exciting, and understandable reality. In addition to appropriate plant selection, a landscape architect can facilitate the selection of paving surfaces that are smooth enough to accommodate unsure feet and wheelchairs and curtail the glare often experienced by older users.

Larger spaces become manageable when, in their capable hands, the garden is separated as if by magic into areas for larger groups and activities, spaces for socializing in smaller groups, and still other places for privacy. In

Figure 19.2 A garden arbor provides places to sit and enjoy the surroundings or meet with friends. *Courtesy of Design Concepts Unlimited, Sausalito, CA.*

this way, the garden can provide a variety of choices in places to visit as well as topics for conversation—birds, flowers, the weather—and the opportunity to walk arm in arm together for exercise.

Wandering loops have gone the way of nurses' stations into the great abyss, replaced with interesting paths that meander through the garden, encouraging residents to walk or join in activities. Today's garden paths offer places to sit and enjoy the surroundings and special areas for visits with family and guests before returning walkers to their point of origin.

Design to Support and Promote Activity

It is often the case that our original vision is a traditional garden. But envisioning gardens in a different way can enlarge the activity program and available activity spaces. In most care settings activities are visualized as occurring only inside, where activity spaces are in short supply. But by broadening our vision we can move many activities outside. Outside environmental settings can be seen as a series of rooms designed to accommodate a variety of uses. Meals and food preparation can be turned into picnics and barbeques. Snap beans grown in the garden can be "snapped" while sitting on the porch enjoying the nice weather. Outside spaces can be designed to accommodate familiar outside activities such a gardening, as well as art programs and other "inside" activities. Porches can be designed for activities other than just rocking. Special lunches on the porch benefit residents and are as easy as good design planning.

The Porch

Porches are more than places to spend a tranquil afternoon. They are transition spaces and increasingly important in long-term-care settings as a means of getting people outside. They don't require steps, and a porch without steps means one less impediment to reaching the garden. Regardless of the health benefit, many older persons are reluctant to step outside. Many are afraid of falling, and others are just afraid. Logic isn't a strategy that often works, but with coaxing, and perhaps the promise of lemonade or cookies, some will give it a try. One of the beauties of the porch is that it effectively blurs the line between indoors and outdoors, and helps to ease reluctant residents into the outside. Sometimes it takes a few days, sometimes a few weeks, and sometime even a few months, but when we are able to make elders comfortable on the porch, the success rate is much higher in getting them into the garden.

Porches are nostalgic. They provide a place to gather and encourage a sense of community. The porch is an outdoor room—a perfect place to sip morning coffee and enjoy the treats of the garden.

Figure 19.3 Porches provide outdoor gathering spaces and are a stepping-stone to the garden. *Courtesy of Francis E. Parker Memorial Home, Piscataway, NJ. Landscape Architect: Dirt-Works PC, New York, NY.*

Figure 19.4 Porches support many activities and are lovely places to dine. *Courtesy of Francis E. Parker Memorial Home, Piscataway, NJ. Landscape Architect: DirtWorks PC, New York, NY.*

Rocking chairs make it a nice spot to relax, read a book, or do a little bird-watching. With a table and chairs, it's a nice place for a special lunch or for craft projects. Wicker furniture with waterproof finishes and a variety of water-resistant fabrics for cushions make the setting even cozier. A chest or a bench with convenient storage underneath for often-used items encourages greater use of the porch.

As dementia progresses, people with Alzheimer's disease become less capable of initiating behavior—even walking through the door. Working together to develop creative strategies to encourage mobility, exercise, and walking will benefit residents and caregivers. Even early morning walks are an opportunity to spend time outdoors, and the porch is an ideal transition space that eases them one step closer to that goal.

Here's the Garden—Where Are the People?

A garden will never be successful if it is not used, so why aren't older adults outside? Policies and staff concerns, as often as the garden design, keep residents from going outside. This is most frequently true in Alzheimer's settings, where doors to the garden may be locked. Concern that a resident may fall, be injured, or wander away means that in addition to being physically safe and secure, gardens must be *perceived* as safe and secure by staff, family, and residents. If the garden is not secure or designed to support safe, independent mobility, staff won't feel comfortable letting residents outside on their own.

Is the garden visible, the design as physically safe as possible, and secure so that leaving is not a concern? Visibility of the garden from inside, as well as access to the outside is important for residents and staff in long-term care settings.

Concern is understandable, and strategies for increasing staff comfort should be explored. Design interventions such as large, strategically placed windows allow greater visibility. Increased visibility often helps staff comfort levels, but if residents are to have free access to the outside, it is our challenge and responsibility to ensure the outside spaces are as safe and secure as they can possibly be. Implementing shared risk policies, and encouraging outside activities that include a staff person can also give more individuals access to the garden. Sheltered pavilions provide shaded places where activities such as painting can be taken outside. Shalom Village in Ontario, Canada, makes daily use of the pavilion in its beautiful garden in warmer weather.

Recognizing the part the wonders of nature play in healing environments has inspired an increasing number of windows in healthcare settings. Large

Figure 19.5 Visibility of residents in the garden is important to ensure safety and increase staff comfort levels. *Courtesy of Francis E. Parker Memorial Home, Piscataway, NJ. Landscape Architect: DirtWorks PC, New York, NY.*

Figure 19.6 Sheltered pavilions at Shalom Village provided a shaded place where activities can take place outside. *Courtesy of Shalom Village, Hamilton, Ontario, Canada. Landscape Architect: Visionscapes, Burlington, Ontario, Canada. Photographer: Virginia Burt.*

windows provide sunlight, abundant views, and a colorful invitation to the garden. Flowers, groves of trees, mountains, birds, and animals and other interesting sights bring the outside into the interior spaces, encouraging people to go into the garden for a closer look.

Safety and Security

Falling is the most common safety concern because of the risk of serious fractures in elderly individuals. Adequately addressing safety means accommodating diminished physical capacity. Uniform, level, nonslip paving surfaces, free of glare, minimize the risk of falls. Walkways should be wide enough to accommodate wheelchairs and people passing with ease. Slightly contouring the edges of the pathway to cause little or no drop-off eases walking, and providing strong contrast between the paved surface and its immediate surroundings helps to clearly distinguish the edge of the walking

Figure 19.7 Residents enjoy the garden daily as well as for special events. *Courtesy of Shalom Village, Hamilton, Ontario, Canada Landscape Architect: Visionscapes, Burlington, Ontario, Canada. Photographer: Virginia Burt.*

path, improving visibility and the ease of walking. A recent study from Yale University[3] indicates that visual acuity and lack of exercise are factors most associated with many falls in the elderly population. Features to encourage exercise must be included in the overall design plan. Handrails provide additional security for frail residents and serve as a guide to return confused residents to the point where they started. New surfaces, such as 2 ft. × 2 ft. UltraSoft pavers, provide a firm surface for walking, but are much softer for fragile bones in case of a fall.

Glare Control

Glare increases the possibility of falls and is particularly hazardous for frail older adults. In designing outdoor spaces it's important to remember that most adults past the age of 50 begin to experience increased sensitivity to glare and reflection from shiny surfaces. Older eyes don't adjust quickly enough to compensate for the higher brightness levels of light reflected from bright white concrete walkways. Paving material in a medium or darker color value reduces glare. Concrete can be colored before it is poured or tinted after. A deeper value adobe color, for example, is much more effective than a light tint of pink.

   Glare can be further reduced by selecting residential outdoor furniture with nonreflective finishes. Benches and chairs allow frequent opportunities to sit and contribute to both real and perceived safety, encouraging residents to be increasingly mobile. Furniture for outdoor settings is notoriously oversized, making it especially important to have someone with a smaller frame test the seating to ensure that it is appropriately sized for older users—both for comfort and for ease of sitting and rising.

Figure 19.8 Glare can be further reduced by selecting residential outdoor furniture with non-reflective finishes. *Courtesy of Pleasant Bay Nursing and Rehabilitation Center, Brewster, MA. Landscape Architect: DirtWorks PC, New York, NY. Photographer: Design Concepts Unlimited, Sausalito, CA.*

Activity Gets People into the Garden

While designers and developers are responsible for an abundance of pretty gardens, the assumption that they will be used is not always a belief borne out in reality. Most gardens are landscaped for visual appeal, but it's activity that gets people into the garden. The most successful gardens are developed as an active collaboration between designers and staff to support a strong activity program. This is especially true in Alzheimer's settings, where programmed activity is inextricably tied to the success of the garden. As their ability to initiate behavior diminishes, even for activities they once loved, such as spending time in the garden, the staff must be challenged to include therapeutic programs and activity in the care plan to ensure continued use of the garden.

There are many opportunities for socializing and other activities in pleasant outdoor settings: picnics, barbeques, music groups and concerts, ice cream socials, croquet, theme parties and tea parties, garden club meetings, bird-watching, or simply time spent relaxing under a big tree.

Figure 19.9 Gardening is a beneficial activity for many residents. *Courtesy of the Life Enrichment Center, Kings Mountain, NC.*

Tai chi, yoga, chair exercises, and garden walks provide physical activity and exercise. Recent studies suggest that physical activity may reduce the risk of early cognitive decline. Long-term regular physical activity, including walking, is associated with significantly better cognitive function and less cognitive decline in older women.[4] Similar results in a study on men suggested that walking is associated with a reduced risk of dementia and that promoting active lifestyles in physically capable men could help late-life cognitive function.[5]

A well-designed environment provide many benefits beyond fulfilling the basic biological and psychological need to get outside. Outdoor spaces offer unique opportunities for a wide range of stimulating, potentially life-enriching activities, such as assisting someone who has been a lifetime gardener to maintain a small outside gardening plot. Raised planting beds that are wheelchair accessible can provide additional opportunities to garden. Accessible gardens can also be created on an enclosed terrace or a porch by using several large pots of plants and chairs grouped in the center for conversation.

TIPS FOR A SUCCESSFUL GARDEN

- Select a sunny location.
- Test your soil first; take a sample to your local agricultural extension service to find out exactly what it needs to grow flowers and vegetables best.
- Plan carefully: tomatoes, cucumbers, and beans are great; corn takes too much space and uses too much water.
- Make certain all plants are nonpoisonous.
- Provide adaptive tools/planting areas and work surfaces.
- Provide plenty of places to sit down.
- Include sources for electricity and water and storage for tools, fertilizer, and other necessities.
- Ensure restrooms are close by.

Meaningful activities that stimulate long-term memories of home life or professional skills are plentiful: mowing the grass, raking leaves, hanging clothes on the line, checking the mail, raising the flag, cleaning and refilling the birdbath, filling bird feeders, walking the dog, and various types of gardening.

Simply getting outdoors is therapeutic in the most basic sense and is even more significant for those who have lost much of what they were once able to do.

Figure 19.10 Meaningful activities such as checking the mail stimulate long-term memory of home life. *Courtesy of the Francis E. Parker Memorial Home, Piscataway, NJ. Landscape Architect: Dirt-Works PC, New York, NY.*

Simple Pleasures and Sensory Stimulation

Gardens are a lovely and interesting way to provide a source of sensory stimulation and avoid monotony. Being in the garden makes my heart sing! Weather, wildlife, flowers, plants, and trees give a sense of the seasons—a virtual symphony of sight, sound, light, color, fragrance, birds, and other small animals. Interesting focal points such as birdhouses and feeders, garden ornaments, weather vanes, and vegetable and flower gardens all motivate people to go outdoors.

Scents, sounds, and sights in the garden can create a strong connection to pleasant memories. Wild violets growing under a hundred-year-old apple tree takes me back to my grandmother's garden where I played as a child. For others it's walks along a country road or in a park with friends. While the sense of smell is diminished in some, it remains strong for others. One whiff of lilac is all it takes to transport me back to my mother's garden. Lilac is known as the "flower of memory," perhaps because the gentle scent of lilacs has the uncanny ability to evoke fond memories, moments long locked away. That may be why we see lilacs used in so many special care settings.

Many summer evenings when I was growing up, we ate outside on the back porch, and picked mint for the iced tea from the garden. Nothing is as refreshing as the fragrance of mint, with the pungent smell of menthol in its stems and leaves, and it's ridiculously easy to grow. It grows in any kind of soil, in either full sun or part shade. Water it regularly and keep pinching off sections for the kitchen, which causes new growth. Easy to plant, easy to water, it works well in raised planters or a container garden. It's fragrant

Figure 19.11 Raised beds, such as these in a beautiful garden in Sebastopol, California, make gardening easy and fun. *Courtesy of Design Concepts Unlimited: Sausalito, CA. Photographer: Anastasia Dellas.*

and easy to pick and use in tea. All in all, growing mint is a productive and meaningful activity choice for gardeners.

Attract butterflies to your garden by planting butterfly bush, a beautiful, fragrant plant that attracts beautiful butterflies. Butterflies are attracted to black-eyed Susans as well. A word of caution: pick the location with care. Just as we—and the butterflies—are attracted, so are the bees.

Nature's Chirping Chorus

Drawing birds to your surroundings is its own reward. Birds are a constant source of color, song, and activity for bird watchers. Goldfinches are fun to watch—they hang upside down to eat. Birdhouses, bird feeders, and bird-baths attract a variety of feathered friends and their brilliant colors, and they provide a variety of associated tasks and activities.

Many gardeners plant foliage and flowers to attract birds and butterflies, and some put out food and water just so they can relax and watch them play. It doesn't take a great deal of time or effort. Adding a feeder or two, birdhouses, and a supply of fresh water will do the trick.

Figure 19.12 Bird-houses and bird feeders attract a variety of feathered friends. *Courtesy of the Francis E. Parker Memorial Home, Piscataway, NJ. Landscape Architect: DirtWorks PC, New York, NY.*

There are many blooming plants that hummingbirds love, including cardinal flower, firebush, coral honeysuckle, pineapple sage, and bee balm. Plant these and hummingbirds will regularly visit the garden, and residents will be rewarded with the beauty of the flowers and the beauty and activity of these little whirling wonders. Hummingbird feeders hold a nectar-type liquid that can be bought or prepared. Red is a color hummingbirds love, and food coloring can be added to attract them.

Cardinals like safflower seeds and peanuts. Sparrows like anything with corn in it. Sunflower seeds seem to please most birds, but investigating what bird species thrive on what foods is an activity in itself, as is preparing bird delicacies and filling feeders. Birding can be a pleasant diversion for older adults and the source for multiple inexpensive and entertaining activities, including educational programs. Supplying food for birds is another activity that's easy and fun. Two of my favorite recipes for making "breakfast for the birds" are:

- Take large shredded wheat biscuits and tie a narrow ribbon or yarn around each piece of cereal. Hang the little packages from tree branches. After the birds have eaten the cereal, leave the colorful ribbon—the birds will use it in future nest building in the spring.
- Take bagels, preferably stale ones, and split them in half. Spread each with peanut butter. Press the peanut butter into a shallow pan of birdseed. Allow the peanut butter to dry for a few days to attach the seed to the bagel, then hang the bagel halves from trees and bushes.

Horticultural Therapy

Gardening adds years
to your life
and life to your years.

Anonymous

Gardening—getting your hands in the soil—can be therapeutic and stimulating. It's good for the soul—an easy way to calm the anxious mind, awaken the senses, revitalize the spirit and an ideal activity for the young and the old to share.

A garden project in Virginia began when the activity director enlisted the residents' help in planting geraniums in hanging pots along the front walkway to replace artificial flowers. She imported a dozen preschoolers from a nearby day care center to pitch in. The next project expanded on that idea when a class of second-graders was invited to work with residents at an Alzheimer's assisted living facility to plant a garden of vegetables,

Figure 19.13 Gardening—getting your hands in the soil—can be therapeutic and stimulating. *Courtesy of Duncaster, a Life Care Retirement Community, Bloomfield, CT, and Design Concepts Unlimited, Sausalito, CA.*

flowers, and herbs. The seniors helped the children plant the flowers and water the plants. One of the seven-year-old gardeners was overheard commenting proudly, "We planted salad. I mean lettuce. Then we watered them."

A 77-year-old gentleman sat in a wheelchair and directed an eight-year-old boy who did the digging and planting. "They are nice young boys," he said of the boys who planted flowers at his feet. They all liked basketball and talked about sports. The children were a welcome addition to gardening day.[6]

The official name for this kind of project is horticultural therapy, or using gardening to help people both physically and emotionally. The healing art of horticultural therapy often complements other therapies. Particularly in places where people feel dependent, plants can give residents a sense of purpose and the opportunity to be in the caregiver role for a change.

At Medford Leas Continuing Care Retirement Community in Medford, New Jersey, the nurse manager of the dementia unit has noticed that residents are more engaged when they are outside in the garden. The garden

Figure 19.14 The garden is an ideal setting for concerts and socializing together in beautiful surroundings. *Courtesy Medford Leas Continuing Care Retirement Community, Medford, NJ. Landscape Architect: Design for Generations, LLC, Medford, NJ.*

creates opportunities for residents to talk about the flowers, the colors, the butterflies, and the vegetables being grown and is an ideal setting for people to meet and enjoy time together. The residents are more relaxed—even their facial expressions and posture changes—and an additional benefit is they now have more volunteers involved.[7]

Accommodating the Need for Privacy

In settings where most living spaces are shared, places of solitude may be hard to find inside, making private areas in the garden treasured by residents and family alike. It is a rare outdoor space that can provide for everyone's needs, but private spaces are needed as much as areas for group activities. Accommodating the need for privacy may actually encourage socialization.

Gardens can also be a calming influence for anxious visitors or family members like me. More than once after visiting my mother I left visibly upset. I would have been so grateful for a quiet, private spot to sit for a few minutes and quiet my emotions before getting into my car on the busy freeway. The privacy of the garden would have been perfect. Gardens may also provide a sense of comfort for families who are facing placement of a loved one. Care staff may find the garden an inviting place for lunch or for a break from the intensity and stress of caregiving.

Accommodating the need for privacy may actually encourage socialization.

Indoor Atriums and Gardens: Bringing the Outside Environment Inside

Outdoor environments provide the potential for numerous casual and organized events, which can complement ongoing indoor activities. They offer opportunities for residents to both observe and participate in activity and observe changes in seasonal landscapes. Now indoor atriums and parks are being designed to bring the magic of the garden inside, with some of the same opportunities for casual and organized events. From the west coast in Oregon to the east coast in Connecticut, these newly developed spaces are infusing the interior with light, lifting spirits, and allowing residents to experience being in an outside environment when it's far too cold to be outside.

Trees fill the new park at Duncaster Continuing Care Retirement Community (Bloomfield, CT). A café with coffee, cocoa, and sweets is open for residents, staff, and guests. Caleb, the resident golden retriever, dances from one person to the next dispensing happy greetings. He's a well-fed happy camper who loves making everyone smile with his antics.

Figure 19.15 The interior park at the new Caleb Hitchcock Health Center is a beautiful place to meet and greet friends. *Courtesy of Duncaster, a Life Care Retirement Community, Bloomfield, CT, and Design Concepts Unlimited. Architect: Ewing Cole, Philadelphia, PA.*

Figure 19.16 The interior park and gazebo provide places to walk and relax in the interior garden. *Courtesy of Alpine Court, Eugene, OR. Architect: LRS Architects, Inc., Portland, OR.*

Spaces like this are wonderful, especially in colder northern climates where being outside in late fall and winter may not be possible. They are designed as an alternative to the garden in cold or inclement weather, not to take the place of going outside in warmer weather. The trees, plants, and high light levels create a remarkably pleasant environment. Interior landscaping keeps humidity levels at an optimal range for human comfort and health, as well as for maintenance. The interior plants improve indoor air quality,[8] in addition to supporting a positive and very alive ambiance.

Research shows that plant-filled rooms contain 50 to 60 percent fewer airborne molds and bacteria than rooms without plants. According to Dr. Billy Wolverton of the Environmental Research Laboratory of the John C. Stennis Space Center in Mississippi, plants clean contaminated air by absorbing pollutants into their leaves and transmitting the toxins to their roots, where they are transformed into a source of food for the plant. While the higher light levels and abundance of plants improve our lives, it is important to recognize that the light in these interior settings is not sufficient to replace the direct sunlight necessary to stimulate vitamin D synthesis.

The Alzheimer's Memory Gardens

In 1998 eight Alzheimer's Memory Gardens were designed and built across the United States through a partnership between the Alzheimer's Association and the American Society of Landscape Architects. The National Alzheimer's Garden Project was a demonstration project to show the benefits of a variety of gardens in settings ranging from adult day care to assisted living to public parks for persons with Alzheimer's disease. While the Portland Memory Garden was one of the most ambitious in size and complexity, it represents the inspiring commitment and caring of each of the garden sites across the country. Commitment, community (enlisting the help and support of the community), creativity, and imagination were common elements that ensured the success of each garden. *All who contributed to these gardens hope they will become not just places to evoke memories, but places to make them.*

The Portland Memory Garden in Portland, Oregon, a 20,000-square-foot manicured park outlined by a handful of mature Douglas fir trees, is one of only two memory gardens in the United States located in a public park; the other is the Alzheimer's Memory Garden in Macon, Georgia. The Portland Memory Garden was a collaborative effort that brought together the local Alzheimer's Association and ASLA chapters with the Center of Design for an Aging Society, Legacy Health Systems, the American Horticultural Therapy Association, Portland State University's Institute on Aging, and the Portland Parks and Recreation department.

Though anyone can enjoy the garden, the Memory Garden was built to benefit those with dementia or Alzheimer's disease. The single entrance and

Figure 19.17 Designed for those with Alzheimer's disease, the Portland Memory Garden is a neighborhood park that is enjoyed by people of all ages. *Courtesy of the Center of Design for an Aging Society, Portland, OR.*

the fenced garden allow caregivers to let people in their care walk freely. Sidewalks designed to form loops keep walkers from becoming confused by dead ends or turns and make the park easy to navigate. Many of the beds of roses and geraniums sit waist-high, so walkers do not have to bend or stoop to see, touch, or smell the plants.

Coral bells, marigolds, cosmos, and other old-fashioned plants were selected to enrich the garden and evoke memories.

The past seems a little foggy to a 93-year-old user who has dementia, but a walk around the garden helps her recollect some of it. The garden's curves remind her of the hills that surrounded her childhood home in central Oregon. The manicured greens remind her of the tidy gardens she saw when she visited Japan more than a decade ago. Memories come and go, but the Memory Garden has triggered countless memories for those who have visited since it opened.

Individuals, foundations, clubs, and garden societies in Portland raised over $600,000 in cash donations, materials, and labor contributions. Local businesses and craftspeople contributed time and materials; high school students in an "at risk program" donated countless hours digging, planting, and caring for the garden; two Boy Scouts worked on their Eagle Scout projects at the site assembling and installing seventeen wood and iron benches; and neighbors gave their time and encouragement. Restrooms and a storage building for maintenance supplies and equipment are being completed. This garden is indeed an ongoing demonstration of community caring and contributions.

While we continue to struggle with the fine lines between safety and freedom, privacy and isolation, and with the consequences of immobility and functional decline, there is new interest in quality care and issues of quality of life.[9] When they are well designed, gardens are a practical intervention that can encourage exercise and mobility and minimize feelings of isolation and vulnerability from loss of capabilities. They can provide activities that give participants a sense of purpose while helping those with cognitive impairment remain connected to nature and the world around them. It's most important to implement gardens and outdoor spaces early when their use can have the greatest impact and then ensure they don't go unused. *Gardens are ultimately about quality of life.*

What Does Success Look Like?

Courtesy of Design Concepts Unlimited, Sausalito, CA

*High mental and physical function and active engagement in life keeps older adults
flourishing in the mainstream of life.*

What Does Success Look Like and How Will You Know?

Careful design planning for the environments we create may prove to be one of the most valuable interventions in allowing individuals to function more independently and improving quality of life.

Elizabeth Brawley,
*Designing for Alzheimer's Disease:
Strategies for Creating Better Care Environments*

As resident care becomes more person-centered or resident-focused, settings are altering their physical spaces to support resident needs. So what differentiates successful facilities from less successful ones? The primary indicator is a fundamental desire for change—to be different. Some care settings show a strong willingness to really look at issues, question basic assumptions, and decide what and how things might be different—how they might be improved. They then make necessary changes—they aren't afraid to change what they do or how they do it, if it improves the relationships and quality of life for their residents. Successful settings truly focus on their residents and design and build environments that support their philosophy of care.

Success doesn't start with the physical environment. While it's easy to fall in love with a beautiful building, it's not always as easy to fit the program into the structure. Too many projects are built only to make caregivers struggle to mold programs to fit the building. Designing the activity program comes before the building design. The architectural design responds to and accommodates the program—the activity spaces, work-spaces, and the variety of therapeutic, recreational, and social needs as well as living accommodations of residents and staff. The design for the physical environment is based on meeting program needs. Identifying, describing, organizing, and designing the varied and often complex activity-based programs to be included can begin before the architectural design team is on the scene.

It is still important to make a clear distinction between the programs and needs (recreational and therapeutic activities) defined by the staff and the program describing spaces and space adjacencies referenced by architects and designers. Because the same word (program) is used to refer to these very different concepts, those involved in planning often hear very different things based on their areas of expertise and may make questionable decisions if they misunderstand the context. Make the distinction, make the distinction again, and continue to clarify the use of the word *program* to eliminate confusion and ensure the success of the design for all parties—planners and users.

The best projects start by defining goals, articulating what's important, and looking at the organizational and the staffing components. Then comes the hard work of figuring out how to maximize the way the building can support your goals. Providers must be clear in conveying to architects how they want particular features to work and what results they expect to achieve. When there is a clear understanding of the project goals it is far easier to achieve good design solutions. This step may take some time. A lot of hard work must be done before the pencil is put to paper designing. This step also provides the foundation for post-occupancy evaluation.

As we struggle—and I don't use the term loosely—to design programs and environments for wonderful older adults, it would be wise to remind ourselves that their struggles are greater than ours. One day, however, they will also be ours; we will be faced with the same difficulties and needs.

I keep a quote from a very wise teacher and compassionate advocate for persons with Alzheimer's disease in view and refer to it often during the design process. Tom Kitwood said, "We are all faced with a series of great opportunities brilliantly disguised as insoluble problems." It seems to put a different perspective on the difficulty of balancing so many critical needs in one healing home environment.

First Impressions Count

First impressions count. Families care how a setting looks, but they care even more about how well it cares for people. They want to know how you help mom with mobility problems and with maintaining muscle strength. They are concerned about whether she is happy and dealing with the many challenges of aging. What kinds of meaningful activities are available and what opportunities does she have to stay socially engaged with neighbors and fellow residents? Is mom eating well, and if not why not? They want to know if the food is appetizing and tasty—how her nutritional needs are being met.

Residents and their families want and expect responsive ways to deal with aging. With increasing reliability, evidence-based design is confirming that healthcare environments themselves can have a significant positive impact. Abundant natural light, access to outside gardens and views, individual control over light levels, sound, and temperature, and features to accommodate family, friends, and social experiences are all things we get at home. They also contribute to person-centered care and resident-healthy environments. Architecture and the environment support living and aging with dignity and programs that encourage staying actively and socially engaged with life. These things matter.

Hands-On Learning

Architects and designers must spend time in long-term-care settings—not as observers, but as hands-on participants. This can be both an enlightening and heartbreaking experience for designers and architects unfamiliar and inexperienced with long-term care, particularly the special needs associated with Alzheimer's disease and dementia. Too often, for example, lighting is designed by people with 20/20 vision, acoustics by someone who thinks the decibel level of a rock concert is great, and mobility issues by people who travel on roller blades—all great experiences but their sensitivity can easily be distorted.

Most design professionals are resistant and unused to such an intimate experience as working in an eldercare setting. It can be emotionally overwhelming and leave one feeling quite vulnerable, but ultimately it is an incredibly valuable experience. With design projects in the hands of creative, experienced professionals with "real" firsthand understanding of the problems, we can expect to see dramatically better solutions.

Suzi Kennedy recently completed a new adult day care center, the Life Enrichment Center in Kings Mountain, North Carolina, whose design was immeasurably enhanced by the sensitivity of their architect Roger Holland. Roger worked daily, hand in hand with the staff, in the nearby Shelby center for more than two weeks. He worked, played, entertained, prepared meals, discussed current events, and read stories. He observed the difficulty of not having necessary items within arm's reach and the necessity of having bathrooms close by. He arranged flowers for the dining tables under careful instruction from program participants, and led a couple of Clydesdales—yes, the very ones—who came to visit the center.

The outstanding building design is a result of the architect's better understanding of the needs of the participants, the program, and the staff. Six large skylights in the living room and dining room and beautiful Palladian

Figure 20.1 Skylights and beautiful Palladian windows infuse interior spaces with light. *Courtesy of the Life Enrichment Center, Kings Mountain, NC. Architect: Holland, Hamrick & Patterson, PA, Shelby, NC. Interior Design: Design Concepts Unlimited, Sausalito, CA.*

windows throughout the building infuse the interior spaces with light. Two sets of French doors offer easy access to the porch and high visibility to the large secured garden.

The environment can have a great impact on behavior. A large percentage of participants and residents in every care setting today are persons with Alzheimer's disease or dementia. In long-term care design, the designer's perspective and talent can be applied to one of the most challenging human conditions. We can learn to use the environment to maintain and enhance independence instead of taking away choices.

Teamwork Pays

A participatory design process brings a team of people together to talk about common concerns and clarify design objectives. With clear objectives designers can approach challenges creatively. Systematic design reviews provide ongoing opportunities to pick up missing details, improve on design solutions, and ultimately determine if the design will function

Figure 20.2 A participatory design process brings a team of people together to talk about common concerns and clarify design objectives. *Courtesy of Design Concepts Unlimited, Sausalito, CA.*

the way it should. This process helps to avoid errors; it's much easier and far less costly to make changes to plans in the paper stage rather than during or after construction.

The participatory process tends to stimulate positive attitudes and behavior and helps to relieve staff anxieties about otherwise unknown changes ahead. Team members become invested in the project, creating a desire by staff to take better care of the resulting design.

Evidence-Based Design

True evidence-based design holds the promise of a bright and exciting future for healthcare architecture and design. It requires the courage and willingness of both healthcare and design professionals to "step out of the box" when designing and building new care settings, and the willingness of all planners to spend more time at the outset of the design process to ensure the total well-being of future residents and the best performance by staff. Having access to the latest research findings on the relationship between the design of the physical environment and the health, economic, and staffing outcomes is also a must.[1] The effort is worth it, for it will mean higher levels of performance and superior results in the development and final design.

Evidence-based design is the deliberate attempt to base design decisions on the best available research findings. For the past fifteen years the Center for Health Design's mission has been to improve the quality of healthcare and promote life-enhancing healthcare environments by demonstrating the value of evidence-based design. It is great news that the term *evidence-based design* has finally made it into the healthcare vernacular.[2]

Evidence-based design for healthcare architecture has been called the natural parallel and analog to evidence-based medicine. Together with informed clients, evidence-based designers make critical decisions on the basis of the best available information from credible research and the evaluation of completed projects.

The best evidence-based projects address serious unanswered questions rather than simply applying routine or readily available knowledge as the basis for design. Design informed by research can test hypotheses about design interventions and intended outcomes. The hypotheses must be stated in advance, during the design phase, and paired with sound methodology to measure results. The evidence-based process should be applied to the concepts or design issues centrally important to the project.[3] It is possible for a well-conceived evidence-based project to test important concepts or hypotheses and still yield poor outcomes.

Most of us doing healthcare design have developed a strong functional perspective in our work and welcome the emergence of solid foundations on which to base important design decisions. Research encourages us to test innovative and interesting ideas that continually evolve into better designs. The knowledge that important design concepts have been tested and that there are data to inform our designs should be a strong support.[4] The Center of Health Design and its Pebble Project partners are good examples of practitioners who collaborate with researchers and enlightened clients to expand our knowledge of the relationship between design and outcomes.

Pebble Project Initiative

When you toss a pebble into a pond it creates a ripple effect, and that's what the Center for Health Design hoped its Pebble Research Project would create in the healthcare community. The objective of the Pebble Project is to provide documented examples of healthcare environments whose designs have made a difference in the quality of care and financial performance of healthcare institutions. In the interest of clinical improvement, patient/resident and family satisfaction, organizational change, and financial performance, participants have gathered credible data, shared results, and published success stories. The design industry has begun taking a scientific, evidence-based approach to design, rather than simply relying on intuition.

Using research findings to improve design comes naturally for many design professionals. But architects and designers are rarely taught about research methods, and most feel they do not have the training to fully understand, much less perform, serious research. It's the data gathering and post-occupancy research that is frequently a problem. As healthcare decision makers develop a taste for evidence-based design, architects should try to convince them of the value of post-occupancy data for comparison. The best results come from an unbiased, third-party evaluation.

A strong case made for design linked to evidence of positive outcomes often provides justification for some of the costly decisions made in the building design. Good evidence-based architecture and design blends the rich experience of the designers with creative inspiration and design decisions based on insightful interpretation of a broad range of research results. The trend toward research-informed design is likely to profoundly transform design in the healthcare field.

Post-Occupancy Evaluation

Post-occupancy evaluation is a periodic, systematic evaluation of the completed project—a measurement and review process. The true test of the design of any healthcare setting is how it performs over time. Post-occupancy evaluations provide an opportunity to answer questions about programming changes that may be of concern and design issues that may appear to clash with programming objectives. The data gathered in a post-occupancy evaluation is made available to the facility and can be invaluable for improving residential settings. The greater benefit, however, is the information that can be used by the next generation of care providers to improve the process. The evaluation also sends an important message to residents and their families of continued interest in their needs.

Carefully documenting these evaluations allows care providers not only to measure progress toward their goals but to examine the reasons for success or failure in achieving these goals. We are able to learn, move forward, and build on our strengths while avoiding the mistakes of the past.

Post-occupancy evaluations and related research investigations have identified common environmental design principles that support people with a higher quality of life. There is general agreement among researchers, design professionals, and operators that small group settings, meaningful environmental stimulation, and residential-style settings are all beneficial. Post-occupancy evaluations can be used to determine if further design elements that are being incorporated into care settings are truly enhancing residents' quality of life.

A greater effort should be made to share valuable information from evaluations with colleagues, as well as with regulators, to promote building codes that put residents first. We can collectively improve state of the art of healthcare design by making post-occupancy evaluations more widely available. Some ideas work, some work differently than what we anticipated and can be adapted or used for another purpose, and some, sadly, just don't work. Too often we have been guilty of promoting ideas without testing or research to determine whether and how successfully they are working for the desired goals. Sometimes we hang on to ideas too long without evidence of success instead of continuing to search for better and more productive solutions.

Life-Enhancing Environmental Design: We've Come a Long Way

Our thoughts about what constitutes good design have changed and continue to change. We've come a long way in an amazingly short time. While there is still work to be done in developing better strategies and better designs to meet the needs of a burgeoning aging population and the rising demands of baby boomers, it is nice to be reminded of what we've done well and what we've done right.

It wasn't so long ago that we expected long-term-care residents to find their way through a maze of endlessly long corridors. Today, current cluster building design has dramatically reduced, if not eliminated, lengthy corridors. Rows of shared rooms organized along double-loaded corridors have been become private rooms with large windows and private bathrooms, clustered in smaller neighborhoods.

The central nurses' station is disappearing and being replaced with smaller decentralized workstations. Great rooms and gathering spaces are being infused with large quantities of natural light, and lighting in general is slowly improving with larger quantities and better quality indirect lighting. We're beginning to see residents allowed, even encouraged, to spend time outside. Amazingly creative and beautiful gardens are being designed along with programs for outdoor spaces to encourage their use.

"It is critical to recognize that what currently exists is not synonymous with what is possible."[6]
Uriel Cohen

Unappealing interior design and metal furniture covered in vinyl has been replaced by more attractive, better-designed, and more appropriate seating. The beautiful colors and residential-style Crypton fabrics look and feel like fabrics from home and have brought previously drab spaces alive. The innovative and functional aspects of Crypton fabrics have literally changed the complexion of interior spaces in healthcare settings.

Despite shifts in principles and expectations for long-term care, too many senior living facilities in the United States are still designed on a peculiar traditional design aesthetic of eighteenth-century décor for everyone over 65. Eighteenth-century style just doesn't reflect "home" to most residents, as is evident by the personal objects many bring into care settings.[5] If it's appropriate, use it, but our thinking is evolving, and in many parts of the country this style will look even more foreign to the next generation. Perhaps most important, the overuse of this design generalization doesn't celebrate or even respect the diversity of our aging population.

As we find better ways to enhance healthcare environments, test solutions, and continue to be innovative in our design, our thoughts about what constitutes good design will continue to evolve and change. Uriel Cohen makes an observation in *Holding on to Home* that we should always keep in mind: "It is critical to recognize that what currently exists is not synonymous with what is possible."[6]

> *The gift of design is a very special opportunity to contribute to people's lives, especially in healthcare environments and in moments of profound need.*

Evidence-based design is moving forward, and we must do everything possible to base our design decisions on hard data or plausible theories, and to test theories by measuring the outcomes associated with our design interventions. Kirk Hamilton is right to remind us that we have a moral and ethical obligation not to knowingly practice in an arbitrary fashion.[7] The gift of design is a very special opportunity to contribute to people's lives, especially in healthcare environments and in moments of profound need.

Courtesy of the Life Enrichment Centers, Shelby, NC

Nothing can replace the person-to-person sensitivity of dedicated staff caregivers.

Thank You

References

PREFACE

1. Hooyman, N., and A. Kiyak. *Social Gerontology: A Multidisciplinary Perspective,* 5th edition. Boston: Allyn and Bacon (1999).
2. American Senior Housing Association (ASHA). *The State of Seniors Housing.* Washington, DC (2004).
3. Congress of the United States Office of Technology Assessment. *Special Care Units for People with Alzheimer's and Other Dementias* (1992).
4. Butler, R. "Why Survive? Author Revisits His Pulitzer Prize–Winning Book." *Aging Today,* vol. XXIV, no. 4 (July–August 2003): 3–6.
5. Levingson, C. "High Rate of Dementia in Assisted Living." *Aging Today,* vol. XXV, no. 5 (October 2004).

CHAPTER 1

1. Crimmins, E., S. Reynolds, and Y. Saito. "Trends in the Health and Ability to Work Among the Older Working Age Population." *Journal of Gerontology,* vol. 54B, no. 1 (March 1999): S31–S40.
2. Institute for Research on Women and Gender, Difficult Dialogues Program. *Aging in the 21st Century Consensus Report.* Stanford, CA: Stanford University (2002).
3. Federal Interagency Forum on Aging-Related Statistics. *Older-Americans 2000: Key Indicators of Well-Being* (2000).

4. Lee, R. "Intergenerational Relations and the Elderly." In *Between Zeus and the Salmon: The Biodemography of Longevity,* ed. K. W. Wachter and C. E. Finch. Washington, DC: National Academy of Sciences Press (1997): 212–233.
5. Friedland, R., and L. Summer. *Demography is not Destiny.* Washington, DC: National Academy on an Aging Society (1999).
6. Friedland, R. "Life Expectancy in the Future: A Summary of a Discussion Among Experts." *North American Actuarial Journal* (October 1998).
7. Institute for Research on Women and Gender, Difficult Dialogues Program. *Aging in the 21st Century Consensus Report.* Stanford, CA: Stanford University (2002).
8. Ibid.
9. Ibid.
10. Velkoff, V., and K. Kinsella. *An Aging World: 2001.* U.S. Census Bureau and the National Institute on Aging (December 13, 2001).
11. *A Profile of Older Americans: 2002.* U.S. Department of Health and Human Services.
12. Velkoff, V., and K. Kinsella. *An Aging World: 2001.* U.S. Census Bureau and the National Institute on Aging (December 13, 2001).
13. Armas, G., Associated Press. "World's Senior Population Up Sharply." *San Francisco Chronicle* (December 13, 2001) A2.
14. Velkoff, V., and K. Kinsella. *An Aging World: 2001.* U.S. Census Bureau and the National Institute on Aging (December 13, 2001).

15. National Academy on an Aging Society and Merck Institute of Aging and Health. *The State of Aging and Health in America.* Gerontological Society of America (November 2002): 8.

16. U.S. Census Bureau. *Population Projections of the United States by Age, Sex, Race, Hispanic Origin, and Nativity: 1999–2100* (January 2000).

17. Jackson, J. S., and S. Sellers. "Health and the Elderly." In *Health Issues in the Black Community,* 2nd ed., ed. R. Braithwaite and S. E. Taylore. San Francisco, CA: Jossey Bass Inc. (2001): 81–96.

18. Cutler, D. "Walking the Tightrope on Medicare Reform." *Journal of Economic Perspectives,* vol. 14, no. 2 (Spring 2001): 45–56.

19. Hayflick, L. *How and Why We Age.* New York: Ballantine Books (1994).

20. AARP Andrus Foundation and Dana Alliance for Brain Initiatives. *Staying Sharp: Quality of Life* (2002).

21. AARP Andrus Foundation and Dana Alliance for Brain Initiatives. *Staying Sharp: Chronic Health Issues* (2002).

22. National Academy on an Aging Society. *Challenges for the 21st Century: Chronic and Disabling Conditions* (November 1999).

23. National Academy on an Aging Society and Merck Institute of Aging and Health. *The State of Aging and Health in America.* Gerontological Society of America (November 2002): 8.

24. National Academy on an Aging Society. *Challenges for the 21st Century: Chronic and Disabling Conditions* (November 1999).

25. Robert Wood Johnson Foundation. *Chronic Care in America: A 21st Century Challenge* (1996).

26. Centers for Disease Control and Prevention (October 25, 2002).

27. Federal Interagency Forum on Aging-Related Statistics. *Older-Americans 2000: Key Indicators of Well-Being* (2000).

28. Hughes, S., R. Seymour, R. Campbell, N. Pollak, G. Huber, and L. Sharma. "Impact of the Fit and Strong Intervention on Older Adults with Osteoarthritis." *The Gerontologist,* vol. 44, no. 2 (April 2004): 217–228.

29. National Center for Health Statistics Data Warehouse in Trends in Health and Aging—Hypertension. *www.cdc.gov/nchs/agingact.htm.*

30. AARP Andrus Foundation and Dana Alliance for Brain Initiatives. *Staying Sharp: Chronic Health Issues* (2002).

31. AARP Andrus Foundation and Dana Alliance for Brain Initiatives. *Staying Sharp: Depression* (2002).

32. Reynolds, C., G. Alexopoulos, and I. Katz. "Geriatric Depression: Diagnosis and Treatment." *Generations,* vol. XXVI, no. 1 (Spring 2002).

33. AARP Andrus Foundation and Dana Alliance for Brain Initiatives. *Staying Sharp: Depression* (2002).

34. McGuire, L. "Depression Hinders the Immune System in Older Adults." *Journal of Abnormal Psychology* (February 2002).

35. American Society on Aging. "Diabetes: A $98 Billion a Year Illness Hitting 7 Million U.S. Elders." *Aging Today,* vol. XXIII, no. 3 (May–June 2002).

36. Hoga, P., T. Daallan, and N. Kolva. "Economic Cost of Diabetes in the U.S. in 2002." *Diabetic Care,* vol. 26, no. 3 (2003): 917–932.

37. American Society on Aging. "Diabetes: A $98 Billion a Year Illness Hitting 7 Million U.S. Elders." *Aging Today,* vol. XXIII, no. 3 (May–June 2002).

38. Manning, A. "One-Third of Americans Born in 2000 Will Get Diabetes: Minorities Face Even Greater Risk." *USA Today* (June 16, 2003).

39. National Institute on Aging. "Osteoporosis: The Bone Thief." *Age Page* (October 2000).

40. National Institute on Aging. "Osteoporosis: The Bone Thief." *Age Page* (October 2000).

41. Mayo Clinic. "Osteoporosis Is an Emerging Problem in Men." *Mayo Clinic Health Letter,* vol. 20, no. 3 (March 2002): 4.

42. Marcus, R., D. Feldman, and J. Kelsey, ed. *Osteoporosis: Translating Research into Clinical Practice.* San Diego: Academic Press (2001).

43. Carmona, R. C. *Bone Health and Osteoporosis: A Report of the Surgeon General.* Washington, DC: U.S. Department of Health and Human Services (October 14, 2004).

44. "Medical Essay: Stroke." *Supplement to Mayo Clinic Health Letter* (February 2002).

45. Torassa, U. "The Facts About Strokes." *San Francisco Chronicle* (August 18, 2002).

46. "Medical Essay: Stroke." *Supplement to Mayo Clinic Health Letter* (February 2002).

47. U.S. Department of Health and Human Services. *Healthy People 2000: The State of Aging and Health* (2000).

48. *Gerontology News,* vol. 30, no. 10 (November 2002).

49. National Center for Chronic Disease Prevention and Health Promotion. "Preventing the Diseases of Aging." *Chronic Disease Notes & Reports,* vol.

12, no. 3. U.S. Centers for Disease Control and Prevention (1999).

50. U.S. Department of Health and Human Services. *Healthy People 2000: The State of Aging and Health* (2000).

CHAPTER 2

1. AARP Andrus Foundation. *Staying Sharp: Memory Loss and Aging* (2002): 3.
2. Torpy, J. "Dementia." *The Journal of the American Medical Association* (September 22/29, 2004).
3. Alzheimer's Association. *What Is Alzheimer's Disease?* (2004).
4. Alzheimer's Disease Education & Referral Center. *Alzheimer's Disease Fact Sheet* (March 2004).
5. Alzheimer's Association. *From Hopeless to Hopeful: 2004 National Public Policy Program to Conquer Alzheimer's Disease.* (2004): 21–24.
6. Eastman, P. "Closer to a Cure for Alzheimer's." *AARP Bulletin,* vol. 45, no. 7 (July/August 2004): 12–14.
7. Herbert, L., P. Scherr, J. Bienias, D. Bennett, and D. Evans. "Alzheimer's Disease in the U.S. Population: Prevalence Estimates Using the 2000 Census." *Archives of Neurology,* vol. 60, no. 8 (2003): 1119–1122.
8. Alzheimer's Association. *From Hopeless to Hopeful: 2004 National Public Policy Program to Conquer Alzheimer's Disease.* (2004): 13.
9. Alzheimer's Association. *From Hopeless to Hopeful: 2004 National Public Policy Program to Conquer Alzheimer's Disease.* (2004): 3.
10. National Institute on Aging, National Institutes of Health, and the U.S. Department of Health and Human Services. *2003 Progress Report on Alzheimer's Disease* (2004): 1–5.
11. Watari, K., and M. Gatz. "Dementia: A Cross Cultural Perspective on Risk Factors." *Generations,* vol. XXVI, no. 1 (Spring 2002): 32–38.
12. National Institute on Aging, National Institutes of Health, and the U.S. Department of Health and Human Services. *2003 Progress Report on Alzheimer's Disease* (2004).
13. Alzheimer's Disease Education & Referral Center. *Alzheimer's Disease Fact Sheet* (March 2004).
14. Alzheimer's Association. *Partnering With Your Doctor.* California Department of Health Services and the Alzheimer's Association (2003).
15. Weiner, A. "Mild Cognitive Impairment: Interview with Dr. Ronald Petersen, Mayo Clinic." *Early Alzheimer's: An International Newsletter on Dementia,* vol. 3, no. 4 (2001).
16. National Institute on Aging, National Institutes of Health, and the U.S. Department of Health and Human Services. *2003 Progress Report on Alzheimer's Disease* (2004): 43.
17. Salmon, D., R. Thomas, M. Pay, A. Booth, C. Hofstetter, L. Thal, and R. Katzman. "Alzheimer's Disease Can be Accurately Diagnosed in Very Mildly Impaired Individuals." *Neurology,* vol. 59, no. 7 (2002): 1022–1028.
18. Alzheimer's Association. *From Hopeless to Hopeful: 2004 National Public Policy Program to Conquer Alzheimer's Disease* (2004).
19. Peterson, D. A. "Stem Cells in Brain Plasticity and Repair." *Current Opinions in Pharmacology,* vol. 2, no. 1 (2002): 34–42.
20. National Institute on Aging, National Institutes of Health, and the U.S. Department of Health and Human Services. *2003 Progress Report on Alzheimer's Disease* (2004): 40–41.
21. Crowley, G. "The Disappearing Mind." *Newsweek* (June 24, 2002).
22. AARP Andrus Foundation. *Staying Sharp: Memory Loss and Aging* (2002).
23. Alzheimer's Association. *Alzheimer's Disease Fact Sheet* (2004).
24. Alzheimer's Association. "Divine Gifts to Science." *Advances,* vol. 19, no. 1 (Spring 1999).
25. Ibid.
26. Larson, E., M. Shadlen, L. Wang, W. McCormick, J. Bowen, L. Teri, and W. Kukull. "Survival after Initial Diagnosis of Alzheimer's Disease." *Annals of Internal Medicine,* vol. 140, no. 7 (April 6, 2004): 501–509.

CHAPTER 3

1. Zeisel, J., and P. Raia. "Nonpharmacological Treatment for Alzheimer's Disease: A Mind-Brain Approach." *American Journal of Alzheimer's Disease and Other Dementias,* vol. 15, no. 6 (November/December 2000): 331–340.
2. Eberhard, J., and B. Patoine. "Architecture with the Brain in Mind." *Cerebrum, The Dana Forum on Brain Science,* vol. 6, no. 2 (Spring 2004): 71–84.
3. Alzheimer's Association. *From Hopeless to Hopeful: 2004 National Public Policy Program to Conquer Alzheimer's Disease* (2004).

4. Cohen-Mansfield, J. "Nonpharmacologic Interventions for Inappropriate Behaviors in Dementia: A Review, Summary, and Critique." *American Journal of Geriatric Psychiatry,* vol. 9, no. 4 (Fall 2001): 361–381.

5. Zeisel, J., N. Silverstein, J. Hyde, S. Levkoff, M. P. Lawton, and W. Holmes. "Environmental Correlates to Behavioral Health Outcomes in Alzheimer's Special Care Units." *The Gerontologist,* vol. 43, no. 5 (October 2003): 697–711.

6. Campion, E. "When a Mind Dies." *New England Journal of Medicine* (1996): 334, 791.

7. Zeisel, J., N. Silverstein, J. Hyde, S. Levkoff, M. P. Lawton, and W. Holmes. "Environmental Correlates to Behavioral Health Outcomes in Alzheimer's Special Care Units." *The Gerontologist,* vol. 43, no. 5 (October 2003): 697–711.

8. Ibid.

9. Norman, D. *The Design of Everyday Things.* New York: Doubleday/Currency (1988).

10. Lynch, K. *The Image of the City.* Cambridge, MA: MIT Press (1960).

11. Zeisel, J., and M. Tyson. "Alzheimer's Treatment Gardens." In *Healing Gardens,* edited by C. Cooper Marcus and M. Barnes. New York: John Wiley and Sons (1999).

12. Corcoran, M., and L. Gitlin. "Environmental Influences on Behavior of the Elderly with Dementia: Principles for Intervention in the Home." *Occupational Therapy Physical Therapy Geriatrics,* vol. 9, no. 3/4 (1991): 5–21.

13. Gitlin, L., J. Liebman, and L. Winter. "Are Environmental Interventions Effective in the Management of Alzheimer's Disease and Related Disorders?" *Alzheimer's Care Quarterly,* vol. 4, no. 2 (2003): 85–107.

14. Cohen-Mansfield, J. "Nonpharmacologic Interventions for Inappropriate Behaviors in Dementia," *American Journal of Geriatric Psychiatry,* vol. 9, no. 4 (Fall 2001): 361–381.

15. Bell, V., and D. Troxel. *The Best Friends Approach to Alzheimer's Care.* Baltimore: Health Professions Press (1997).

16. Zeisel, J., and P. Raia. "Nonpharmacological Treatment for Alzheimer's Disease: A Mind-Brain Approach." *American Journal of Alzheimer's Disease and Other Dementias,* vol. 15, no. 6 (November/December 2000): 331–340.

17. Coste, J. K. *Learning to Speak Alzheimer's.* Boston: Mariner–Houghton Mifflin Company (2004): 204.

18. Zeisel, J., and P. Raia. "Nonpharmacological Treatment for Alzheimer's Disease: A Mind-Brain Approach." *American Journal of Alzheimer's Disease and Other Dementias,* vol. 15, no. 6 (November/December 2000): 331–340.

19. Pallat, B. "Liberty, Justice and Design-for-All: Designing for Cognitive Disabilities." *Interiors & Sources,* vol. 11, no. 4 (April 2004): 71–73.

Chapter 4

1. Horowitz, A., and C. Stuen. "Aging and Vision Loss: A Critical Health Care Issue." *Home Care Council of New York City Report* (Winter 1996).

2. Desai, M., L. Pratt, H. Lentzner, and K. Robinson. "Trends in Vision and Hearing Among Older Americans." *Aging Trends,* no. 2. Hyattsville, MD: National Center for Health Statistics (2001): 1–8.

3. Keller, B., J. L. Morton, V. S. Thomas, and J. F. Potter. "The Effect of Visual and Hearing Impairments on Functional Status." *Journal of the American Geriatrics Society,* vol. 47 (1999): 1319–1325.

4. Rovner, B., and M. Ganguli. "Depression and Disability Associated with Impaired Vision: The MoVIES Project." *Journal of the American Geriatrics Society,* vol. 46 (1998): 617–619.

5. Tinetti, M., S. K. Inouye, T. M. Gill, and J. T. Doucette. "Shared Risk Factors for Falls, Incontinence and Functional Dependence: Unifying the Approach to Geriatric Syndromes." *JAMA,* vol. 273 (1995): 1348–1353.

6. The Lighthouse Inc. *The Lighthouse National Survey on Vision Loss: The Experiences, Attitudes and Knowledge of Middle-Aged and Older Americans.* New York: The Lighthouse Inc. (1995).

7. Horowitz, A., E. Balistreri, C. Stuen, and R. Fangmeier. "Vision Impairment Among Nursing Home Residents: Implications for Physical and Cognitive Functioning." *46th Annual Scientific Meeting of the Gerontological Society of America* (November 1993).

8. The Lighthouse Inc. *The Lighthouse National Survey on Vision Loss: The Experiences, Attitudes and Knowledge of Middle-Aged and Older Americans.* New York: The Lighthouse Inc. (1995).

9. Noell, E. "Daylighting Design: The Challenges of New Legislation, Evolving User Demands, and Our Physical and Mental Well-Being." In *Energy, Environment and Architecture.* Washington, DC: American Institute of Architects (1992): 159–167.

10. McFarland, R., and M. Fisher. "Alterations in Dark Adaptation as a Function of Age." *Journal of Gerontology,* vol. 10 (1955): 424–428.

11. Noell-Waggoner, E. "Light: An Essential Intervention for Alzheimer's Disease." *Alzheimer's Care Quarterly,* vol. 3, no. 2 (2002): 343–352.

12. Desai, M., L. Pratt, H. Lentzner, and K. Robinson. "Trends in Vision and Hearing Among Older Americans." *Aging Trends,* no. 2. Hyattsville, MD: National Center for Health Statistics (2001): 1–8.

13. Ibid.

14. National Advisory Eye Council. *Report of the Retinal Diseases Panel: Vision Research: A National Plan, 1994–1998.* Bethesda, MD: U.S. Department of Health and Human Services (1993): Publication NIH 93-3186.

15. Faye, E., and W. Stappenbeck. *Changes in the Aging Eye.* New York: Lighthouse International (2000).

16. Age-Related Eye Disease Study Research Group. "A Randomized, Placebo-Controlled Clinical Trial of High-Dose Supplementation with Vitamins C and E, Beta Carotene, and Zinc for Age-Related Macular Degeneration and Vision Loss AREDS." Report no. 8. *Archives of Ophthalmology,* vol. 119 (October 2001): 1417–1436.

17. Faye, E., and W. Stappenbeck. *Changes in the Aging Eye.* New York: Lighthouse International (2000).

18. Age-Related Eye Disease Study Research Group. "A Randomized, Placebo-Controlled Clinical Trial of High-Dose Supplementation With Vitamins C and E, Beta Carotene, and Zinc for Age-Related Macular Degeneration and Vision Loss AREDS." Report no. 8. *Archives of Ophthalmology,* vol. 119 (October 2001): 1417–1436.

19. Mayo Clinic. "Supplements May Slow Age-Related Macular Degeneration." *Mayo Clinic Health Letter,* vol. 20, no. 3 (March 2002).

20. Faye, E., and W. Stappenbeck. *Changes in the Aging Eye.* New York: Lighthouse International (2000).

21. Desai, M., L. Pratt, H. Lentzner, and K. Robinson. "Trends in Vision and Hearing Among Older Americans." *Aging Trends,* no. 2. Hyattsville, MD: National Center for Health Statistics (2001): 1–8.

22. Faye, E., and W. Stappenbeck. *Changes in the Aging Eye.* New York: Lighthouse International (2000).

23. Rosenfeld, I. "I Can See Clearly Now!" *Parade Magazine* (August 11, 2002): 3.

24. Faye, E., and W. Stappenbeck. *Changes in the Aging Eye.* New York: Lighthouse International (2000).

25. Rosenfeld, I. "I Can See Clearly Now!" *Parade Magazine.* (August 11, 2002): 3.

26. Desai, M., L. Pratt, H. Lentzner, and K. Robinson. "Trends in Vision and Hearing Among Older Americans." *Aging Trends,* no. 2. Hyattsville, MD: National Center for Health Statistics (2001): 1–8.

27. Mayo Clinic. "Circadian Rhythms: How Your Body's Internal Clock Affects Your Health." *Mayo Clinic Women's Healthsource,* vol. 6, no. 10 (October 2002): 4–5.

28. Rea, M., M. Figueiro, and J. Bullough. "Circadian Photobiology: An Emerging Framework for Lighting Practice and Research." *Lighting Research Technology,* vol. 34, no. 3 (2002): 177–190.

29. Rea, M. "Light—Much More Than Vision." The Fifth International LRO Lighting Research Symposium—Lighting and Human Health (November 3–5, 2002).

30. Figueiro, M., J. Bullough, and M. Rea. *Spectral Sensitivity of the Circadian System.* Lighting Research Center (2003).

31. Chen, C., P. Sloane, and T. Dalton. *Lighting and Circadian Rhythms and Sleep in Older Adults.* Electric Power Research Institute (January 2003).

32. Roberts, J. "Light Interactions with the Human Eye as a Function of Age." Fifth International Lighting Research Symposium—Light and Human Health (November 3–5, 2002).

33. Brainard, G. "Photoreception for Regulation of Melatonin and the Circadian System in Humans." The Fifth International LRO Lighting Research Symposium—Lighting and Human Health (November 3–5, 2002).

34. Klein, D., R. Moore, and S. Reppert, eds. *Suprachiasmatic Nucleus: The Mind's Clock.* Oxford: Oxford University Press (1991).

35. Brainard, G. "Photoreception for Regulation of Melatonin and the Circadian System in Humans." The Fifth International LRO Lighting Research Symposium—Lighting and Human Health (November 3–5, 2002).

36. Wetterberg, L. *Light and Biological Rhythms in Man.* Stockholm: Pergamon Press (1993).

37. Van Someren, E. "Circadian Rhythms and Sleep in Human Aging." *Chronobiology International,* vol. 17, no. 3 (2000): 233–243.

38. Ancoli-Israel, S., and D. Kripke. "Now I Lay Me Down to Sleep: The Problem of Sleep Fragmentation in Elderly and Demented Residents of Nursing Homes." *Bulletin of Clinical Neurosciences,* vol. 54 (1989): 127–132.

39. Ancoli-Israel, S., M. Klauber, D. Jones, D. Kripke, J. Martin, W. Mason, R. Pat-Horenczyk, and R. Fell. "Variations in Circadian Rhythms of Activity, Sleep, and Light Exposure Related to Dementia in Nursing Home Patients." *American Sleep Disorders Association and Sleep Research Society,* vol. 20, no. 1 (1997): 18–23.

40. Illuminating Engineering Society of North America. *Lighting and the Visual Environment for Senior Living* RP-28-98 (1998): 40.

41. Berson, D. "Strange Vision: Ganglion Cells as Circadian Photoreceptors." *Trends in Neurosciences,* vol. 26, no. 6 (June 2003).

42. Berson, D., F. Dunn, and M. Takao. "Phototransduction by Retinal Ganglion Cells That Set the Circadian Clock." *Science,* vol. 295 (February 8, 2002).

43. Hall, C. "Secret to Body's 24-hour Time Clock Is the Eye." *San Francisco Chronicle* (February 8, 2002).

44. Moran, M., T. Thompson, and A. Nies. "Sleep Disorders in the Elderly." *American Journal of Psychiatry,* vol. 145, no. 11 (1988): 1369–1378.

45. National Commission on Sleep Disorders Research. *Wake Up America: A National Sleep Alert.* Submitted to the U.S. Congress and to the Secretary of the U.S. Department of Health and Human Services (1993).

46. Noell-Waggoner, E. "Let There Be Light, or Face the Consequences: A National Concern for Our Aging Population." The Fifth International LRO Lighting Research Symposium—Lighting and Human Health (November 3–5, 2002).

47. Bliwise, D. "Sleep in Normal Aging and Dementia." *Sleep,* vol. 16, no. 1 (1993): 40–81.

48. Figueiro, M. "Research Recap." *Lighting Design and Architecture* (June 2003): 8–11.

49. Skene, D., and D. Swaab. "Melatonin Rhythmicity: Effect of Age and Alzheimer's Disease." *Exp. Gerontology,* vol. 38 (2003): 199–206.

50. Van Someren, E. "Circadian Rhythms and Sleep in Human Aging." *Chronobiology International,* vol. 17, no. 3 (2000): 233–243.

51. Chen, C., P. Sloane, and T. Dalton. *Lighting and Circadian Rhythms and Sleep in Older Adults.* Electric Power Research Institute (January 2003).

52. Bliwise, D. "Sleep in Normal Aging and Dementia." *Sleep,* vol. 16, no. 1 (1993): 40–81.

53. Van Someren, E., E. Hagebeuk, C. Lijzenga, P. Scheltens, S. DeRooji, C. Jonker, A. Pot, M. Mirmiran, and D. Swaab. "Circadian Rest-Activity Rhythm Disturbances in Alzheimer's Disease." *Biological Psychiatry,* vol. 40 (1996): 259–270.

54. Chen, C., P. Sloane, and T. Dalton. *Lighting and Circadian Rhythms and Sleep in Older Adults.* Electric Power Research (January 2003).

55. Bliwise, D. "Sleep in Normal Aging and Dementia." *Sleep,* vol. 16, no. 1 (1993): 40–81.

56. Chen, C., P. Sloane, and T. Dalton. *Lighting and Circadian Rhythms and Sleep in Older Adults.* Electric Power Research Institute (January 2003).

57. Brainard, G., J. Hanifin, J. Greeson, B. Byrne, G. Glickman, E. Gerner, and M. Rollag. "Action Spectrum for Melatonin Regulation in Humans: Evidence for a Novel Circadian Photoreceptor." *Journal of Neuroscience,* vol. 21, no. 16 (2001): 6405–6412.

58. Figueiro, M., G. Eggleston, and M. Rea. "Effects of Light Exposure on Behavior of Alzheimer's Patients—a Pilot Study." The Fifth International LRO Lighting Research Symposium—Lighting and Human Health (November 3–5, 2002).

59. National Safety Council. *National Safety Council Accidental Facts* (1988).

60. Greenspan, S., E. Myers, et al. "Fall Severity and Bone Mineral Density as Risk Factors for Hip Fractures in Ambulatory Elderly." *Journal of the American Medical Association,* vol. 271, no. 2 (1994): 128.

61. Holick, M. "Vitamin D: A Required Supplement or a Sunshine Hormone." The Fifth International LRO Lighting Research Symposium—Lighting and Human Health (November 3–5, 2002).

62. Noell-Waggoner, E. "Let There Be Light, or Face the Consequences: A National Concern for Our

Aging Population." The Fifth International LRO Lighting Research Symposium—Lighting and Human Health (November 3–5, 2002).

63. Simon, N. "Your Health: Here Comes the Sun." *AARP Bulletin,* vol. 45, no. 6 (June 2004): 14.

64. Holick, M., and E. Jung. *Biologic Effects of Light.* Boston: Kluwer Academic Publishing Company (1999).

65. Gilchrest, B. "Sunscreens: A Public Health Opportunity." *The New England Journal of Medicine,* vol. 329, no. 6 (1993).

66. Holick, M. "Vitamin D—New Horizons for the 21st Century." McCollum Award Lecture. *American Journal of Clinical Nutrition* (1994): 619–630.

67. Simon, N. "Your Health: Here Comes the Sun." *AARP Bulletin,* vol. 45, no. 6 (June 2004): 14.

68. Elias, M. "Patients in Sunny Rooms Need Fewer Pain Drugs, Study Hints." *The Arizona Republic* (2004): A20.

69. Miller, N. "Light and Dark: The New Drugs." *Architectural Lighting* (June 2004): 19–21.

70. Ibid.

71. Brainard, G. "Photoreception for Regulation of Melatonin and the Circadian System in Humans." The Fifth International LRO Lighting Research Symposium—Lighting and Human Health (November 3–5, 2002).

72. Miller, N. "Lighting for Seniors: Obstacles in Applying the Research." The Fifth International LRO Lighting Research Symposium—Lighting and Human Health (November 3–5, 2002).

73. Anderson, L. "The Art of Seeing: Lighting for Aging Vision and Health." *The Third International Lighting Research Symposium—Lighting for Aging Vision and Health.* New York: Lighting Research Institute (1995): 167–174.

74. Noell-Waggoner, E. "Let There be Light, or Face the Consequences: A National Concern for Our Aging Population." The Fifth International LRO Lighting Research Symposium—Lighting and Human Health (November 3–5, 2002).

Chapter 5

1. Weeks, K. "Lighting Up." *Contract* (April 2003): 46–47.

2. Lovette, G. "Natural Light Control: Why We Should Care." *Design and Window Coverings* (March 2004): 22–26.

3. Miller, N. "Light and Dark: The New Drugs." *Architectural Lighting* (2004): 19–21.

4. Miller, N. "Lighting for Seniors: Obstacles in Applying the Research." The Fifth International LRO Lighting Research Symposium—Light and Human Health (November 3–5, 2002): 171–173.

5. Lovette, G. "Natural Light Control: Why We Should Care." *Design and Window Coverings* (March 2004): 22–26.

6. Ibid.

7. Noell-Waggoner, E. "Lighting Solutions for Contemporary Problems of Older Adults." *Psychological Nursing and Mental Health Services,* vol. 42, no. 7 (July 2004): 14–20.

8. Noell-Waggoner, E. "Let There Be Light, or Face the Consequences: A National Concern for our Aging Population." The Fifth International LRO Lighting Research Symposium—Light and Hu-man Health (November 3–5, 2002): 157–167.

9. Brainard, G. "Photoreception for Regulation of Melatonin and the Circadian System in Humans." The Fifth International LRO Lighting Research Symposium—Light and Human Health (November 3–5, 2002).

10. Roberts, J. "Light Interactions with the Human Eye as a Function of Age." The Fifth International LRO Lighting Research Symposium—Light and Human Health (November 3–5, 2002): 115–125.

11. Gotti, M. B., "Trends in Healthcare Lighting." *FacilityCare* (July, August 2003): 14–15.

12. Noell-Waggoner, E. "Lighting Solutions for Contemporary Problems of Older Adults." *Psychological Nursing and Mental Health Services,* vol. 42, no. 7 (July 2004): 14–20.

13. Noell-Waggoner, E. "Light: An Essential Intervention for Alzheimer's Disease." *Alzheimer's Care Quarterly,* vol. 3, no. 4 (Fall 2002): 343–352.

14. Noell-Waggoner, E. "Lighting Solutions for Contemporary Problems of Older Adults." *Psychosocial Nursing and Mental Health Services,* vol. 42, no. 7 (July 2004).

15. Benya, J. "Design Report." *Architectural Lighting,* vol. 18, no. 1 (Jan/Feb 2003).

16. Snyder, L. "Lighting Efficiency: Obstacles and Opportunities." *Building Operating Management* vol. 51, no. 3 (March 2004).

17. Audin, L. "Keeping Up with Lighting Technology." *Building Operating Management* (August 2003).

18. Benya, J. "Design Report." *Architectural Lighting,* vol. 18, no. 1 (Jan/Feb 2003).

19. Graf, S. and S. Stancavage. "Beyond Bad Lighting." *Building Operating Management,* vol. 51, no. 9 (September 2004): 43–50.

20. Snyder, L. "Lighting Efficiency: Obstacles and Opportunities." *Building Operating Management,* vol. 51, no. 3 (March 2004).

21. Audin, L. "Keeping Up with Lighting Technology." *Building Operating Management* (August 2003).

22. Graf, S., and S. Stancavage. "Beyond Bad Lighting." *Building Operating Management,* vol. 51, no. 9 (September 2004): 43–50.

23. Gotti, M. B. "Trends in Healthcare Lighting: Ask the Pros." *FacilityCare.* (July/August 2003): 14–16.

24. Noell-Waggoner, E. "Light: An Essential Intervention for Alzheimer's Disease." *Alzheimer's Care Quarterly,* vol. 3, no. 4 (2002): 343–352.

25. Walitdky, P. "Trends in Healthcare Lighting: Ask the Pros." *FacilityCare* (July/August 2003): 14–16.

CHAPTER 6

1. Louderback, J. "TechSmart: A Sound Solution." *USA Weekend Magazine* (October 17–19, 2003): 4.

2. Cruickshanks, K., T. Wiley, T. Tweed, et al. "Prevalence of Hearing Loss in Older Adults in Beaver Dam, Wisconsin: The Epidemiology of Hearing Loss Study." *American Journal of Epidemiology,* vol. 148 (1998): 879–886.

3. Hearing Society for the Bay Area. *Growing Community* (October 2004).

4. Yueh, B., N. Shapiro, and P. Shelkelle. "Screening and Management of Adult Hearing Loss in Primary Care." *Journal of the American Medical Association,* vol. 289, no. 15 (April 16, 2003): 1976–1985.

5. Parmet, S. "Adult Hearing Loss." *Journal of the American Medical Association,* vol. 289, no. 15 (April 16, 2003): 2020.

6. Yueh, B., N. Shapiro, and P. Shelkelle. "Screening and Management of Adult Hearing Loss in Primary Care." *Journal of the American Medical Association,* vol. 289, no. 15 (April 16, 2003): 1976–1985.

7. Mulrow, C., C. Aguilar, J. Endicott, et al. "Association Between Hearing Impairment and the Quality of Life of Elderly Individuals." *The Journal of the Geriatric Society,* vol. 38 (1996): 45–50.

9. Yueh, B., N. Shapiro, and P. Shelkelle. "Screening

and Management of Adult Hearing Loss in Primary Care." *Journal of the American Medical Association,* vol. 289, no. 15 (April 16, 2003): 1976–1985.

10. Gonick, J. "Logic Escapes as Hearing Tunes Out." *San Francisco Chronicle* (September 12, 2003): J20–22.

11. Ibid.

12. Appollonio, I., C. Carabellese, L. Frattola, and M. Trabucchi. "Effects of Sensory Aids on the Quality of Life and Mortality of Elderly People: A Multivariate Analysis." *Age and Aging,* vol. 25 (1996): 89–96.

13. Horowitz, A. "The Relationship Between Vision Impairment and the Assessment of Disruptive Behaviors Among Nursing Home Residents." *The Gerontologist,* vol. 17, no. 5 (1997): 620–628.

14. Peters, C., J. Potter, and S. Scholer. "Hearing Impairment as a Predictor of Cognitive Decline in Dementia." *Journal of the American Geriatric Society,* vol. 36 (1988): 981–986.

15. Bess, F., M. Lichtenstein, S. Logan, M. Burger, and E. Nelson. "Hearing Impairment as a Determinant of Function in the Elderly." *Journal of the American Geriatric Society,* vol. 37 (1989): 123–128.

16. Weinstein, B., and L. Amsel. "Hearing Loss and Senile Dementia in the Institutional Elderly." *Clinical Gerontologist,* vol. 4 (1986): 3–15.

17. Yueh, B., N. Shapiro, and P. Shelkelle. "Screening and Management of Adult Hearing Loss in Primary Care." *Journal of the American Medical Association,* vol. 289, no. 15 (April 16, 2003): 1976–1985.

18. Desai, M., L. Pratt, H. Lentzner, and K. Robinson. "Trends in Vision and Hearing Among Older Americans." *Aging Trends,* no. 2. Hyattsville, MD: National Center for Health Statistics (March 2001): 1–8.

19. Wallhagen, M., W. Strawbridge, R. Cohen, and G. Kaplan. "An Increasing Prevalence of Hearing Impairment and Associated Risk Factors over Three Decades of the Alameda County Study." *The American Journal of Public Health,* vol. 87 (1997): 440–442.

20. Mazer, S. "Tuning In to the Sound Environment." *Design* (March 2002).

21. Mazer, S. "What Is at Stake in the Sound Environment?" *HealthcareDESIGN* (November 2001): 32–37.

22. Mazer, S. "Sound Advice: Seven Steps for Abating Hospital Noise Problems." *Health Facilities Management* (May 2002).

23. Ulrich, R., and C. Zimring. *The Role of the Physical Environment in the Hospital of the 21st Century: A Once-in-a-Lifetime Opportunity.* Concord, CA: Center for Health Design (September 2004).

24. Dubbs, D. "Ceiling Tile Study Shows How Noise Impacts Patients and Staff." *Health Facilities Management* (September 2004).

25. Dubbs, D. "Acoustical Ceilings: Performance, Aesthetics Improve." *Facilities Design & Management* (February 2003): 20.

26. Kroll, K. "Blocking the Talk: Acoustics in the Workplace." *Building Operating Management,* vol. 50, no. 12 (December 2003): 40–42.

27. American Society of Interior Designers. *Better Sound Solutions* (2004): 26.

28. Dubbs, D. "Sound Effects." *Health Facilities Management* (September 2004).

29. Mazer, S. "What Is at Stake in the Sound Environment?" *HealthcareDESIGN* (November 2001): 32–37.

30. Mazer, S. "Speaking with Susan Mazer." *FacilityCare* (July/August 2002).

31. Ulrich, R., and C. Zimring. *The Role of the Physical Environment in the Hospital of the 21st Century: A Once-in-a-Lifetime Opportunity.* Concord, CA: Center for Health Design (September 2004).

32. Bogardus, S., B. Yueh, and P. Shekelle. "Screening and Management of Adult Hearing Loss in Primary Care." *Journal of American Medical Association,* vol. 289 (April 16, 2003): 1987.

33. Mazer, S. "What Is at Stake in the Sound Environment?" *HealthcareDESIGN* (November 2001): 32–37.

34. Appollonio, I., C. Carabellese, L. Frattola, and M. Trabuchi. "Effects of Sensory Aids on the Quality of Life and Mortality of Elderly People: A Multivariate Analysis." *Age and Aging,* vol. 25 (1996): 89–96.

35. Desai, M., L. Pratt, H. Lentzner, and K. Robinson. "Trends in Vision and Hearing Among Older Americans." *Aging Trends,* no. 2 Hyattsville, MD: National Center for Health Statistics (March 2001): 1–8.

36. Hearing Society for the Bay Area. *Providing Communication Access to People Who are Hard of Hearing or Deaf.*

37. Louderback, J. "TechSmart: A Sound Solution." *USA Weekend Magazine* (October 17–19, 2003): 4.

38. Mazer, S. "Tuning In to the Sound Environment." *Design* (March 2002).

39. LeJeune, B., S. Steinman, and J. Mascia. "Enhancing Socialization of Older People Experiencing Loss of Both Vision and Hearing." *Generations,* vol. XXVI, no. 1 (Spring 2003): 95–97.

CHAPTER 7

1. Thompson, A. "Preventing Falls Among Elders—a $20 Billion a Year Challenge." *Aging Today* (September/October 2002): 10.

2. Gill, T., C. Williams, and M. Tinetti. "Environmental Hazards and the Risk of Nonsyncopal Falls in the Homes of Community-Living Older Persons." *Medical Care,* vol. 38, no. 12 (2000): 1174–1183.

3. Seely, D., W. Browner, M. Nevitt, H. Genant, J. Scott, and S. Cummings. "Which Fractures Are Associated with Low Appendicular Bone Mass in Elderly Women?" *Annals of Internal Medicine,* vol. 115 (1991): 837–842.

4. McGarry, N. "An Ounce of Prevention: Halting Injuries, Fatalities for Elders." *Aging Today* (November/December 1999): 9–10.

5. Center for Disease Control and Prevention National Center for Injury Prevention and Control. *Falls in Nursing Homes* (1999).

6. McGarry, N. "An Ounce of Prevention: Halting Injuries, Fatalities for Elders." *Aging Today* (November/December 1999): 9–10.

7. Trotto, N. "They All Fall." *Contemporary Long Term Care* (April 2001): 38–42.

8. Riggs, B., and L. Melton, eds. *Osteoporosis: Etiology, Diagnosis, and Management,* 2nd ed. New York: Raven Press (1995): 239.

9. Riggs, B., and L. Melton. "The Worldwide Problem of Osteoporosis: Insights Afforded by Epidemiology." *Bone,* vol. 17, no. 5 (November 1995): 505S–511S.

10. Kron, M., S. Loy, E. Sturm, T. Nikolaus, and C. Becker. "Risk Indicators for Falls in Institutionalized Frail Elderly." *American Journal of Epidemiology,* vol. 158 (2003): 645–653.

11. Le Postollec, M. "Taking Steps to Prevent Falls." *Advance,* vol. 4, no. 1 (January/February 2001): 74–76.

12. National Center for Health Statistics. *Health, United States, 2004* (2004).

13. Kavanaugh, K., and B. Tate. "Recognizing and Helping Older People with Vision Impairments." *Geriatric Nursing,* vol. 17 (1996): 68–71.

14. Brown, J., "Treat Urge to Prevent Injury." *Journal of the American Geriatrics Society,* vol. 48, no. 7 (July 2000).

15. *Accident Facts.* National Safety Council, Chicago (1992).

16. Tideiksaar, R. *Falls in Older People: Prevention and Management,* 3rd ed. Baltimore, MD: Health Professions Press (2002).

17. Peterson, E. "Strides in Research on Fear of Falling." *Maximizing Human Potential,* vol. 7, no. 3 (Winter 2000).

18. Lachman, M., J. Howland, S. Tennstedt, A. Jette, S. Assman, and E. Peterson. "Fear of Falling and Activity Restriction: The Survey of Activities and Fear of Falling in the Elderly (SAFE)." *Journal of Gerontology: Psychological Sciences,* vol. 53B, no. 1 (2004): 43–50.

19. Kleinfield, N. "Health Workers Helping Elderly Face Their Fear of Falling." *San Francisco Chronicle* (March 6, 2003): G10.

20. Gillespie, L., et al. "Interventions for Preventing Falls in Elderly People." *Cochrane Library,* issue 3 (2002).

21. Rubenstein, L., R. Kenny, M. Eccles, F. Martin, and M. Tinetti. "Evidence-Based Guideline for Falls Prevention: Summary of the Bi-National Panel." *Generations,* vol. XXVI, no. 4 (Winter 2002–3): 38–41.

22. National Academy on an Aging Society and Merck Institute of Aging and Health. *The State of Aging and Health in America.* Gerontological Society of America (November 2002): 5.

23. Rubenstein, L., R. Kenny, M. Eccles, F. Martin, and M. Tinetti. "Evidence-Based Guideline for Falls Prevention: Summary of the Bi-National Panel." *Generations,* vol. XXVI, no. 4 (Winter 2002–3): 40.

24. Tinetti, M., et al. "A Multifactorial Intervention to Reduce the Risk of Falling Among Elderly People Living in the Community." *New England Journal of Medicine,* vol. 331, no. 13 (1994): 821–827.

25. Shumway-Cook, A., et al. "The Effect of Multidimensional Exercises on Balance, Mobility, and Fall Risk in Community-Dwelling Older Adults." *Physical Therapy,* vol. 77, no. 1 (1997): 46–57.

26. Tinetti, M., et al. "A Multifactorial Intervention to Reducing the Risk of Falling Among Elderly People Living in the Community." *New England Journal of Medicine,* vol. 331, no. 13 (1994): 821–27.

27. Berg, K., and D. Kairy. "Balance Interventions to Prevent Falls." *Generations,* vol. XXVI, no. 4 (Winter 2002–3): 75–78.

28. White, F. "Preventing Falls, Promoting Fitness." *Nursing Homes* (September 1998): 20–25.

29. Wright, A., "Steady on Your Feet." *AARP Bulletin,* vol. 42, no. 10 (November 2001): 20–21.

30. Kruger, J., D. Brown, D. Galuska, and D. Buchner. "Strength Training Among Adults Aged 65 Years and Older—United States, 2001." Centers for Disease Control and Prevention (January 23, 2004).

31. Devereux, J. "Work Related Stress and Musculoskeletal Disorders." Second European Ergonomics Conference and Trade Show, Brussels (April 24, 2004).

32. Fiatarone, M., et al. "Exercise Training and Nutritional Supplementation for Physical Frailty in the Oldest Old." *New England Journal of Medicine,* vol. 330 (1994): 1769–75.

33. Associated Press. "Exercise Works Wonders for Frail Elderly, Study Says." *San Francisco Chronicle* (June 23, 1994): A6.

34. McCarthy, M. "Getting a Lift from Lifting." *Provider* (August 2003): 36–37.

35. McNamee, G. "Wandering Soles." *Modern Maturity,* vol. 44W, no. 5 (September/October 2001): 74–79.

36. Hilleras, P., A. Jorm, A. Herlitz, and B. Winblad. "Activity Patterns in Very Old People: A Survey of Cognitively Intact Subjects Aged 90 Years and Older." *Age Ageing,* vol. 28 (1999): 147–152.

37. Marcus, B., P. Dubbert, L. Forsyth, et al. "Physical Activity Behavior Change: Issues in Adoption and Maintenance." *Health Psychology,* vol. 19, suppl. 1(2000): 32–41.

38. Conn, V., K. Burks, S. Pomroy, S. Ulbrich, and J. Cochran. "Older Women and Exercise: Explanatory Concepts." *Women's Health Issues,* vol. 13, no. 4 (July/August 2003): 158–166.

39. Rose, D. "Results of Intervention Research: Implications for Practice." *Generations,* vol. XXVI, no. 4 (Winter 2002–3): 60–65.

40. Day, M., et al. "Randomized Factorial Trial of Falls Prevention Among Older People Living in Their Own Homes." *British Medical Journal*, vol. 325 (2002): 128–133.

41. Kleinfield, N. "Health Workers Helping Elderly Face Their Fear of Falling." *San Francisco Chronicle* (March 6, 2003): G10.

42. Ivry, J. "Aging in Place: The Role of Geriatric Social Work." *Families in Society*, vol. 76 (1995): 76–85.

43. Wagnild, G. "Growing Old at Home." *Journal of Housing for the Elderly*, vol. 14 (2001): 71–84.

44. Overton, J., and J. Pynoos. "Injury-Proofing Elders' Homes." Published by *Aging Today* (November/December 1999): 10.

45. Lachman, M., J. Howland, S. Tennstedt, A. Jette, S. Assman, and E. Peterson. "Fear of Falling and Activity Restriction: The Survey of Activities and Fear of Falling in the Elderly (SAFE)." *Journal of Gerontology: Psychological Sciences*, vol. 53B, no. 1 (2004): 43–50.

46. Cummings, R. G., et al. "Home Visits by an Occupational Therapist for Assessment and Modification of Environmental Hazards: A Randomized Controlled Trial." *Journal of the American Geriatric Society*, vol. 47, (1999): 1397–1402.

47. Rose, D. "Results of Intervention Research: Implications for Practice." *Generations*, vol. XXVI, no. 4 (Winter 2002–3): 60–65.

48. California Department of Aging. *Home Modifications Fact Sheet* (2002).

49. Gill, T., C. Williams, and M. Tinetti. "Environmental Hazards and the Risk of Nonsyncopal Falls in the Homes of Community-Living Older Persons." *Medical Care*, vol. 38, no. 12 (2000): 1174–1183.

50. Ibid.

CHAPTER 8

1. Tofle, R. B., B. Schwarz, S. Yoon, and A. Max-Royale. *Color in Healthcare Environments*. San Francisco: The Coalition for Health Environments Research (2003).

2. Ibid.

3. Ibid.

4. Arditi, A., and K. Knoblauch. "Choosing Effective Display Colors for the Partially Sighted." *Society for Information Display International Symposium Digest of Technical Papers*, vol. XXV (May 1994): 32–35.

5. Arditi, A., and K. Knoblauch. "Effective Color Contrast and Low Vision." In *Functional Assessment of Low Vision*. B. Rosenthal and R. Cole, eds. St. Louis, MO: Mosby (1996): 129–135.

6. Goselin, K. "Color Grows Up." *Interiors & Sources* (May 2003): 80–82.

7. Windle, L. "Paint: Fresh Look at the Bottom Line." *Building Operating Management* (November 2003): 57–58.

8. Zimmerman, G. "Low-VOC Paints Are More Than Just 'Green.'" *Building Operating Management*, vol. 51, no. 4 (April 2004): 39–42.

CHAPTER 9

1. Fauble, F. "Emerging Trends in Healthcare Design." *FacilityCare*, vol. 9, no. 1 (January/February 2004): 8.

2. Beattie, S., and R. Guess. "Flooring Choices for Healthcare Applications." *Interiors and Sources* (October 1996): 108–111.

3. Perritt, M., D. McCune, and S. McCune. "The Effect of Floor Texture and Patterns for the Older Client: An Empirical Study." *International Conference Abstracts of the Interior Design Educators Council* (2004).

4. Perritt, M., D. McCune, and S. McCune. "The Effect of Floor Texture and Patterns on Walking Time and Stability of Persons With Alzheimer's Disease." *International Conference Abstracts of the Interior Design Educators Council* (2003).

5. Dickinson, J., J. Shroyer, and J. Elias. "The Influence of Commercial-Grade Carpet on Postural Sway and Balance Strategy Among Older Adults." *The Gerontologist*, vol. 42, no. 4 (2002): 552–559.

6. Maddox, E. "Carpet Trends in Healthcare Facilities." *FacilityCare*. (August 1998): 20–21.

7. Pence, A. "New HEPA Filter Vacuum Cleans Your Carpet and Then Some." *San Francisco Chronicle* (Saturday, October 19, 2002): E5.

8. Taylor, M. "Designing a Flooring System for your Healthcare Facility." *FacilityCare* (May/June 2001): 17–19.

9. Ibid.

10. Brawley, E., and M. Taylor. "Designing for Senior Care Environments." *Interiors & Sources* (March 2003): 64–67.

11. Carpet and Rug Institute. *Often-Held Myths Surrounding Carpet Are Dispelled by the Carpet and Rug Institute* (August 2001).
12. Brawley, E., and M. Taylor. "Designing for Senior Care Environments." *Interiors & Sources* (March 2003): 64–67.
13. Ibid.
14. Maddox, E. "Carpet Trends in Healthcare Facilities." *FacilityCare* (August 1998): 20–21.
15. Fauble, F., and B. Erwin. "Defining the Healing Environment Through Product Development." *Healthcare Design* (May 2004): 45–50.
16. Taylor, M. "Designing a Flooring System for your Healthcare Facility." *FacilityCare* (May/June 2001): 17–19.
17. Piper, J. "Flooring: Back to Basics." *Building Operating Management,* vol. 50. no. 8 (August 2003): 49–50.
18. Weinhold, V. "Flooring Options: Carpet Now a Major Contender." *Health Facilities Management* (May 1992): 96.
19. Barbacci, D. "Carpet Concerns in Fast-growing Healthcare Environments." *FacilityCare* (March 1999): 13–14.
20. Pence, A. "New HEPA Filter Vacuum Cleans Your Carpet and Then Some." *San Francisco Chronicle* (October 19, 2002): E5.
21. Coombs, R. "HEPA Filtration." *FacilityCare.* (September/October 2001): 7.

Chapter 10

1. Perkins, B., D. Hoglund, D. King, and E. Cohen. *Building Type Basics for Senior Living.* New York: John Wiley and Sons (2004).
2. Kozlowski, D. "Getting a Grip on Green Products." *Building Operating Management* (May 2003): 57–58.
3. Collins & Aikman. *Creating Harmony Between Industry and Nature* (2003).
4. Perkins, B., D. Hoglund, D. King, and E. Cohen. *Building Type Basics for Senior Living.* New York: John Wiley and Sons (2004).
5. "Greening the Workplace: Special Report." *EnvironDesign Journal* (Spring 2003): 18.
6. "Measuring Sustainability." *Building Operating Management,* vol. 51, no. 5 (May 2004): 103.
7. Taylor, M. "Promoting Wellness with Floorcovering." *FacilityCare.* (November/December 2003).
8. Ryan, M. "Sustainable Carpet Choices." *Building Operating Management,* vol. 50, no. 7 (July 2003): 43–49.
9. "Measuring Sustainability." *Building Operating Management,* vol. 51, no. 5 (May 2004): 103.
10. Sellers, K. "Carpet Recycling." *FacilityCare.* (May/June 2000): 37.
11. Ryan, M. "Sustainable Carpet Choices." *Building Operating Management,* vol. 50, no. 7 (July 2003): 43–49.
12. Burnett, L. "Healing Environments?" *Contract* (September 2004): 60–62.

Chapter 11

1. Boyd, C. "Residents First: A Long-Term Facility Introduces a Social Model That Puts Residents in Control." *Health Progress,* vol. 75, no. 7 (1994): 34–39.
2. Lustbader, W. "The Pioneer Challenges: A Radical Change in the Culture of Nursing Homes." In *Qualities of Caring: Impact on Quality of Life,* ed. N. Noelker and Z. Harel. Rochester, NY: Springer Publishing Company (2000).
3. Maher, V. "Legal and Policy Issues in Long-Term Care." In *Health Care Management: Long Term Care: Concept and Reality,* ed. H. Jolt and M. Leibovici. Philadelphia: Hanley & Belfs, Inc. (1997).
4. Fagan, R. M. "Pioneer Network: Changing the Culture of Aging in America." In *Culture Change in Long-Term Care,* ed. A. Weiner and J. Ronch vol. 2. New York-London-Oxford: Haworth Social Work Practice Press (2002).
5. McNamara, S. "Eldercare at a Crossroads." *Democrat & Chronicle* (Rochester, NY, August 8, 1999): 1A, 6A.
6. Ibid.
7. Fagan, R. M. "Pioneer Network: Changing the Culture of Aging in America." In *Culture Change in Long-Term Care,* ed. A. Weiner and J. Ronch vol. 2. New York-London-Oxford: Haworth Social Work Practice Press (2002).
8. Fagan, R. "Recreating Our Nursing Homes Through Culture Change." *Elders with Illness* (April 2000): 21.
9. Fagan, R. M. "Turning the Tables: Who Directs Care at Your Community? Staff or Residents?" *Assisted Living Today* (October 2002): 36–38.
10. Ibid.

11. Ibid.
12. Ibid.
13. Meyers, S. Jewish Home and Hospital, Bronx, New York, in a taped discussion with Mrs. Beatrice Taishoff about her ethical will. In 2001, Mrs. Taishoff was 99 years old and lived in the Jewish Home (November 2001).
14. Willging, P. "Long-Term Care Needs to Change Its Focus." *Nursing Home Magazine* (February 2004: 16.
15. Fagan, R. M. "Turning the Tables: Who Directs Care at Your Community? Staff or Residents?" *Assisted Living Today* (October 2002): 36–38.
16. Providence Mount St. Vincent. *An Alternative to Nursing Homes: Impacting Resident Functional and Health Decline.* Seattle: Sisters of Providence (1994).
17. Ransom, S. *Eden Alternative: The Texas Project.* Institute for Quality Improvement in Long-Term Care. IQILTHC Series Report 2000-4 (2000).
18. Dannefer, D., and P. Stein. *Systemic Change in Long Term Care.* Report to the New York State Department of Health. Warner Graduate School, University of Rochester (1999).
19. Dannefer, D., and P. Stein. *From the Top to the Bottom, From the Bottom to the Top: Systemically Changing the Culture of Nursing Homes.* Report to the van Ameringen Foundation. Warner Graduate School, University of Rochester (2002).

CHAPTER 12

1. Volzer, R. "Designing for the Long Term." *Interiors* (August 2000): 32.
2. Regnier, V. *Design for Assisted Living: Guidelines for Housing the Physically and Mentally Frail.* New York: John Wiley and Sons (2002).
3. Ibid.
4. "Culture Change Now." *Action Pact Newsletter* (May 2004).

CHAPTER 13

1. Lawton, M. P., and J. Bader. "Wish for Privacy by Young and Old." *Journal of Gerontology*, vol. 25, no. 1 (1970): 48–54.
2. Regnier, V. *Design for Assisted Living: Guidelines for Housing the Physically and Mentally Frail.* New York: John Wiley & Sons (2002).

3. Sanford, J. "Toileting: Impact of the Physical Environment." American Association of Homes and Services for the Aging Annual Meeting, Nashville, TN (October 2004).
4. Alden, A. "Rethinking Bathroom Design." *Nursing Homes Magazine* (March 2004): 15–19.
5. Sanford, J. *Best Practices in the Design of Toileting and Bathing Facilities for Assisted Transfers.* Washington, DC: U.S. Access Board (2001).
6. Alden, A. "Rethinking Bathroom Design." *Nursing Homes Magazine* (March 2004): 15–19.
7. Sanford, J. *Best Practices in the Design of Toileting and Bathing Facilities for Assisted Transfers.* Washington, DC: U.S. Access Board (2001).
8. Alden, A. "Rethinking Bathroom Design." *Nursing Homes Magazine.* (March 2004): 15–19.
9. Ibid.
10. Foltz-Gray, D. "Rough Waters." *Contemporary Long Term Care* (September 1995): 66–70.
11. Sloane, P., J. Rader, A. Barrick, B. Hoeffer, S. Dwyer, D. McKenzie, et al. "Bathing Persons with Dementia." *The Gerontologist*, vol. 35, no. 5 (1995b): 672–678.

CHAPTER 14

1. AARP Andrus Foundation and Dana Alliance for Brain Initiatives. *Staying Sharp.* Washington, DC (2002).
2. Federal Interagency Forum on Aging Related Statistics *Older Americans 2000: Key Indicators of Well-Being.* Hyattsville, MD (2000).
3. Burgener, S., R. Shimmer, and L. Murrell. "Expression of Individuality in Cognitively Impaired Elders." *Journal of Gerontological Nursing,* vol. 19, no. 4 (1993): 13–22.
4. Davis, D., and A. Bush-Brown. *Hospitable Design for Healthcare and Senior Communities.* New York: Van Nostrand & Reinhold (1994): 16.
5. Danes, S. "Creating an Environment for Community." *Alzheimer's Care Quarterly*, vol. 3, no. 1 (Winter 2002): 61–66.
6. Calkins, M. "The Nursing Home of the Future: Are You Ready?" *Nursing Homes Magazine,* vol. 51, no. 6 (June 2002): 42–47.
7. von Faber, M., A. Bootsma-van der Wiel, E. van Exel, J. Gussekloo, A. Lagaay, E. van Donger, D. Knook, S. an der Geest, and R. Westendorp. "Successful Aging in the Oldest Old: Who Can

Be Characterized as Successfully Aged?" *Archives of Internal Medicine,* vol. 161, no. 22 (December 10–24, 2001): 2694–2700.

8. Koepke, D. "Tapping the Spirit." *Journal on Active Aging,* vol. 2, no. 6 (November/December 2003): 40–45.

9. Hales, D. "Why Prayer Could Be Good Medicine." *Parade Magazine* (March 23, 2003): 4–5.

10. Ibid.

11. Koenig, H. "Religion and Medicine IV: Religion, Physical Health and Clinical Implications." *International Journal of Psychiatry in Medicine,* vol. 31 (2002a): 321–336.

12. Kirby, S., P. Coleman, and D. Daley. "Spirituality and Well-Being in Frail and Nonfrail Older Adults." *Journal of Gerontology: Psychological Sciences,* vol. 59B, no. 3 (May 2004): P123–P129.

13. Alzheimer's Association. "Keeping the Faith: Religion, Spirituality Play Central Roles in Lives Affected by Alzheimer's." *Advances,* vol. 22, no. 2 (Summer 2002): 6–7.

14. Bell, V., and D. Troxel. *A Dignified Life.* Deerfield, FL: Health Communications (2002).

7. Rabig, J. "The Green House Project: An Alternative Model of Elder Care." Unpublished paper (2003).

8. " 'Green Houses' Incubating the Future of Long Term Care." *Culture Change Now,* vol. 2 (2003): 14–15.

9. Ibid.

10. Schwarz, B. *Nursing Home Design: Consequences of Employing the Medical Model.* New York: Taylor and Francis (1996).

11. Rabig, J. "The Green House Project: An Alternative Model of Elder Care." Unpublished paper (2003).

12. Alexander, C., M. Silverstein, and S. Ishikawa. *A Pattern Language: Towns, Buildings, Construction.* New York: Oxford University Press (1977).

13. "Long-Term Care Checks Out of Heartbreak Hotel." *Culture Change Now,* vol. 2 (2003): 16.

14. Thomas, W. "Expert Opinion: The Green House Project." *snalfnews.com* (8/13/04).

15. Volzer, R. "Home Is Where the 'Hearth' Is . . ." *Nursing Homes Long Term Care Management,* vol. 52, no. 10 (October 2003): 47–49.

16. Thomas, W. "Expert Opinion: The Green House Project." *snalfnews.com* (8/13/04).

CHAPTER 15

1. Sahyoun, N., L. Pratt, H. Lenzer, A. Dey, and K. Robinson. "The Changing Profile of Nursing Home Residents: 1985–1997." *CDC Aging Trends.* Baltimore: National Institutes on Aging, No. 4 (2001).

2. Kane, R. L. "The Evolution of the American Nursing Home." In *The Future of Long Term Care: Social Policy Issues,* ed. R. Binstock, L. Cluff, and O. von Mering. Baltimore: Johns Hopkins University Press (1996): 145–168.

3. Rabig, J. "The Green House Project: An Alternative Model of Elder Care." Unpublished paper (2003).

4. Ibid.

5. Lachman, M., M. Ziff, and A. Spiro. "Maintaining a Sense of Control in Later Life." In *Aging and Quality of Life,* ed. R. Abeles, H. Giff, and M. Ory. Baltimore: Johns Hopkins University Press (1994): 216–232.

6. Avorn, J., and E. Langer. "Induced Disability in Nursing Home Patients: A Controlled Trial." *Journal of the American Geriatrics Association,* no. 30 (1982): 182–188.

CHAPTER 16

1. Winik, L. W. "How Much Can I Give?" *Parade Magazine* (January 29, 1995): 4–6.

2. National Adult Day Services Association. *Standards and Guidelines for Adult Day Services.* Washington, DC: National Council on Aging (1997).

3. Welch, C. "The Many Benefits of Adult Day Care." *Side by Side.* Santa Barbara, CA: Alzheimer's Association (Fall 2002): 6.

4. George G. Glenner Alzheimer's Family Centers. *Sharing the Caring Newsletter* (Fall/Winter 2004).

5. Zarit, S., M. Stephens, A. Townsend, and R. Greene. "Stress Reduction for Family Caregivers: Effects of Adult Day Care Use." *Journal of Gerontology: Social Sciences,* vol. 53B (1998): S267–S277.

6. Travis, S., and A. Stemmel. "Predictors of the Likelihood to Provide Intergenerational Activities in Child and Adult Day Care Centers." In *Intergenerational Programs: Understanding What We Have Created,* ed. V. S. Kuehne. New York: Haworth Press (1999): 101–116.

7. Salari, S. "Intergenerational Partnerships in Adult Day Centers: Importance of Age-Appropriate Environments and Behaviors." *The Gerontologist,* vol. 42, no. 3 (2002); 321–333.

8. Moore, K. "Dementia Day Center: Does the Physical Setting Matter?" *Alzheimer's Care Quarterly,* vol. 3, no. 1 (2002): 67–73.

9. Lawton, M. P., and L. Nahemow. "Ecology and the Aging Process." In *Psychology of Adult Development and Aging,* C. Eisdorfer and M. P. Lawton. Washington, DC: American Psychological Association (1973).

10. Lawton, M. P., M. Fulcomer, and M. Kleban. "Architecture for the Mentally Impaired." *Environment and Behavior,* vol. 16, no. 6 (1984): 730–757.

11. Moore, K. *Dementia Day Care Facility Development Workbook.* Milwaukee: Center for Architecture and Urban Planning Research (2002).

12. National Adult Day Services Association. *Standards and Guidelines for Adult Day Services.* Washington, DC: National Council on Aging (1997).

13. Moore, K. "Dementia Day Center: Does the Physical Setting Matter?" *Alzheimer's Care Quarterly,* vol. 3, no. 1 (2002): 67–73.

14. Moore, K. *Dementia Day Care Facility Development Workbook.* Milwaukee: Center for Architecture and Urban Planning Research (2002).

15. Williams, B., and P. Roberts. "Friends in Passing: Social Interaction at an Adult Day Care Center." *International Journal of Aging and Human Development,* vol. 41, no. 1 (1995): 63–78.

16. Reifler, B. *Partners in Caregiving: The Adult Day Services Program,* vol. 11, no. 1 (March 2001).

CHAPTER 17

1. The Gerontological Society of America. *Gerontology News,* vol. 32, no. 9 (September, 2004).

2. Gearon, C. J. "Planetree: 25 Years Older." *Hospitals & Health Networks,* vol. 76, no. 10 (October 2002).

3. Gilpin, L., and M. Schweitzer. "Twenty-Five Years of Planetree Design." *Healthcare Design,* vol. 3, no. 3 (September 2003): 13–16.

4. Frampton, S. "Introduction: The Emergence of Patient-Centered Care and the Planetree Model." *Putting Patients First: Designing and Practicing Patient-Centered Care,* ed. S. Frampton, L. Gilpin, and P. Charmel. San Francisco: Jossey-Bass (2003).

5. Ibid.

6. Ford, C., and L. Gilpin. "Informing and Empowering Diverse Populations." In *Putting Patients First: Designing and Practicing Patient-Centered Care,* ed. S. Frampton, L. Gilpin, and P. Charmel. San Francisco: Jossey-Bass (2003): 43.

7. Lindheim, R. "New Design Parameters for Healthy Places." *Places,* vol. 2, no. 4 (1985): 17–27.

8. Gilpin, L., and M. Schweitzer. "Twenty-Five Years of Planetree Design." *Healthcare Design,* vol. 3, no. 3 (September 2003): 13–16.

9. Arneil, B., and K. Frasca-Beaulieu. "Healing Environments: Architecture and Design Conductive to Health." In *Putting Patients First: Designing and Practicing Patient-Centered Care,* ed. S. B. Frampton, L. Gilpin, and P. Charmel. San Francisco: Jossey-Bass (2003): 163–164.

10. Martin, D., et al. "Randomized Trial of a Patient Centered Hospital Unit." *Patient Education and Counseling,* vol. 34 (1998): 125–133.

11. Gilpin, L. "The Importance of Human Interaction." In *Putting Patients First: Designing and Practicing Patient-Centered Care,* ed. S. Frampton, L. Gilpin, and P. Charmel. San Francisco: Jossey-Bass (2003): 9.

12. Mooney, B. "Patient Paradise." *Advance for Nurses—New England,* vol. 2, no. 25. (December 9, 2002).

13. Ibid.

14. Donnarumma, L. "An Interview with Steven Horowitz, MD." *Planetalk* (April 2004).

15. Handzo, G., and J. C. Wilson. "Spirituality." In: *Putting Patients First: Designing and Practicing Patient-Centered Care,* ed. S. Frampton, L. Gilpin, and P. Charmel. San Francisco: Jossey-Bass (2003): 103.

16. Spatz, M., and D. Storby. "Human Touch." In: *Putting Patients First: Designing and Practicing Patient-Centered Care,* ed. S. Frampton, L. Gilpin, and P. Charmel. San Francisco: Jossey-Bass (2003): 105–116.

17. Ulrich, R. S. "Effects of Health Facility Interior Design on Wellness: Theory and Recent Scientific Research." *Journal of Health Care Design,* vol. 3 (1991): 97–109.

18. Ulrich, R. S. "Aesthetic and Affective Response to Natural Environments." In *Human Behavior and the Environment,* ed. I. Altman and J. F. Wohlwill, vol. 6. New York: Plenum (1983).

19. Ulrich, R. S. "Biophilia, Biophobia, and Natural

Landscapes." In *The Biophilia Hypothesis,* ed. S. A. Kellert, and E. O. Wilson. Washington, DC: Island Press/Shearwater (1993).

20. Ulrich, R., and L. Gilpin. "Healing Arts: Nutrition for the Soul." In *Putting Patients First: Designing and Practicing Patient-Centered Care,* ed. S. Frampton, L. Gilpin, and P. Charmel. San Francisco: Jossey-Bass (2003): 124.

21. Gilpin, L., and M. Schweitzer. "Twenty-Five Years of Planetree Design." *Healthcare Design,* vol. 3, no. 3 (September 2003): 13–16.

Chapter 18

1. Antonucci, T., and H. Akiyama. "Stress and Coping in the Elderly." *Journal of Applied and Preventive Psychology,* vol. 2 (1993): 201–208.

2. Lunney, J., J. Lynn, D. Foley, S. Lipson, and J. Guralnik, "Patterns of Functional Decline at the End of Life." *Journal of the American Medical Association,* vol. 289, no. 18 (May 14, 2003): 2387–2392.

3. "Physicians Urged to Use Hospice Principles to Relieve Suffering in Other Care Settings." *End of Life Care.* San Francisco: Hospice By the Bay (Summer 2001).

4. Teno, J., B. Clarridge, V. Casey, L. Welc, T. Wetle, R. Shield, and V. Mor. "Family Perspectives on End-of-Life Care at the Last Place of Care." *Journal of the American Medical Association,* vol. 291, no. 9 (January 7, 2004): 88–93.

5. Yun, D. "Hospice Helps Sick Finish Life with Care." *San Francisco Chronicle* (Friday, October 1, 2004): F1–2.

6. Alive Hospice Community Report. Nashville, TN: Alive Hospice, Inc. (2003).

7. Mitchell, S., D. Kiely, and M. Hamel. "Dying with Advanced Dementia in the Nursing Home." *Archives of Internal Medicine,* vol. 164, no. 3 (2004): 321–326.

8. Hospice Foundation of America. "Living with Grief: Alzheimer's Disease." *Eleventh Annual Living With Grief Teleconference* (April 28, 2004).

9. Mayo Clinic. "Palliative Care." *Mayo Clinic Health Letter,* vol. 20, no. 2 (February 2002): 4.

10. Fried, T., C. van Doorn, J. O'Leary, M. Tinetti, and M. Drickamer. "Older Persons' Preferences for Site of Terminal Care." *Annals of Internal Medicine,* vol. 131 (1999): 109–112.

11. Ibid.

12. Mezey, M., N. Dubler, E. Mitty, and A. Brody. "What Impact Do Setting and Transitions Have on the Quality of Life at the End of Life and the Quality of the Dying Process?" *The Gerontologist,* vol. 42, Special Issue III (2002): 54–67.

13. National Center for Assisted Living, 2001.

14. Mezey, M., N. Dubler, E. Mitty, and A. Brody. "What Impact Do Setting and Transitions Have on the Quality of Life at the End of Life and the Quality of the Dying Process?" *The Gerontologist,* vol. 42, Special Issue III (2002): 54–67.

15. Zimmerman, S., P. Sloane, L. Hanson, L. Churchill, J. Eckert, and K. Magaziner. "End-of-Life Care in Residential Care and Nursing Homes." Unpublished manuscript, University of North Carolina, Chapel Hill (2001).

16. Miller, S., P. Gozalo, and V. Mor. Hospice "Enrollment and Hospitalization of Dying Nursing Home Patients." *American Journal of Medicine,* vol. 111, no. 1 (July 2001): 38–44.

17. Magaziner, J., P. German, S. Zimmerman, H. Hebel, L. Burton, and A. Gruber-Baldini. "The Prevalence of Dementia in a Statewide Sample of New Nursing Home Admissions Aged 65 and Older: Diagnosis by Expert Panel." Epidemiology of Dementia in Nursing Homes Research Group. *The Gerontologist,* vol. 40 (2000): 663–672.

18. Kayser-Jones, J., E. Schell, W. Lyons, A. Kris, J. Chan, and R. Beard. "Factors That Influence End-of-Life Care in Nursing Homes: The Physical Environment, Inadequate Staffing, and Lack of Supervision." *The Gerontologist,* vol. 43, Special Issue II (2003): 76–84.

19. Nightingale, F. *Notes on Nursing: What It Is and What It Is Not.* Philadelphia: Edward Stern, Churchill Livingston, Inc. (1859, 1946).

20. Maher, L. "Dignified Departures." *Contemporary Long Term Care* (December 2000).

21. SNALF Expert Opinion. *SNALFnews.com* (December 13, 2001).

Chapter 19

1. Campbell, S., D. Kripke, J. Gillian, and J. Hrubovcak. "Exposure to Light in Healthy Elderly Subjects and Alzheimer's Patients." *Psychology and Behavior,* vol. 42 (1988): 141–144.

2. Brawley, E. "Therapeutic Gardens for Individuals

with Alzheimer's Disease." *Alzheimer's Care Quarterly,* vol. 3, no. 1 (Winter 2002): 7–11.

3. Gill, T., C. Williams, and M. Tinetti. "Environmental Hazards and the Risk of Nonsyncopal Falls in the Homes of Community-Living Older Persons." *Medical Care,* vol. 38, no. 2 (2000): 1174–1183.

4. Weuve, J., J. Kang, J. Manson, M. Breteler, J. Ware, and F. Grodstein. "Physical Activity, Including Walking, and Cognitive Function in Older Women." *Journal of the American Medical Association,* vol. 292, no. 12 (September 22–29, 2004): 1454–1461.

5. Abbot, R., L. White, G. Ross, K. Masaki, J. Curb, and H. Petrovitch. "Walking and Dementia in Physically Capable Elderly Men." *Journal of the American Medical Association,* vol. 292, no. 12 (September 22–29, 2004): 1447–1453.

6. Simpson, E. "Project Lets Seniors with Alzheimer's Be the Caregiver." *The Virginian-Pilot Newspaper* (May 22, 2001).

7. Carman, N., and J. Carman. "The Care and Use of a Special Needs Garden: Making the Most of Planned Activities in the Garden." *Memory Care Professional* (October 2003): 30–31.

8. Gilhooley, M. "Green Green Grass of Work." *Facilities Design & Management,* vol. 21, no. 9 (October 2002): 26–29.

9. Brawley, E. "Gardens of Memories." *Alzheimer's Care Quarterly,* vol. 5, no. 2 (2004): 154–164.

CHAPTER 20

1. Levin, D. "If You Like the Magazine, You'll Love the Conference." *Healthcare Design* (May 2003).

2. Hamilton, K. "The New Evidence-Based Designers." *Interiors and Sources,* vol. 11, no. 1 (January 2004): 58–59.

3. Hamilton, K. "Certification for Evidence-Based Projects." *Healthcare Design,* vol. 4 (May 2004): 37–41.

4. Hamilton, K. "The New Evidence-Based Designers." *Interiors and Sources,* vol. 11, no. 1 (January 2004): 58–59.

5. Volzer, R. "Designing for the Long-Term." *Interiors* (August 2000): 32.

6. Cohen, U., and G. Weisman. *Holding on to Home.* Baltimore: The Johns Hopkins University Press. (1991).

7. Hamilton, K. "Healthcare Spending Dilemmas." *Contract* (September 2002): 86.

Resources

CHAPTER 1

Administration on Aging
www.aoa.gov
Publication: *A Profile of America's Older Americans*

Alliance for Aging Research
202-293-3650
Fax: 202-785-8574
www.agingresearch.org

American Society on Aging (ASA)
Market Street
San Francisco, CA
www.asa.org

American Association of Retired Persons
601 E Street, NW
Washington, DC 20049
800-775-6776
www.aarp.org

AARP Andrus Foundation
601 E Street, NW
Washington, DC 20049
800-775-6776
www.andrus.org

American Chronic Pain Association
916-632-0922
Fax: 916-632-3208
www.theacpa.org

American Heart Association
National Center
7272 Greenville Avenue
Dallas, TX 75231
214-373-6300
800-553-6321 (Stroke Connection)
www.amhrt.org

Depression and Related Affective Disorders Association (DRADA)
www.med.jhu.edu/drada

Family Caregiver Alliance
690 Market Street, Suite 600
San Francisco, CA 94104
415-434-3388
Fax: 415-434-3508
www.caregiver.org

Gerontological Society of America (GSA)
1030 15th Street, NW, Suite 250
Washington, DC 20005-1503
202-842-1275

Institute for Research on Women and Gender
Difficult Dialogues Program
Stanford University
556 Salvatierra Walk
Stanford, CA 94305-8640
Publication: *Aging in the 21st Century Consensus Report*

Mayo Clinic Stroke Center
www.strokefreeforlife.com
Publication: *Stroke Free for Life,* by Dr. David Wiebers

Merck Institute of Aging and Health
202-842-0525
Publication: *The State of Aging and Health in America*
(November 2002)

National Academy on an Aging Society
Publication: *The State of Aging and Health in America*
(November 2002)

National Council on Aging (NCOA)
202-479-1200
Fax: 202-479-0735
www.ncoa.org

National Foundation for Depressive Illness
800-239-1265
www.depression.org

National Institute on Aging (NIA)
P.O. Box 8057
Gaithersburg, MD 20898-8057
301-496-1752
800-222-2225
800-222-4225 TTY
www.nih.gov/nia
Publication: *An Aging World: International Population Reports* (November 2001)

National Institute of Mental Health
301-443-4513
Fax: 301-443-4279
www.nimh.nih.gov

National Institute of Neurological Disorders and Stroke
NIH Neurological Institute
P.O. Box 5801
Bethesda, MD 20824
800-352-9424
www.ninds.nih.gov/health_and_medical/disorders/stroke.htm

National Mental Health Association
703-684-7722
800-969-6642
Fax: 703-686-5968
www.nmha.org

National Stroke Association
96 Inverness Drive East, Suite 1
Englewood, CO 80112-5112
303-649-9299
800 STROKES
www.stroke.org

NIH Osteoporosis and Related Bone Diseases National Resource Center
1232 22nd Street, NW
Washington, DC 20037
800-624-BONE
http://www.osteo.org
Publication: book and video about exercise for older people

U.S. Census Bureau
301-457-3030
Publication: *An Aging World: International Population Reports* (November 2001)

U.S. Department of Health and Human Services
Publication: *A Profile of Older Americans: 2002*
www.SeniorsSuperStores.com
Health aids such as lighted canes and large-print keyboards
www.armchairfitness.com
Armchair exercise videos for seniors, without loud music

Chapter 2

AARP Andrus Foundation
www.andrus.org
Publication: *Staying Sharp* series

Alliance for Aging Research
202-293-2856
Fax: 202-785-8574
www.agingresearch.org

Alzheimer's Association
225 N. Michigan Avenue, Suite 1700
Chicago, IL 60601-1676
800-272-3900
Fax: 312-335-1100
Benjamin Green-Field Library
312-335-9602
www.alz.org

Public Policy Office
1319 F Street, NW, Suite 710
Washington, DC 20004-1106
202-393-7737
202-393-2109
www.alz.org/Advocacy/overview.asp

Safe Return Program—Safe Return is a nationwide identification program created for individuals afflicted with Alzheimer's disease and related dementia (800-272-3900).

Maintain Your Brain: How to Live a Healthy Lifestyle Program

Alzheimer's Disease Education and Referral Center (ADEAR)
P.O. Box 8250
Silver Spring, MD 20907-8250
800-438-4380
Fax: 301-495-3334
www.alzheimers.org
Publication: *2003 Progress Report on Alzheimer's Disease*

The Alzheimer's Store
www.alzstore.com

Dana Alliance for Brain Initiatives
www.dana.org
Publication: *Staying Sharp* series

Eldercare Locator
800-677-1116
www.eldercare.gov

Family Caregiver Alliance
690 Market Street, Suite 600
San Francisco, CA 94104
415-434-3388
Fax: 415-434-3508
www.caregiver.org

Gerontological Society of America (GSA)
1275 K Street, NW, Suite 350
Washington, DC 20005
202-842-1275
Fax: 202-842-1150
www.geron.org

National Alliance for Caregiving
www.caregiving.org

National Association of Area Agencies on Aging (N4A)
1730 Rhode Island Avenue, NW
Suite 1200
Washington, DC 20036
202-872-0888
Fax: 202-872-0057
www.N4A.org

National Council on the Aging (NCOA)
(National Adult Day Services Association)
409 Third Street, SW
Washington, DC 20024
202-479-1200
202-479-0735
www.ncoa.org

National Institute on Aging (NIA)
(Information Center)
P.O. Box 8057
Gaithersburg, MD 20898-8057
301-496-1752
800-222-2225
800-222-4225 (TTY)
www.nia.nih.gov

National Institutes of Health
www.nih.gov

National Library of Medicine
8600 Rockville Pike
Bethesda, MD 20894
888-346-3656
www.nlm.nih.gov

Publications

Bell, V. and D. Troxel. *The Best Friends Approach to Alzheimer's Care*. Baltimore: Health Professions Press (1997).

Gwyther, L. *Caring for People with Alzheimer's Disease: A Manual for Facility Staff*. Washington, DC: Alzheimer's Association and American Health Care Association (2001).

Sifton, C. B. *Navigating the Alzheimer's Journey*. Baltimore: Health Professions Press (2004).

Snowden, D. *Aging With Grace: What the Nun Study Teaches Us About Leading Longer, Healthier, and More Meaningful Lives.* New York: Bantam Books (2001).

CHAPTER 3

Academy of Neurosciences for Architects
American Institute of Architects
1735 New York Avenue, NW
Washington, DC 20006-5292
Fax: 202/626-7399

Adaptive Environments
374 Congress Street, Suite 301
Boston, MA 02210
(617) 695-1225
www.adaptiveenvironments.org

Harvard University Graduate School of Design
Executive Education Program
1033 Massachusetts Avenue—5th Floor
Cambridge, MA 02138
Assisted Living: Design of Facilities for the Frail Elderly or Alzheimer's

InformeDesign
Clearinghouse for design and human behavior re-search.
www.informedesign.umn.edu

Publications

Bell, V., and D. Troxel. *The Best Friends Approach to Alzheimer's Care.* Baltimore: Health Professions Press (1997).

Bell, V., and D. Troxel. *The Best Friends Staff.* Baltimore: Health Professions Press (2001).

Bell, V., and D. Troxel. *The Best Friends Book of Alzheimer's Activities.* Baltimore: Health Professions Press (2004).

Brawley, E. *Designing for Alzheimer's Disease: Strategies for Creating Better Care Environments.* New York: John Wiley and Sons (1997).

Hellen, C. *Alzheimer's Disease: Activity-Focused Care.* Boston: Butterworth-Heinemann (1998).

CHAPTER 4

Center of Design for an Aging Society
9027 NW Bartholomew Drive
Portland, OR 97229
503-292-2912
503-296-5285
www.centerofdesign.org

Centers for Disease Control and Prevention (CDC)
U.S. Department of Health and Human Services
www.cdc.gov/nchs

Electric Power Research Institute
3412 Hillview Avenue
Palo Alto, CA 94304
800-313-3774
www.epri.com

International Association of Lighting Designers (IALD)
Merchandise Mart, Suite 9-104
200 World Trade Center
Chicago, IL 60654
Chicago, IL
312-527-3677

Lighthouse Information and Resource Service
Lighthouse International
111 East 59th Street
New York, NY 10022-1202
800-829-0500
www.lighthouse.org
The Lighthouse has many information brochures and booklets for consumers and professionals about vision impairment; it also has educational videotapes about age-related vision loss for health and human service workers and older adults.
See especially the executive summary of *The Lighthouse National Survey on Vision Loss: The Experiences, Attitudes and Knowledge of Middle-Aged and Older Americans.*

Lighting Research Center
Rensselaer Polytechnic Institute
Troy, NY 12180
518-687-7100

Lighting Research Office
3559 Birch Tree
Cleveland Heights, OH 44121
216-570-2686
Fax: 216-382-6424
www.lightingresearchoffice.org

National Eye Institute
301-496-5248
www.nei.nih.gov

National Institute on Aging (NIA)
P.O. Box 8057
Gaithersburg, MD 20898-8057

301-496-1752
800-222-2225
800-222-4225 TTY
www.nih.gov/nia

National Institutes of Health
888-644-6226
www.ods.od.nih.gov/factsheets/cc/vitd.html
Publications: Fact sheet on Vitamin D

Prevent Blindness America
800-331-2020
www.preventblindness.org

Websites on Age-Related Macular Degeneration
www.amd.org
www.retinopathy.org
www.glaucoma.org

CHAPTER 5

Center of Design for an Aging Society
9027 NW Bartholomew Drive
Portland, OR 97229
503-292-2912
503-296-5285
www.centerofdesign.org

Electric Power Research Institute
3412 Hillview Avenue
Palo Alto, CA 94304
800-313-3774
www.epri.com

Energy Design Resources
www.energydesignresources.com
Download *Skylighting Guidelines*

Illuminating Engineering Society of North America
120 Wall Street, 17th Floor
New York, NY 10005
www.iesna.org
Publications:
IESNA/ANSI: RP-28-2001 *Lighting and the Visual Environment for Senior Living*
Lighting Education Fundamentals: ED-100
RP-5-99 *Daylighting*

International Association of Lighting Designers (IALD)
Merchandise Mart, Suite 9-104
200 World Trade Center
Chicago, IL 60654
312-527-3677

International Commission on Illumination
www.cie.co.at/cie

Lawrence Berkeley National Laboratories
www.lbnl.gov
Download *Tips for Daylighting with Windows*

Lighting Research Center
Rensselaer Polytechnic Institute
21 Union Street
Troy, NY 12180
www.lrc.rpi.edu

Lighting Research Office
3559 Birch Tree
Cleveland Heights, OH 44121
216-570-2686
Fax: 216-382-6424
www.lightingresearchoffice.org
Publication: *Fifth International LRO Light Research Symposium—Light & Human Health: Final Report*

MechoShade Systems Inc.
42-03 35th Street
Long Island City, NY 11101
718-729-2020
Fax: 718-727-2941
www.mechoshade.com

CHAPTER 6

American Society of Interior Designers
608 Massachusetts Avenue, NE
Washington, DC 20002-6006
202-546-3480
www.asid.org
Publication: *Better Sound Solutions: Applying Occupant and Building Performance Measurement and Design to Improve Office Acoustics*

American Speech-Language-Hearing Association (ASHA)
1080 Rockville Pike
Rockville, MD 29852
800-638-8255
www.asha.org

American Tinnitus Association
www.ata.org

Better Hearing Institute
800-327-9355
703-684-3393
www.betterhearing.org

Center for Health Design
1850 Gateway Boulevard, Suite 1083
Concord, CA 94520
925-521-9404
www.healthdesign.org
Publication: *The Role of the Physical Environment in the Hospital of the 21ˢᵗ Century: A Once-in-a-Lifetime Opportunity*

Deafness Research Foundation (DRF)
1050 17th Street, NW, Suite 701
Washington, DC 20036
202-289-5850
www.drf.org

General Technologies
7417 Winding Way
Fair Oaks, CA 95628
800-328-6684
www.devices4less.com
Assistive listening devices

Healing Healthcare Systems
100 West Grove Street, Suite 245
Reno, NV 89509
775-827-0300
800-348-0799
www.healinghealth.com

Hearing Society for the Bay Area
49 Powell Street, Suite 400
San Francisco, CA 94102
415-693-5870
415-824-1055 (TTY)
www.hearingsociety.org

National Academy on an Aging Society
1030 15th Street, NW, Suite 250
Washington, DC 20005
202-408-3375
www.agingsociety.org/profiles.htm

National Association of the Deaf
814 Thayer Avenue
Silver Spring, MD 20910-4500
301-587-1788
301-587-1789 (TTY)

National Campaign for Hearing Health
Washington, DC
www.hearinghealth.net

National Center for Health Statistics
Trends in Health and Aging
www.cdc.gov/nchs/agingact.htm
Publication: *The Changing Profile of Nursing Home Residents: 1985–1997*

National Organization for Hearing Research Foundation
225 Haverford Avenue, Suite 1
Narberth, PA 19072
610-664-3155
www.nohrfoundation.org

Occupational Safety and Health Administration
www.osha.gov

Self Help for Hard of Hearing People (SHHH)
7910 Woodmont Avenue, Suite 1200
Bethesda, MD 20814
301-657-2248
301-657-2249 (TTY)
www.shhh.org
www.hearingloss.org

Sound Associates, Inc.
424 West 45th Street
New York, NY 10036
212-757-5679
1-888-772-7686
www.soundassociates.com

Wise Ears!
Office of Health Communication & Public Liaison
National Institute on Deafness & Other Communication Disorders
31 Center Drive, MSC 2320
Bethesda, MD 20892-2320
301-496-7243
www.nih.gov/nidcd/heath/wise

Chapter 7

Active Living by Design
www.activelivingbydesign.org

Administration on Aging (AOA)
www.aoa.dhhs.gov
www.aoa.dhhs.gov/elderpage.html
www.healthfinder.gov

Ageless Design
12633 159th Court North
Jupiter, FL 33478
www.agelessdesign.com
Publication: Warner, M. "The Complete Guide to Alzheimer's Proofing Your Home." West Lafayette, IN: Purdue University Press (1998).

The Alzheimer's Store
www.alzstore.com

American Association of Retired Persons (AARP)
www.aarp.org
www.aarp.org/confacts/fitness/resolve.html

American Geriatrics Society (AGS)
www.americangeriatrics.org
www.americangeriatrics.org/education/forum/falling.shtml

American Society on Aging (ASA)
833 Market Street, Suite 511
San Francisco, CA 94103-1824
www.asaging.org

American Society of Consultant Pharmacists
www.ascp.com

Boston University Roybal Center for the Enhancement of Late-Life Function
www.bu.edu/roybal

Centers for Disease Control and Prevention (CDC)
U.S. Department of Health and Human Services
www.cdc.gov/nipc/falls
www.cdc.gov/ncipc/duip/spotlite/falls.htm
www.cdc.gov/ncipc/duip/spotlite/falfacts.htm

Community and Home Injury Prevention Program for Seniors (CHIPPS)
San Francisco Department of Public Health
415-554-2924
www.dph.sf.ca.us/CHPP/inj-chip.htm

Edward R. Roybal Centers for Research on Applied Gerontology
www.applied-gerontology.org
www.applied-gerontology.org/BUBrief.pdf

Edward R. Roybal Institute for Applied Gerontology
5151 State University Drive
Los Angeles, CA 90032-8913

323-343-4724
Fax: 323-343-6410
Publication: *A Fall Can Change Your Life: Seven Home Remedies to Prevent Falls*

Health Canada
www.hc-sc.gc.ca/english/lifestyles/injury

Human Kinetics
P.O. Box 5076
Champaign, Il 61825-5076
www.humankinetics.com
Publications: Rose, Debra. *FallProof: A Comprehensive Balance and Mobility Program,* 2003
www.activeliving.info
Active Living Partners: Activate Sedentary Older Adults

International Council on Active Aging
3307 Trutch Street
Vancouver, BC V6L 2T3
Canada
866-335-9777
604-734-4466
Fax: 604-708-4464
www.icaa.cc
Publication: *The Journal on Active Aging*

National Alliance for Home Modifications and Senior Independence
www.hmemods.org

National Council on Aging (NCOA)
300 D Street, SW, Suite 801
Washington, DC 20024
202-479-1200
www.ncoa.org

National Institute on Aging (NIA)
P.O. Box 8057
Gaithersburg, MD 20898-8057
301-496-1752
800-222-2225
800-222-4225 (TTY)
www.nih.gov/nia
www.nih.gov/data/publist.asp
www.nia.nih.gov/exercisebook
Publication: *Exercise: A Guide from the NIA*
Age Pages fact sheets

National Resource Center on Aging and Injury (NRCAI)
Center on Aging
San Diego State University
San Diego, CA 92182
www.olderadultinjury.org

National Resource Center on Supportive Housing and Home Modification
University of Southern California
Andrus Gerontology Center
3715 McClintok Avenue, #228
Los Angeles, CA 90089-0191
213-740-1364
http://homemods.org

On Lok's 30th Street Senior Services
225 30th Street
San Francisco, CA 94131
415-550-2210
www.onlok.org

Partnership for Prevention
www.prevent.org
Publication: *Creating Communities for Aging Adults*

Pioneer Network
P.O. Box 18448
Rochester, NY 14618
585-271-7570
www.PioneerNetwork.net

Senior Injury Prevention Program (SIPP)
San Francisco Department of Public Health
www.dph.sf.ca.usm

The Hartford House
www.thehartford.com/AARPins/hartfordhouse/

Centers for Disease Control and Prevention (CDC)
National Center for Injury Prevention and Control
U.S. Department of Health and Human Services
www.cdc.gov/ncipc/duip/spotlite/falls.htm
Publication: *Tool Kit to Prevent Senior Falls*

Walkable Communities, Inc.
www.walkable.org

CHAPTER 8

Coalition for Health Environments Research (CHER)
1701 Jackson Street, #803
San Francisco, CA 94109
415-359-1818
www.cheresearch.org

Crypton Super Fabrics
800-279-7866
www.cryptonfabric.com
www.cryptoncare.com

Lighthouse International
111 East 59th Street
New York, NY 10022-1202
212-821-9200
800-829-0500
Fax: 212-821-9707
212-821-9713 (TTY)
www.lighthouse.org

Publications
Effective Color Contrast: Designing for People with Partial Sight and Color Deficiencies
Making Text Legible: Designing for People with Partial Sight

Products
Radiance
Paint with energy-efficient features
www.radiancecomfort.com

Scrubtough
A scrubbable, tough, durable water-based paint for interior walls from the Scuffmaster Architectural Finish line by Wolf Gordon
www.scuffmaster.com

CHAPTER 9

Carpet and Rug Institute
P.O. Box 2084
Dalton, GA 30722
800-882-8846
www.carpet-rug.com

International Facility Management Association (IFMA)
1 East Greenway Plaza, Suite 1100

Houston, TX 77046-0194
713-623-4362
www.ifma.org

InVista
170 Town Park Drive, Suite 400
Kennesaw, GA 30144
www.invista.com

U.S. Environmental Protection Agency (EPA)
401 M Street, SW
Washington, DC 20460
202-260-2080
Fax: 202-260-6257

CHAPTER 10

Center for Excellence for Sustainable Development
1617 Cole Blvd.
Golden, CO 80401
800-357-7732

DuPont Carpet Reclamation Program
170 Town Park Drive, Suite 400
Kennesaw, GA 30144
800-4DUPONT
www.antron.dupont.com

EnvironDesign
840 U.S. Hwy. One, Suite 330
North Palm Beach, FL 33408
561-627-3393
www.environdesign.com

Green Building Alliance
64 S. 14th Street
Pittsburgh, PA 15203
412-431-0709
www.gbapgh.org

Green Building Information Council
130 Lewis Street
Ottawa, Ontario
Canada K2P 0S7
613-769-1242

Green Resource Center
www.greenresourcecenter.org

Green Construction in Healthcare
www.healthybuilding.net/healthcare

Health Care Without Harm
1755 S Street, NW, Suite 6B
Washington, DC 20009
www.noharm.org
www.hcwh.;org/healthyBuilding/Issue

Healthy Building Network
2425 18th Street, NW
Washington, DC 20009
www.healthybuilding.net

InVista
170 Town Park Drive, Suite 400
Kennesaw, GA 30144
www.invista.com

U.S. Environmental Protection Agency (EPA)
401 M Street, SW
Washington, DC 20460
202-260-2080
Fax: 202-260-6257

U.S. Green Building Council (USGBC)
1015 18th Street, NW, Suite 805
Washington, DC 20036
202-82-USGBC
www.usgbc.org

CHAPTER 11

Action Pact, Inc.
5122 W. Washington Blvd.
Milwaukee, WI 53208
414-476-8758
www.culturechangenow.com

Crestview Homes Inc. Wheelchair Buffet
Bethany, MO
660-425-3128
www.idealnursinghome.com

Eden Alternative
742 Turnpike Road
Sherburne, NY 13460
907-747-4888
Fax: 607-674-6732
www.edenalt.com

Green House Project
535 West 34th Street, Suite 404A
New York, NY 10001

646-792-2960
www.thegreenhouseproject.com

Institute for the Future of Aging Services
American Association of Homes and Services for the Aging
2519 Connecticut Avenue, NW
Washington, DC 20008-1520
888-508-9441
www.aahsa.org

Institute for Quality Improvement in Long Term Health Care
601 University Drive
San Marcos, Texas 78666

Live Oak Living Center
Greenridge Heights
2150 Pyramid Drive
El Sobrante, CA 94803

The Pioneer Network
P.O. Box 18648
Rochester, NY 14618
www.PioneerNetwork.net
Publications: *Getting Started: A Pioneering Approach to Long Term Care Culture Change*

Planetree
130 Division Street
Derby, CT 06418
203-732-1366
www.planetree.org

Providence Mount St. Vincent Home
4831 35th Avenue SW
Seattle, WA 98126-2799
206-937-3700
www.providence.org/Long_Term_Care/Mount_St_Vincent

Wellspring Innovative Solutions
2149 Velp Avenue, Suite 500
Green Bay, WI 54303
920-434-0123
www.wellspringis.org

Publications
Sifton, C. B. "Educating Caregivers for Person-Centered Dementia Care." *Alzheimer's Care Quarterly* (July/September 2004).

Stone, R., S. Reinhard, B. Bowers, D. Zimmerman, C. Phillips, C. Hawes, J. Fielding, and N. Jacobson. *Evaluation of the Wellspring Model for Improving Nursing Home Quality* (August 2002).

Weiner, A., and J. Ronch, eds. *Culture Change in Long-Term Care,* vol. 2. New York-London-Oxford: Haworth Social Work Practice Press (2002).

CHAPTER 13

Cornice Lighting Systems, Inc.
52 Torbay Road
Markham, Ontario L3R 1G6
Canada
866-248-8735

InPro Corporation
Grab bars in colors and textures
580 W 18766 Apollo Drive
Muskego, WI 53150
800-222-5556
www.inprocorp.com

MechoShade Systems Inc.
42-03 35th Street
Long Island City, NY 11101
718-729-2020
www.mechoshade.com

Publications
Alden, A. "Rethinking Bathroom Design." *Nursing Homes Magazine* (March 2004).

Barrick, A., J. Rader, B. Hoeffer, and P. Sloane. *Bathing Without a Battle: Personal Care of Individuals With Dementia.* New York: Springer Publishing Company (2002).

Barrick, A., and J. Rader. "Bathing Without a Battle." *Alzheimer's Care Quarterly,* vol. 1, no. 4, (2000).

Regnier, V. *Design for Assisted Living: Guidelines for Housing the Physically and Mentally Frail.* New York: John Wiley & Sons (2002).

Sanford, J. *Best Practices in the Design of Toileting and Bathing Facilities for Assisted Transfers.* Washington, DC: U.S. Access Board (2001).

Sanford, J. "Time to Get Rid of Those Old Gray Grab Bars and Get Yourself a Shiny New Pair." *Alzheimer's Care Quarterly,* vol. 3, no. 1 (Winter 2002).

CHAPTER 14

Center to Study Human-Animal Relationships and Environments (CENSHARE)
200 Oak Street, SE, Suite 350
Minneapolis, MN 55455
612-626-1975

Eden Alternative
742 Turnpike Road
Sherburne, NY 13460
907-747-4888
Fax: 607-674-6732
www.edenalt.com

Federal Interagency Forum on Aging Related Statistics
3311 Toledo Road, Room 6227
Hyattsville, MD 20782
301-458-4460
Fax: 301-458-4037
www.agingstats.gov

Alzheimer's Association
225 N. Michigan Avenue, Suite 1700
Chicago, IL 60601-1676
800-272-3900
www.alz.org
Program: *Memories in the Making*

Publications

Eisenhandler, S. *Keeping the Faith in Late Life.* New York: Springer Publishing Company (2003).

Gwyther, L. *You Are One of Us: Successful Clergy/Church Connections to Alzheimer's Families.*

Durham, NC: Duke University Medical Center (1995).

Thomas, W. *Life Worth Living.* VanderWyk and Burnham (1996).

Thomas, W., and L. Strohmeier. *Learning from Hannah: Secrets for a Life Worth Living.* VanderWyk and Burnham (1999).

CHAPTER 15

Eden Alternative
742 Turnpike Road
Sherburne, NY 13460
907-747-4888
Fax: 607-674-6723
www.edenalt.com

Green House Project
535 West 34th Street
Suite 404A
New York, NY 10001
646-792-2960
www.thegreenhouseproject.com

Publications

Thomas, W. H. *Learning From Hannah: Secrets for a Life Worth Living.* Acton, MA: VanderWyk & Burnham (1999).

Thomas, W. H. *Life Worth Living: The Eden Alternative in Action.* Acton, MA: VanderWyk & Burnham (1996).

CHAPTER 16

National Adult Day Services Association, Inc.
722 Grant Street, Suite 1
Herndon, VA 20170
800-558-5301
703-345-8630
Fax: 703-435-8631
www.nadsa.org

National Council on Aging (NCOA)
(National Adult Day Services Association)
409 Third Street, SW
Washington, DC 20024
202-479-1200
Fax: 202-479-0735
www.ncoa.org

Partners in Caregiving
Wake Forest School of Medicine
Wake Forest University
Medical Center Boulevard
Winston-Salem, NC 27157-1087
336-716-2648

Publications

Alden, A., G. Betrabet, K. Moore, and G. Weisman. *Designing a Better Day: Annotated Bibliography of Adult Day Care Literature from 1990–1998.* Milwaukee: Center for Architecture and Urban Planning Research (1999).

Bell, V., and D. Troxel. *The Best Friends Approach to Alzheimer's Care.* Baltimore: Health Professions Press (1997).

Bell, V., and D. Troxel. *The Best Friends Staff.* Baltimore: Health Professions Press (2001).

Bell, V., and D. Troxel. *The Best Friends Book of Alzheimer's Activities.* Baltimore: Health Professions Press (2004).

Hellen, C. *Alzheimer's Disease: Activity-Focused Care.* Boston: Butterworth-Heinemann (1998).

Moore, K. D. *Dementia Day Care Facility: Development Workbook.* Milwaukee: Center for Architecture and Urban Planning Research (2000).

Moore, K., L. Geboy, G. Weisman, and S. Mleziva. *Designing a Better Day: Planning and Design Guidelines for Adult and Dementia Day Centers.* Milwaukee: Center for Architecture and Urban Planning Research (2002).

Chapter 17

Planetree
130 Division Street
Derby, CT 06418
203-732-1366
www.planetree.org

Publications
Frampton, S., L. Gilpin, and P. Charmel. *Putting Patients First: Designing and Practicing Patient-Centered Care.* San Francisco: Jossey-Bass (2003).

Chapter 18

Alive Hospice
1718 Patterson Street
Nashville, TN 37203
615-327-1085
800-327-1085
www.alivehospice.org

American Academy of Hospice and Palliative Medicine
www.aahpm.org

Americans for Better Care of the Dying
www.abcd-caring.com

American Hospice Foundation
www.americanhospice.org

Center for Gerontology and Health Care Research
www.chcr.brown.edu

Center to Improve Care of the Dying
George Washington University
www.gwu.edu/~cicd

Hospice by the Bay
1540 Market Street, Suite 350
San Francisco, CA 94102
415-626-5900
www.citysearch.com/sfo/hospicebythebay

Hospice Foundation of America
2001 S. Street, NW #300
Washington, DC 20009
800-854-3402
Fax: 202-638-5312
www.hospicefoundation.org

Missoula Demonstration Project: The Quality of Life's End
www.missoulademonstration.org

National Hospice & Palliative Care Organization
www.nhpo.org

Pain Medicine & Palliative Care
Beth Israel Medical Center
www.stoppain.org

Partnership for Caring: America's Voice for Dying
www.partnershipforcaring.org

Chapter 19

Ageless Design, Inc.
12633 159th Court North
Jupiter, FL 33478
561-745-0210

American Horticultural Therapy Association
909 York Street
Denver, CO 80206-3799

American Society of Landscape Architects (ASLA)
636 Eye Street, NW
Washington, DC 20001-3736
202-898-1185
Therapeutic Garden Design—Professional Interest Group—ASLA members with shared interest in creating therapeutic garden and sharing knowledge.
www.asla.org

Audubon Society
700 Broadway
New York, NY 10003
212-979-3000
Fax: 212-979-3188
www.audubon.org
Audubon At Home Program is about simple things we all can do to create a healthier place to live for our families, our communities, birds, plants and other wildlife—making the yard bird friendly, plants for birds and wildlife—and resource lists.

Bird Villas and Feeders
905 Woodside Drive
Kings Mountain, NC 28086
866-852-7854
www.tommysbirdvillas.com

Butterfly Garden Club of America
P.O. Box 629
Burgin, KY 40310

Chicago Botanic Garden
1000 Lake Cook Road
Glencoe, IL 60022
847-835-8250
www.chicago-botanic/HortTherapy.html

Cornell University
Cornell Lab of Ornithology
www.birds.cornell.edu/program/allaboutbirds

CSSI Resilient Surfacing Products
715 Fountain Ave.
Lancaster, PA 17601
800-851-4746
Fax: 717-481-2934
www.carlsurf.com/softpave/ultra.html
UltraSoft Pavers—shock and sound-absorbing surfacing systems made from recycled rubber

Horticultural Services Inc.
P.O. Box 1328
Sumner, WA 98390
800-256-0021

Supplies for greenhouse equipment and systems
www.hortservicesinc.com
Greenhouses for therapeutic gardening—including design consultation and construction of greenhouses and internal systems

Horticulture as Therapy
Order from:
Homewood Health Center
150 Delhi Street
Guelph, Ontario N1E 6K9
Canada

Hummingbirds
www.birds-n-garden.com
Feeders and baths

U.S. Fish and Wildlife Services
800-344-9453
Publication: *For the Birds: The ABCs of Attracting Birds*

Publications
Cooper Marcus, C., and M. Barnes. *Healing Gardens.* New York: John Wiley & Sons (1999).

Hewson, M. "Horticulture as Therapy." Self-published (2000).

Rothert, G. *The Enabling Garden: Creating Barrier Free Gardens.* Dallas, TX: Taylor Publishing Company (1994).

Tyson, M. *The Healing Landscape: Therapeutic Outdoor Environments.* New York: McGraw Hill (1998).

Xerces Society with the Smithsonian Institution. *Butterfly Gardening: Creating Summer.* San Francisco: Sierra Club Books (1998).

CHAPTER 20

Center for Health Design
1850 Gateway Boulevard, Suite 1083
Concord, CA 94520
925-521-9404
www.healthdesign.org

Index

A

AARP, 260
Academy of Neuroscience for Architecture, 28
Accessibility:
    for bathroom doorways, 195–196
    for gardening, 285, 287
    for lavatories, 192
    for showers, 188
    for toilets, 186–187
Accessible design, 35, 109–110
Access to home, for aging in place, 109
Acoustical ceiling tiles, 84, 86, 200
Acoustical engineering, 86
Acoustical environment:
    ceilings, 83–84, 86
    defined, 85
    designing, 80–82
    floors, 82
    sound control design for, 82
    sound masking, 86
    standards for, 86–89
    walls, 82, 83
Acoustical wallcoverings, 86–87
Acoustics:
    in bathing environment, 200
    defined, 85
    and flooring choice, 132–133
    and perception of care quality, 84
Activities. *See also* Meaningful activity
    in adult day care, 235–240, 246
    bird feeding, 289
    culture change and levels of, 158
    designing for, 299–300
    food preparation, 177, 178
    in Green House model, 230
    involving families, 205, 208, 209
    as key to initiating change, 152
    normal daily household tasks, 177–178
    in outdoor spaces, 284–286
    religious, 205
    social, 205–209. *See also* Social
        interaction
    therapeutic, 33–34
    volunteering, 207
Activities of daily living (ADLs), 223
    lighting for, 63
    and vision impairment, 39

Activity spaces, xv. *See also* Gathering spaces;
    Social living spaces
    and culture change, 168
    in gardens, 277
    in innovative building designs, 212
    kitchens as, 172, 173, 175
    "Main Street," 168
    outdoor, 275–291, 294–295
    in Planetree model, 252
    in sitting areas, 171–172
    "Town Square," 168, 211
Acute care, 249
ADA, *see* Americans with Disabilities Act
Adaptive Environments, 35
ADLs, *see* Activities of daily living
Adult day care, 233–247
    activities in, 235–240, 246
    benefits of, 237–240
    intergenerational programs in, 240
    at Life Enrichment Centers, 235–236
    need for, 233–234
    physical setting for, 241–247
    programs for, 234–235
    services of, 235, 236
Aesthetics:
    and carpet choice, 136
    and fabrics, 123
    first impressions, 127, 300–301
    and flooring, 129
Age-related changes, 8–9
    chronic health conditions, 8–13
    joint and back pain, 95
    in vision, 40, 63, 64
Age-related hearing loss, 10, 77, 78
Age-related macular degeneration (AMD), 42
Age-related memory loss, 17, 22
Aging, xiii
    demographics of, 4
    effects of, 3
    fear of, 150
    global, 5
    and learning speed, 18
    and memory loss, 17
    normal brain neuron loss in, 20
    perceptions of, 3
    physical and mental experiences of, xiv
    physical changes related to, 7–8

    and prevalence of hearing impairment, 80
    and risk of falls, 98
    in stable living environment, xiii
    as state of mind, 7
    successful, 212
    transformation of attitudes toward, 148
    and variability in health/quality of life, 6–8
    views of, 148
Aging in place, xiii, 107–110
Agitation, 49
AHSA (American Seniors Housing Associa-
    tion), xiii
Airborne pollutants, 133–134, 293
Air-jet tubs, 198
Air quality:
    and floorcoverings, 133–134
    and plants, 293
Alcoves, 172, 219, 220
Aldersgate, 84
Alexander, Christopher, 226, 252
Alive Hospice, 270
Allen House, 170
Alpine Court, 62
Alzheimer's Association, 24, 294
Alzheimer's Association International, 212
Alzheimer's disease, 18–25
    beginning signs of, 18–19
    causes of, 20, 22
    day care for people with, 237
    defined, 18
    detection of, 23–24
    early-onset, 20, 22, 23
    end-of-life care for, 265–267
    environmental influences on, xv
    environment as treatment for, 29–30
    falls associated with, 98
    habilitation therapy for, 34
    impact of, 20
    knowledge about, 20
    late-onset, 20, 23
    Life Skills programs for, 177
    lifestyle and risk of, 24
    and melatonin deficiency, 47
    memory loss with, 19
    mild cognitive impairment vs., 22
    naturally mapped environments for, 30–33
    Nun Study of, 25